# The Final Prison Break:

## Adventures and Misadventures in Synchronicity, Grace and Awakening

*by*

**Mark Pope**

For Mike, the who is Living Awakening w/ me in Birmingham AL this Easter, 2012 Blessings Mark Pope

©2011

*by*

**Mark Pope**

**ISBN-10: 1467910260**
**ISBN- 13: 978-1467910262**

**Library of Congress Control Number: 2011960591**

*Edited by*
**Lux Newman**

*Contributing Editor*
**Marta Adelsman**

*Cover Photograph by*
**Ron Evans**
**Mountain Spirit Gallery**
**ronevansphotography.com**

*Cover design by*
**Lux Newman**

**Printed in the United States of America**

*You get your visions through whatever gates you're granted.*
~ Ken Kesey


*True Love is for everyone, everywhere, always and forever. Such is the only love that liberates. All other, more limited and limiting versions are not love at all, but ego at a masquerade party.*
~ Who cares who said it?

## Dedication

This book is dedicated to the Unvarnished Truth,
though such Unvarnished Truth may appear distorted in its pages.
It is further dedicated to spiritual awakening
and its sometimes merciful, sometimes brutal expressions.
Apparently, this author required both.

# ACKNOWLEGEMENTS

I bear indescribable gratitude to so many individuals that I cannot name them without resembling an award ceremony. Everyone I met served in some way, whether by loving me or hating me. So, if you exist, thank you.

I will mention a few specifically, however. I thank Kathryn Olson, without the support of whom, I would not likely still be living in a body; Ronnie West, whose actual name shall remain unknown, but whose part in this Mystery Play will be partially revealed in the pages to follow; Brugh Joy, whose realization of the nature of the Heart and whose integrity as a spiritual teacher shine forever; Eckhart Tolle and Adyashanti, who have both been invaluable mirrors of unwavering Truth; Hal Vaile and Marian Sears, who have provided sanctuary and friendship for many years; and Lux Newman, whose sudden and synchronistic appearance caused, among other graces, the final obstacles to publishing this book to simply disappear.

The following individuals made financial contributions or pledges to support the publication of this book: Brittany Blondino, Ronnie West, Kathryn Olson, Joe Wolfe, Tyrone Campbell, Brenda Cosse, Marta Adelsman, Ben Montrose, Rosie Douglas, Grace, Doris Hoskins, Carol Dombrose, Brenda Adelman, Dee Rudd, Ron and Leslie Cunningham, Bill and Cynthia Miller, Kerry Bober, Kit Fuchs, Cis Dickson, Hal Vaile, Marian Sears, Kenn and Jeanette Suggs, Gail Green, Mary Lucero, Syhdasa, Patrick and Paula Hicks, Aria Magi, Charles Collins, Kurtis Probst, Barbara Margotta, Edith Stein, Charles (The Master/The Dog...no one knows which?) Siemers, Sandy Bond, Lucile Barbati, Joyce Parker and various anonymous ones.

# A Letter from Mark Pope

I don't really trust memory. The mind can make stuff up and convince us it is true. I did my best to tell these stories as they actually occurred. I did change a few names to protect the guilty or the innocent. If a date is not perfectly in alignment with recorded history, or an event not consistent with someone's memory of how it happened, I apologize...but, not really. I am not recording history here. I am reporting, as best I can recall, the stories of synchronicity, grace and awakening that burst into my egoic delusion and slowly...very slowly... eroded it.

I do hope it is possible to learn from the mistakes of others and avoid some suffering, though you couldn't prove it by me. To that end, I offer these adventures and misadventures, some pointers to the Truth, and some honest confessions of how often I missed the Truth, or misinterpreted It, or distorted It.

Try to overlook the mistakes in language and prose or even grammar. However much I have loved the great writers such as Tom Robbins, or my namesake, Mark Twain, I do not have their training or education or gifts. I am only authorized to write by experiences beyond convention and by assuming permission to do so.

# TABLE OF CONTENTS

## Chapters:

# Chapter 1
## Back Story:
## Disappearing Auras, Rejecting Authority
## and Other Components of My Descent into Darkness

My mother had firecrackers on her breakfast tray the morning after my birth. She felt her baby was destined to live an extraordinary life. I would first become acquainted with the dark side of extraordinary.

I entered the world at 11:34 p.m. on July 3, 1947 in Elmira, New York. My parents were staying at the Mark Twain Hotel. So, they decided to name me Mark.

Although I never discussed it with others, I was sensitive as a child in two particular ways. For one, I could see energy around things. I had never heard the word *aura*. I had seen some pictures in a book of religious figures with halos and wondered if, perhaps, the artist could see this energy. The auras were particularly evident to me when alone and outdoors. Trees and plants appeared to be enclosed in a subtle, vibrating, pulsating energy or light. At times, I would see a field of energy around others, as well. When this energy appeared around people, it was sometimes white, and on other occasions, it would appear light blue, green or yellow. I felt a sense of connection or relationship to life when this light was evident. I could not have told you it was a spiritual experience, because I had no concept of what that meant. It was a pleasant feeling, however, and I privately treasured it.

The other particular sensitivity was empathy. I could feel the emotions of others. Regardless of how adept people were at hiding

1

their emotions, I could often tell how they really felt. This produced a great deal of confusion for me when I was around large numbers of people. In crowds I would often feel a wide range of emotions. This sensitivity wasn't always pleasant, and I didn't know how to control it.

One of my most vivid and informative experiences helps to convey both of these particular sensitivities, and it would lead to an act of theft that would symbolize the experiences I would undergo for the next half-century. It occurred in my third grade classroom at South Houston Elementary School. Classmates had nicknamed me Marco Polo, because I wouldn't stay in my seat. At every opportunity I would wander to the windows and look out at the trees. I could see energy vibrating around the trees, bushes and grass. I sensed that everything in nature was connected to everything else, and this would help reestablish my fading sense of connection to life.

My empathy also drove me to the window. The classroom was loud and wild. Kids threw spitballs and paper airplanes at each other whenever the teacher would leave the room. And some kids seemed cruel and hurtful. I could sense a wide range of emotions. I often felt overwhelmed by this. I kept going to the window to look at the trees, to attempt to regain a sense of balance and a connection, at least to nature. Little by little, the light was dimming though. It would soon slip out of awareness and remain hidden through years of criminal behavior and incarceration. This light would have to wait. My destiny for now was not the light, but the darkness.

I was punished for going to the window. I was taken into the hallway and told by the teacher to bend over and grab my knees. Then, she paddled me with a wooden paddle. One day, it seemed the teacher was intent on breaking me of my wandering ways. She paddled me especially hard. It stung badly and I cried and felt humiliated. That was the day I embarked upon the criminal life. My meager and tentative spiritual awareness slipped from view. I thought, "This world is full of people who will hurt you. They don't care about others. They only care about their rules. Well," I continued to muse, "I refuse to believe in rules made by people who don't care about others. I'll do what I want."

That day after school, I stole a yo-yo. No one else ever knew. I had no regret at all. I had begun a rebellion against the world that would result in enormous pain. I had rejected authority. The yo-yo was a perfect symbol for the ups and downs that were now in store for me.

Psychologists might say that my rebellion was rooted in my relationship with my father. He was the original authority figure. He, too, seemed unaware of my emotional life. From the narrow perspective I had adopted, I saw our relationship as about his imposing rules, my breaking the rules and his punishing me for breaking them. This narrow perspective blocked from awareness the fact that he was showing his love in the only way he was able. By working hard to provide food and a home, he was attempting to give me everything he had been denied.

My father had been abandoned at the age of twelve. He had shined shoes and slept on a barber shop floor during the depression. The military had been the door to a better life. The discipline he learned there had given him a set of principles and a sense of integrity that were guiding him. By imposing rules, he had hoped to teach me what he had learned to value. I missed this altogether. I saw him as unreasonably restrictive, distant and angry.

While visiting my father much later in life, he shared his perspective on what happened that caused me to leave home at twelve years old. It was just as I remembered it except that I didn't know he'd hoped I wouldn't go.

My mother was kind, compassionate and sensitive. She seemed to intuitively sense my more vulnerable times and would offer consolation. She and my dad didn't get along well. Eventually, my parents began divorce proceedings. My mother had what I was told was a nervous breakdown. She was taken to a military sanitarium.

My criminal life accelerated over the next few years. I vandalized vacant homes, stole pop bottles from the open garages of neighbors (worth two cents each, when redeemed at the local 7-11 convenience store). Also, I was suspended from school for three days for a fistfight I had with another student.

At the age of twelve, I stole my first car, loaded my bike in the back and drove until I ran out of gas. I found some money in the car, so when I abandoned it, I hid my bike and took a bus to Dallas, Texas. There I went to the movies and saw *Breakfast at Tiffany's*. The lyrics of the theme song, Henry Mancini's *Moon River*, "...comin' round the bend, my Huckleberry friend..." and... "two drifters out to see the world, there's such a lot of world to see..." struck a chord deep within me. As I left the movie, some 250 miles from home and nearly broke, I felt encouraged to push on in my exploration of the world. I hitchhiked out of Dallas, going north. In Denton, Texas, the police picked me up. The rule-breaker was returned once again to the rule-maker.

Back at home, my father sat me down. "Son," he said, "if you want to live in this house, you have an obligation to follow the rules of the home." He then said, "If you're not willing to do that, there is a duffel bag in the other room. Just pack your stuff and head on back out that door. But if you go, you're on your own from here on out."

My father is 92 years old now. He told this story to me in the spring of 2001 when I was visiting him. He said he had hoped I would be ready to straighten up, and that he never believed I would go. But I did. I felt he didn't love me, and the pain of that belief caused me to pack and leave. I did not return for many years.

After leaving home, I spent the majority of the next four years incarcerated in detention homes and reform school. I entered reform school in 1962. The Gatesville State School for Boys remains in my memory as one of the darkest times of my life. The school was eventually closed down for its brutal practices. The following quote is taken from *The Handbook of Texas On-line: A digital Gateway to Texas History:*

> A class-action lawsuit, filed against the Texas Youth Council, on behalf of juvenile offenders in 1971, marked the beginning of sweeping changes in the Texas juvenile justice system. The school enrolled approximately 1,500 boys and employed over 250 staff members in 1974, when federal judge William Wayne Justice issued a ruling in Morales v. Turman. The judge ruled that a number of practices at Texas Youth Council facilities constituted cruel and unusual punishment that violated the Eighth Amendment to the United States Constitution. Staff members routinely dispensed arbitrary and unnecessary punishments that included beating, solitary confinement, the use of chemical crowd-control devices and the utilization of drugs, instead of psychotherapy, as a means for controlling behavior. Justice also concluded that the

school's staff failed to protect the inmates from violence and personal injury and that most employees lacked proper qualifications and training for supervising troubled youths.

I arrived at Gatesville (the primary facility of the above-mentioned Texas Youth Council) with several other boys from the Houston area in 1962, nine years before the above action by the federal court system. I was placed in the Diagnostic Unit. The guards, dressed in military-like khaki uniforms, informed us that there were rules and that failure to comply with these rules would cause us pain and regret. We were to be up early, shower and dress quickly. There was to be no talking under any circumstances while we were in the diagnostic unit.

We received haircuts. They shaved our heads to the scalp. We were issued old military fatigues on some days and khakis on other days. We were to wear what we were given. We were to march in a straight line to the chow hall and back. After medical exams, vaccinations and orientation, we would be assigned to a Company, depending on physical size and age.

One of my fellow inmates, who had arrived with me from Houston, was a twelve year old black boy. He had stolen a bicycle. His parents had failed to show up in court to ask for his release, so the judge had committed him to the state school. He had cried most of the way there. I had tried to comfort him, but he was inconsolable. The truth was, I was afraid, too. The very first day after our arrival, he tried to tell the guards that he didn't belong there. He begged for his mother and was punished every time he opened his mouth. The guards used what they called *knot sticks* to administer the first level of punishment. Knot sticks were shaped like little baseball bats, about eight inches long. The guards would pop them against the skull of the perpetrator, raising a knot on the skull.

Before the day was up, my little black friend had reached the second level of punishment. He was tied by the wrists to a wire mesh cage, such that his toes could barely touch the ground. But he couldn't learn. He still kept talking, begging for his mother, crying for help. Finally, he reached the third level of punishment.

I was to discover this third level of punishment was very common throughout the system. It was called *racking*. The guards would put on leather gloves, intended to keep the bruising to a minimum, and beat the offender about the face, arms and torso. The offender was expected by the guards and the inmates to stand there and take these beatings without ducking, flinching or crying out. Weakness was considered intolerable by inmates and guards alike. This racking always involved more than one guard, usually two or three. It was always done in the privacy of an office. It wasn't meant to be a secret, however. I think they were using my little black friend to make a statement to all of us, as we could hear him crying out as he was being beaten severely.

This is as good a time as any to admit that, when I arrived in Gatesville at fourteen years old, I was still a bed-wetter. One may easily imagine how ashamed I was about this fact. My anxiety built throughout that first day, as I anticipated what would happen if this were discovered. This became my greatest fear. The humiliation I knew would be mine if I were to wet the bed terrified me. The consequences were unthinkable. It didn't happen. Amazingly, I never wet the bed again. I now know great challenges often result in transformational changes. Such challenges may result in the discovery of inner resources that, until the challenge required it, may have been unimaginable. One never knows what is possible until the circumstance calls it forth.

Within the first few days, while still in the Diagnostic Unit, I decided to attempt an escape. Gatesville had no walls or fences. What I didn't know is that we were far from any town. What I was about to discover was, they did have dogs trained to hunt us down. I passed the word surreptitiously to the others. Several of us agreed we would bolt from the line on the way back from dinner and head through the nearby cornfields. When the time came, my little black friend and I were the only ones to run. He had not even been told about the escape attempt. I suspect he just got caught up in the moment and followed me, since I was the only person showing him any kindness. The last I saw of my little friend was the top of his small, black head, now shaven to the scalp, bobbing up and down amidst the tall rows of corn.

Gatesville is in central Texas, just west of Waco. It was summer and very hot. I was winded in no time. Yet, as far as I could tell, no one was following me. As I continued through the cornfields and into some hills dotted with gnarled cedars, I began to hear dogs barking. As I continued on, stumbling up and down through this hill country, the barks grew louder and louder. Although it hadn't occurred to me that they were hunting me, I began to feel nervous. Suddenly, they appeared...a pack of dogs, maybe ten or twelve. They were vicious looking, and they were heading straight for me, growling and barking. I could see saliva dripping down their jaws. As they closed in on me, those jaws began snapping. The growling grew fiercer. Two or three nipped at my legs. One tore my pants. I froze in panic. That, it turned out, was a good thing. As I stood, glued to the spot, the dogs ceased the nipping and simply stood, encircling me and barking.

Guards arrived soon after on horses. They and the dogs herded me back across a couple of hills to a small, crushed rock road where a jeep awaited me. As mentioned, I never saw my little black friend again. Gatesville was segregated. I'm sure he was eventually assigned to the Riverside Unit, as were all blacks. Judging from my experiences, I am equally sure he suffered greatly before he arrived there.

I was taken to the Major's office, where they racked on me. Then they introduced me to the fourth level of punishment. I was temporarily assigned to a unit called Mountain View, otherwise known as *lock-up*. It resembled the stereotypical prison with high fences topped with barbed wire. Here each inmate was placed in a separate cell. The general population in lock-up was comprised of the toughest and meanest in the system. Silence was the rule here, too. Being in a cell in lock-up was an experience in isolation and loneliness. The days passed slowly with nothing to break the monotony. At night, I wept - very quietly. It would be the last time I would cry for years. The code against weakness forbade it. I was resolved to hide my vulnerable nature. This hiding of my vulnerable side began to give rise to a new mask or persona that outwardly appeared cool and fearless.

Two weeks later, I was released from lock-up. During the following year, I underwent a deepening development of this new, harder, colder aspect of being. I learned to fistfight to protect myself. Really, I just learned to do what I perceived had to be done to survive in this strange and dark world called Gatesville.

After more than a year of incarceration at Gatesville, I was released. Two weeks later, I again stole a car, was arrested and returned to Gatesville. Why would I do this? I'm not certain myself as I look back, more than fifty years later, except to say that I was now identified almost fully with this new persona, which I refer to as the Ice Man. I had been rewarded on the inside for it, in that I had survived and gotten respect, and I was now driven by what might be termed criminal values. I really had no other conscious identity. Perhaps I was simply acting according to what I now believed I was - a criminal - the ultimate rule-breaker.

In 1964, at the age of seventeen, and some fourteen months into my second period of incarceration at Gatesville, I was called to the superintendent's office and told that I was being released early. I was shocked and excited as I had expected to serve many more months. The superintendent who issued this news was named Mark Sills. I would encounter him again, serendipitously, many years later. It would be one of many experiences in *synchronicity* and *grace* that describe my spiritual path of *awakening*. For now, however, that story will have to wait.

My release, it turned out, was conditional. I was required to undergo psychiatric evaluation. This had been arranged by my father and his new wife, Nelle. The evaluation resulted in my being placed in a locked psychiatric ward for emotionally disturbed adolescents at the University of Texas Medical Center's psychiatric unit in Galveston, Texas. Although I rebelled at first, I soon developed an attraction for this place. I would never have admitted this attraction to anyone, however.

The psychiatrist who was assigned to me, Dr. Grace K. Jameson, questioned me in a manner unique to my experience. No one had ever asked me what I was feeling or why I felt as I did. She wanted to know what had made me so angry. When I told her why I thought I was angry, she seemed pleased and asked even more questions. Eventually, she told me she thought I was attempting to punish myself. She said I felt guilty and blamed myself for my parents' divorce. She said that my parents had probably never really loved each other, and that growing up in a home where the parents were at odds with each other had been very difficult on me emotionally.

Dr. Jameson said my father had told her, in a private meeting, he had married my mother because he felt obligated to do so. She had become pregnant with me, and having grown up mostly on his own during the depression, he felt strongly that he should provide better for his own offspring. Dr. Jameson told me he had broken down crying while telling her this. That was a strange idea to me. I had never seen my father express much emotion. I could barely conceive of his crying.

Her theory about me was, as best I can recall, that I had begun to act out or rebel in the belief that it would cause my parents to come together to help me. She said I needed them both emotionally. When my unconscious attempt to cause them to come together failed, I acted out even more. Then, when they separated and my mother had a nervous breakdown, I felt responsible. According to her theory, I proceeded to act out unconsciously, in an attempt to punish myself, believing I had caused the separation and divorce. She was trying to explain that it really wasn't my fault. She said my parents' marriage had never had the love and substance good marriages require.

I thought Dr. Jameson was a nice lady; that she cared about my well-being. I could not relate to her theories though. I thought that everyone else was trying to punish me. The idea that I had unconscious aspects of being was beyond my comprehension. What mattered, though, was that Dr. Jameson communicated a sincere and authentic compassion for me. Although the seeds of her work with me didn't come to immediate fruition, they had been planted. A part of me resonated with her. It was a rare experience for me to encounter an authority figure whom I could respect.

For the next few months, I continued to reside at the adolescent psychiatric unit in Galveston. I met regularly with the psychiatrists, Dr. Jameson and the residents training under her. I also attended occupational therapy sessions and took accelerated high school classes for credit.

The occupational therapist at the treatment facility was a woman named Ann. She was warm, friendly and attractive. I was infatuated. She seemed responsive. Eventually, as I earned the right to leave the hospital, I returned and visited her at her apartment near the medical center. Ann was 26, and I was 17. My experience with women had, until now, been mostly imaginary. However, I was now becoming aware of the fact that women found me attractive. Although I would not know it for years, I was deeply needful of feminine containment. At every possible opportunity, I moved toward intimate relationship with Ann.

The plan for my education was, through completing the accelerated classes for credit at the hospital, I would be able to return to high school and graduate on time, with the class I would have been a part of had I not been sent to reform school. Another trickier part of the plan was that I would return to my father's home while completing my high school education. The first part of the plan was successful. The second was not. I excelled in both the accelerated classes and in high school when I returned. My high school diploma indicates that I graduated 38th in a class of 457 students from South Houston High School in 1965.

Upon my release and return home, my father, the rule-maker, seemed as intent as always on having me accept and embrace his values and rules. And I, the rule-breaker, reacted as always. I moved out. This time however, instead of "punishing myself," I took a job at a K-Mart and rented a bedroom.

Soon thereafter, a new friend, Wendell, introduced me to his mother. She and Wendell offered me the opportunity to live with them until graduation. So, my high school education was finished without too much disruption. There were fistfights at Vicki's Drive-in, the local hangout, alcohol use, and some rather clumsy sexual encounters with girls my own age.

I also began to travel back to Galveston to see Ann, eventually engaging in an affair with her. I continued to see Dr. Jameson. I remember telling her about the affair with Ann as it was happening. Rather than reacting negatively, she smiled warmly and asked me if we were using any kind of protection.

"No," I said. "I don't think I would enjoy that much."

"I understand," said Dr. Jameson. "My husband says the idea of using prophylactics would be about like taking a shower with your socks on." And we laughed. I realize now that had Dr. Jameson reacted differently, I may have placed Ann's career in great jeopardy. As it happens, Ann's career - and more than her career - would be jeopardized by her relationship with me. I was still quite capable of extremely risky behavior, and our relationship would grow closer.

My high school graduation marked the end of the longest period of freedom I had experienced for years. I left the hospital in October of 1964, entering my high school senior year a little late, graduating

May 26, 1965. By the end of June, I was back in jail in Del Rio, Texas.

I had traveled to Mexico to celebrate my graduation with Ronnie West, a friend with whom I had done time in Gatesville. We had ingested some barbiturates, and I had immediately reverted fully back to my old ways, stolen a car and was quickly arrested and placed in the Val Verde County Jail. There I would remain for the next six months awaiting trial.

Once again, although it would still be years before I would recognize it as such, a certain spiritual grace would reach in and help me out of the darkness. My mother, now remarried and healthier, hired a lawyer. The attorney traveled the several hundred miles to Del Rio from Houston and managed to negotiate a plea bargain for me. The felony charge was reduced to a misdemeanor, and I was released for time served. The lawyer's name was Marvin Teague, and he would eventually be appointed to the Texas Court of Criminal Appeals. I remember him as another of the few authority figures I liked. I knew he was a really good person, trying to help me.

However, the word grace was not a part of my vocabulary. I still had a number of appointments with the darkness before I would recognize the light of spiritual awareness, much less this indescribable grace that, in retrospect, has always been flowing into and through my life.

Upon my release from the Val Verde county jail, I returned to Houston. At my mother's home, my sister, Maralyn, greeted me with a gift. She had bought me a black 1951 Plymouth for $60. She had told the seller that it was for her big brother, so maybe he wouldn't get in trouble stealing cars anymore. I was touched.

Maralyn was sixteen years old now and had turned into quite a beauty. She had received instruction as a model and had begun to pose for newspaper ads. She was sensitive and caring. Within the next two years, Maralyn would begin to hear voices in her head. She would be diagnosed with schizophrenia, hospitalized and subjected to a series of shock treatments. I would visit the San Antonio State Hospital where she was receiving the shock treatments. She would cry out to me as I left, begging me to help her, not to leave her there. Outside the hospital, I would kneel beside my car, tears streaming down my face, nauseous.

Maralyn would never overcome this disease. She would spend years living in the streets, panhandling, and in and out of state institutions for the mentally ill. Today she lives in Houston in an impoverished neighborhood known as the "third ward." At sixty-two, she has only a few teeth, has given birth to two children (by two separate fathers), both of whom have been raised by my mother. Maralyn lives in squalid conditions.

Meanwhile, my younger brother, Neal, had become addicted to heroin. He would eventually spend a large portion of his life in prison. Until July of 2011, when my mother passed away, Neal lived with her in Houston. The conditions of their lives had also been extremely impoverished.

During my time in jail in Del Rio, Ann had continued to love and support me. She had written often and sent me spending money. A few months after my release, we were married. I was hungry for the stability she offered. Everything in those days was mostly about me and my needs. I doubt I understood what it meant to love someone. In exchange for the stability she gave me, she received adventure. I do know Ann loved me and attempted in every way she knew to support me through some of the darker days of my life. She risked everything she had and lost it all attempting to help me. I rarely stayed with her except when I needed her help. I divorced her, just before having a spiritual awakening.

From 1966 to 1969, my friend, Ronnie West and I were arrested in Houston, Dallas, Oklahoma City, New Orleans and Phoenix, for charges ranging from vagrancy to burglary and from theft to flight to avoid prosecution, a federal offense. Honestly, I cannot say what my motivations were at the time. Was I needy? Yes, I think I always felt an underlying insecurity, a sense that there might not be enough. Was I angry? Yes, I still rejected authority and almost all authority figures. However, I also clearly remember enjoying the adventure associated with the risk. Something in me felt born to explore the unacceptable; to step outside the boundaries of society.

In Phoenix in 1968, I began to encounter the drug culture. Ronnie had dropped acid (ingested LSD) and loved it. He began to tell me that he was having spiritual experiences and how, as a child, he had wanted to become a priest. I hadn't dropped acid, nor had I had any spiritual experiences, but something began to stir within me when he said that.

I was living under an alias during this time, and had been running from the FBI, who had a "flight to avoid prosecution" warrant out for me. I had jumped bond and failed to appear in court in Dallas on a burglary charge.

One bright, sunshiny day in Phoenix, Arizona, Ronnie and I were pulled over for a traffic violation. This minor offense led to the discovery of my real identity. Along with local law enforcement, the FBI arrived on the scene. We were arrested and transported to the Maricopa County jail pending extradition back to Texas. More than anything, I felt relieved. The running was over. Ronnie and I signed extradition papers, and two Harris County deputies arrived and drove us back to Houston to stand trial.

Ronnie and I spent the next several months in the Harris County jail, waiting for trial. We were held in different areas of the jail and would not see one another again for quite some time. Eventually, I received a two-year sentence and was bench warranted to Dallas to face two burglary charges. Several months later, still in the Dallas county jail, I discovered that the state's case against me had weakened because some of the witnesses could no longer be located. The district attorney eventually offered me two two-year sentences to run concurrently with my two-year sentence from Harris County. That is, all three sentences would begin on the same date. In the most practical terms, this meant I would serve the time of a single two-year sentence but have three felony convictions. This was an excellent offer, and I took it. I caught the *chain* (a vehicle transporting convicts) for the *joint* (the penitentiary).

I had been contemplating the *something* that had stirred within me, while Ronnie talked about the priesthood. Finally, I was admitting to myself that there must be a better way to live. Inwardly, I promised myself I would change when I got out this time. Perhaps this is what set the stage for a spiritual awakening.

## Chapter 2
## The Penitentiary: Meeting a Mystic

I entered the Diagnostic Unit of the Texas Department of Corrections in 1969. I was 22 years old. Prior to this moment in time, I had been arrested dozens of times and locked up for seven of the previous nine years in detention homes, reform school, a locked psychiatric ward and county jails. In the Diagnostic Unit, I underwent a medical exam, my criminal record was reviewed, and I was assigned to a maximum security unit of the Texas penitentiary. I was told I had been classified *incorrigible*. I had to look it up later in the dictionary, where I found it means "cannot be corrected, improved or reformed" or "delinquent; not manageable."

The inmates arriving with me and I were informed that there would be no talking except in direct response to questions from the guards. We were immediately stripped of our street clothes, herded through open showers and given *prison whites* to wear.

My initial impression was of the *light*. The corridors and cells were brightly lit. And the *smell*. The antiseptic in the air was so strong it stung my nostrils. *Clean. White. Light.* I felt like a bug under a microscope with nowhere to run or hide. I had grown so accustomed to darkness, metaphorically speaking, that this much light shocked me. I had no idea that another light, the light of spiritual awareness, would soon break through to me.

Despite the terror, the shock and the extreme sense of vulnerability I felt inwardly, I displayed as little emotion as possible. Throughout the years I had spent locked up, I had learned that, in such places, weakness is despised and often punished severely. Time and time again, in the various institutions where I had been incarcerated, I had witnessed the weak being raped, sodomized, beaten and degraded.

14

So I had somehow learned to push the fear down, in what was perhaps a form of denial, and pull up another part of me - a harder, more detached, less fearful part. Today, at the age of 64, as I peer back through so-called time, I think of this Ice Man part of me with appreciation. I know he saved me.

Within a few days, I was transferred to the maximum security unit where I had been assigned to spend the next two years. For many years, I had heard about how tough the maximum security units of the Texas prison system were. The two I had heard about were Ellis and Eastham, both located in East Texas. In county jails and on the streets, having done time in these units was considered a badge of honor. On the inside, it only meant hard time. I was assigned to the Eastham unit.

The main building at Eastham is traversed by a wide and very long corridor. Along the corridor are wings, extending at right angles from the corridor. Each wing is comprised of cells and a day-room. The wings are called lines and distinguished from one another alphabetically. I was assigned to L line.

Each line was overseen by guards who remained outside the bars. Inside the bars, each line was governed by a building tender. A building tender is an inmate who has been given this status by the guards for keeping the area clean and orderly. These positions were generally held by inmates with lengthy sentences, who were also seen by the warden and the guards as cooperative. I do not know how the prison system in Texas operates today, but in those days building tenders were also expected to impose certain punishments on other inmates.

Building tenders were afforded special privileges in exchange for their cooperative efforts. They were not required to work in the fields. They were allowed better food, and their prison whites were pressed. They were given greater freedom of movement within the building. As you might imagine, building tenders were not always looked upon kindly by the general prison population. A few attempted to keep the respect of their fellow inmates by treating them as fairly as possible. Many were worse than guards and quick to inflict punishments on other inmates in order to maintain their privileged status.

L line was overseen by a building tender named Sonny. Sonny was one of the few who attempted to walk the fine line of pleasing his employers, the guards, on the one hand, and being fair to his charges, the inmates, on the other.

Once I was assigned a cell, Sonny came by to see me. He made the rules clear. Cells were to be kept immaculate. No talking after lights out. The television in the dayroom was under his control. The commissary hours were explained, as were the visitation times.

"The work here," Sonny said, "is hard. Lights on at 5:30 a.m., followed by breakfast at 6:00 a.m. By 6:30 a.m. you will be on trailers on the way to the fields. Remember," he said, "this farm is on the silent system. There is no talking in the cells, no talking in the halls, no talking in the shower, no talking in the chow hall and no talking in the fields. You may talk in the dayroom only, and keep your voice down, there. I've heard you're good people (prison vernacular for one with a good reputation among inmates), Pope. Don't make me enforce the rules."

I never crossed swords with Sonny, and he never treated me ill. I heard he had two 35-year sentences stacked, meaning the sentences were to be served consecutively. The second sentence would begin only after the first sentence is completed. It was not difficult for me to imagine, with that kind of time to serve, one might not care what the other inmates thought about one accepting the controversial position of building tender. The few privileges seemed small consolation for one who would probably not be free again.

My first day at work in the fields brought a pleasant surprise and a decidedly unpleasant realization. The pleasant surprise was an encounter with one of my best friends from reform school. David Boss and I had served some eighteen months together in Gatesville. He was definitely considered good people and had probably been responsible for my decent reputation preceding me with Sonny. There we stood in the field, smile and twinkling eyes to smile and twinkling eyes. But no talking.

It is hard to explain how comforting it was to see him. I could hardly wait to talk to him. But I would have to wait. The silent system was brutally enforced. Talking in the field could result in a punishment that included no shower, no dinner and no sleep. Instead of sleeping, one could be required to stand on the end of a coke box - a wooden box that held 24 cokes in those days - all night. The next morning, the rule-breaker would be expected to return to work and keep up the pace in the field. As it happened, I never had the opportunity to speak with David. Beneath the Ice Man exterior, I grieved this lost opportunity to connect with a friend.

It was winter when I arrived, and our work was clearing the land. This entailed the use of axes. Row after row of convicts worked side-by-side, clearing the thick brush and trees along the Trinity River bottom. Each tree had to be stumped. That is, after the tree was cut down, the stump had to be removed below the surface of the ground. The unpleasant surprise to which I was referring was the difficulty of the work.

Yes, I had heard the work was hard, but no words could have prepared me. I had spent nearly a year in county jails in Houston and Dallas prior to my arrival, and had had no physical exercise during that time. I was in poor, even pitiful shape physically, and was now paying a hellish price. Even with gloves on, my hands blistered within the first hour. By the second hour, the blisters were broken and bleeding. The pain was excruciating. My hands and legs quivered with exhaustion. By midday, my hands were throbbing with sharp pain. There would be no sympathy, and there was no excuse for slowing down. Water breaks were few and ended quickly; time to drink water, and immediately return to work.

Inwardly, I prayed for strength. I considered myself agnostic, so I wasn't sure what or to whom I was praying; but mounting fear and pain made me hope for some source of strength beyond the personal. By mid-afternoon, I was pretty sure I would collapse before quitting time. The convicts on either side of me whispered to me to just keep moving, and they began to help with my swath of brush.

We had been hauled out to the fields that morning by flatbed trailers drawn by tractors. As I attempted to climb back onto the trailer, my legs collapsed beneath me. I rose quickly as two convicts grabbed my arms and pulled me up. They knew. Most everyone had endured a similar introduction to the work ethic in Texas prison farms in the '60s. As we rode toward the building, I knew my mask of bravado was slipping. Everyone else there had endured this trial by fire. A little help was one thing; sympathy for weakness quite another. I would be expected to endure and persevere. And truth be told, I wasn't sure I had it in me. Fear mounted quietly within me.

In the shower, I couldn't hold onto the bar of soap. It stung mercilessly, and my grip was nearly non-existent. The second day was the worst. The broken blisters on my hands made me want to cry out. Vainly, I kept adjusting my grip on the ax to try to take some of the pressure off the most painful blisters. "Grit your teeth, and go on," I told myself. Somehow I did as early words from my father, whom I had rejected absolutely, floated into mind, "That boy can do anything when he makes up his mind."

Day by day, calluses replaced blisters, and my body strengthened. By the third month, I resembled a greyhound. Having lost all body fat, I was now sleek and strong and fast. We were working in the cotton fields, chopping and blocking and eventually picking cotton. I could easily carry my row and help another when it was called for. I had experienced a profound physical transformation more rapidly than I would have dreamed possible.

While undergoing this period of physical transformation, I had the first of two significant encounters with one significant individual. I was given a new position in the line of workers. Now, Michael Lewis worked beside me every day, carrying the row just to my left.

Michael was different from any other inmate I had ever met. To begin with, he seemed at peace. At the same time, despite an inner equanimity, Michael physically struggled with the work. Somewhere, perhaps it was in one of the word power books I had read in jail, I had run across the term "constitutionally inadequate." This is what came to mind as I observed Michael. He looked more like the stereotypical librarian than a convict. Complete with black, horn-rimmed glasses, Michael was slight of build and meek-mannered. His freckled face was so unremarkable, I can only find one word - plain. He appeared out of place, somehow, and was an enigma to me. I was curious about him from the beginning.

The bosses (guards) rode behind us on horses with rifles across their laps. Their obscenities and threats filled the air throughout the day. "Goddammit, you better git on down that row, you sorry old thang." Or, more personally, "You better git your sorry ass down that row, old Lewis."

I often helped Michael a little. Perhaps it was his mysterious manner that caused me to want to help him. I'd like to think I felt some compassion. Although I was largely unconscious and self-centered in those days, I remembered those who had helped me in my first days there. For Michael, every day was still an enormous challenge physically. My recent physical transformation made it easy for me to keep up and help him as well. So I did. Although talking was prohibited, he would whisper, "Thank you," out of the side of his mouth. His voice was soft and had an authenticity to it. At the end of the workday, as we rode back to the building on trailers, I attempted to engage Michael in surreptitious conversation. He would politely decline. Bringing one finger to his lips and turning his face away from any visible bosses, he would shake his head ever so slightly from side to side.

One particularly hot and humid day, we were blocking cotton. That is, we were cutting out a few of the new plants with a hoe, leaving space for the remaining plants to flourish. Salt tablets were passed out at water break to help us stay hydrated. We were pushing hard that day, moving down the rows as fast as we could. I glanced to my left and realized Michael had dropped behind again. As I turned to go back after him, I beheld Michael sitting in the middle of his row with one arm in the air, calling out in a soft and respectful voice, "Laying it down here, boss."

In a maximum security unit of the Texas penitentiary, there are many crimes one can commit and for which one will undoubtedly be punished. The very worst crime is refusal to work. Hard work is the centerpiece of the Texas prison farm system. Punishment for refusal to work is at least debilitating if not brutal. The most likely punishment for refusal to work is to be thrown in the hole (solitary confinement). The hole is a cell that has no bunk, no mattress, no sink, no commode and no light. There is a hole in the floor in which to perform the normal bodily functions. One is fed a slice of bread and water three times a day and given a balanced meal once every three days. The balanced meal, a form of minimal adherence to federal statutes prohibiting cruel and unusual punishment, generally consists of about a tablespoon each of two vegetables and approximately three ounces of meat.

One always returns to work from the hole, weakened and having lost weight. He is, nevertheless, expected to keep up the pace in the fields. The length of time an individual spends in the hole is determined first, by his willingness to return to work; and second, by the evaluation of his attitude by the warden. It is an understatement to say that going to the hole is considered an undesirable experience by the inmates.

Now, let me interpret Michael's statement, "Laying it down here, boss." This is prison vernacular for "I quit." I ran back to where Michael was sitting. The boss began to shout warnings at him.

"Old Lewis, you better git your ass back to work, goddammit! Don't you make me call the captain over here, you sorry thang."

As I approached Michael, I started blocking his row of cotton, and I committed the crime of talking in the field. I whispered, "Come on, Michael, just get up and walk. I'll carry your row." I thought he was exhausted and was offering to do his work and mine in order to keep him from being arrested for this unpardonable crime. The boss ignored my smaller crime of talking, probably in the hope Michael would get up and go back to work. I guessed the boss wasn't particularly anxious to see Michael punished since he never caused problems and was clearly one who lacked physical stamina.

As I turned my head toward Michael, I saw something new in his face. There was an aura, a presence of calm resolve. He looked me straight in the eye and with great force said, "Mark, you don't understand. I know what I'm doing." I thought I saw a trace of a smile on his lips and a glint in his eyes.

The boss was moving toward us on his horse. "Git on back to work, Pope."

I turned away, then back toward Michael. His head was hanging down now. I stumbled, turned again and walked, then jogged back up to the line. I felt confused and, even more, curious. What was it about this guy? He had to know the consequences of quitting. Yet, he seemed altogether unperturbed.

Several days later, I overheard Sonny, the building tender, talking to another building tender. Apparently, the other building tender had the duty of helping feed the prisoners in the hole. He was talking about Michael. He said the warden had offered several times to let Michael out, asking him if he was ready to go back to work. He said Michael always answered the warden, "No, sir. No, thank you, sir."

Alex had concluded that "Lewis is a crazy son of a bitch."

Personally, I was impressed. Although outwardly frail, Michael apparently had some kind of inner strength. Either that or Alex was right - he was just a crazy son of a bitch. Perhaps the strangest part of his behavior was his tendency to be gracious and polite, two traits as rare in a maximum security unit of the Texas penitentiary as one imagines are ice cubes in hell.

Michael Lewis was still in solitary confinement in late summer of 1970, when I was transferred to Jester, a pre-release unit of the Texas Department of Corrections. In this unit, one is required to work only a half-day. Mandatory classes are given in pre-release to prepare the inmate to re-enter society. The classes teach one how to obtain a driver's license, how to get a social security card, how to apply for a job and other such things. Although the classes are regarded with derision by most inmates, the truth is, many inmates need them. After years of incarceration, the toughest of inmates may secretly fear re-entry into the free world.

One day, about two weeks into the six week pre-release program, I was standing in line at the chow hall and glanced up to see new arrivals entering. There among them stood Michael Lewis. Something inside me immediately leapt. Now I could ask him the questions that had been burning within me. There were no rules against talking in pre-release. That night, I finally had my chance. I was particularly curious to know why he appeared so unperturbed with being in prison. Why had he chosen to go to the hole and declined to leave when given the opportunity? Though I couldn't have said it at the time, I wanted to know what his values were. What follows is Michael's explanation to me. He never said I believe this or that or the other thing. He spoke from a point of view of some authority; an inner authority it seemed to me.

"Mark, I am a student of spiritual teachings. These teach one how, among other things, to transcend the mind. Ultimately, we learn that the universe is a single, interconnected system of intelligent energy, of which we are all a part. The goal of these teachings" he said, "is to realize oneself to be united with all creation and its Source.

"We must learn to calm our minds and our emotions, Mark, because what we think and feel is creative. We are always experiencing the results of prior thoughts and feelings. We must also learn to use our minds in a positive and constructive manner regardless of our circumstances. If we can do that, our circumstances will improve as a result.

21

"You and I," continued Michael, "have been experiencing some rather difficult conditions lately. I was tried, found guilty and sentenced to prison, for a crime I did not commit. On the surface, that seems unfair. However, I know I have been reaping the results of past negative thoughts and feelings. In mystical traditions, this is known as the law of cause and effect. This universal law is neither good nor bad. It is simply the law of the universe.

"Among other things, the mystical traditions teach meditation, a technique for transcending the mind. Perhaps someday you'll want to learn this technique, Mark. I chose freely to go to the hole in order to have time to meditate. I didn't eat the small amounts of food they gave me. I dumped them in the hole. They only give you enough to keep the digestive system working, and that keeps you hungry. Fasting is another practice spiritual teachings advocate. After about three days of no food, the digestive system is allowed to rest, and the hunger stops. At that point, the mind naturally calms down, and one may more easily access deeper states of consciousness. In deep meditation we realize more and more that we are united with all life and that life is ultimately fair and very good."

I asked Michael about his personal life. He said he had been an accounting student at the University of Texas when he was arrested for possession of drugs. The drugs, he told me, had belonged to some friends who had been riding in the car with him. The district attorney had wanted to make an example of him. In his campaign for reelection, the D. A. had promised to be tough on crime.

Although I didn't know what one was, I had met my first mystic. Michael Lewis had been convicted and sentenced to five years for a crime he had not committed. Not only was he without resentment, he actually saw the experience as spiritually valuable. I would like to say that I went right to work changing my own attitude; that I really understood what he was telling me. It wouldn't be true. Yes, something was stirring within me. I intuitively sensed the truth behind his words. Yet, it would take a while longer, and one more major crisis, for these seed-thoughts to begin to bear fruit.

A few weeks later, I walked out of the Texas penitentiary. Free again. I will never forget that day. I wore khakis and a plaid shirt furnished by the prison system. They gave me a small brown envelope with $50 cash in it. I stood on the street looking up at the bluest sky I had ever seen. I heard birds chirping and felt the wind on my face. The whole world suddenly seemed more beautiful, more precious and more pregnant with possibility than ever.

Perhaps it was my awareness of the contrast between incarceration and freedom. For some fifteen months, I had not peed without permission. In the fields, we had been required to ask, "Pour it out over here, boss?" I now felt electrified by release from such limitation. Inwardly, I renewed my decision to stay free this time, no matter what it took. I had to find a new way to be in the world.

With this experience of freedom, I felt energy erupting and coursing through me. I was feeling something I had rarely, if ever felt. So rarely had I felt what I now experienced that I had no word for it. I would spend a great deal of my life attempting to replicate the feeling I had that day. I would succeed at times. I would fail miserably at others.

The feeling I had that day was a profound, even ecstatic, gratitude. The light of spiritual awareness was beginning to dawn, but the darkness wasn't done with me yet.

## Chapter 3
## Facing a Life Sentence: Initial Awakening

In the penitentiary, the outside world is referred to as the free world. And whether anyone wants to admit it or not, the idea of stepping out into the free world is not only filled with excitement, it is also frightening and filled with questions.

"How will I make a living? Where will I live? Should I admit to my past when applying for work? Will anyone take a chance on me?"

Fortunately, I had some help waiting for me. My former wife, Ann, and my mother both had offered me a place to stay. Through the grace of a friend of my mother's, and also through some assistance that was given me by the state's Vocational Rehabilitation Program, I was able to attend both the Houston Cocktail Bartender's School in the evenings and San Jacinto Jr. College during the days.

In bartender's school, I had met Pope (his first name). Coincidentally, we shared the same birthday, July 3rd. Pope had long hair and dealt in antiques. He had a tiny apartment furnished with antiques, and he was tuned in to metaphysics and mysticism. His girlfriend, Constance, was equally tuned in. They were planning to attend a lecture on meditation and invited me to come along. We were all eventually initiated in Transcendental Meditation and given our secret mantras, a Sanskrit word or sound, presumably with a mysterious sacred meaning, to be used as a device for focusing attention inwardly.

I recall a Woody Allen movie with a brief scene showing a young man on the phone with a look of desperation asking, "What do I do? I forgot my mantra." In another scene a bearded guru, resembling Maharishi Mahesh Yogi, the founder of Transcendental Meditation, is standing at a urinal. Despite the parody of the newly popular saffron robed "masters" and their teachings, I was served by these teachings and practices. The Transcendental Meditation organization taught their students to view conscious mind activity as clouds rolling by and to focus more and more on the mantra in an effortless fashion.

"Do not resist the conscious thought process," they said. "Just realize when you are identified with thought and let go. Return your attention to the mantra."

Pope, Constance and I practiced meditation. We compared notes on our experiences, and we read and read. We frequented the metaphysical bookstores and ravenously consumed everything we could get our hands on.

My grades at the Jr. College were good. In one class, I excelled. History had never been my favorite subject, but the teacher, Patsy Goss, was so excited about what she taught it was contagious. Since I did well in her class, Patsy Goss took some interest in me and discovered I was in bartender's school at night. She told me that she and her husband owned an old restaurant and nightclub on the San Jacinto River, which they were busy remodeling. They had applied for a liquor license and would need a bartender.

Pope and I graduated from bartender's school. Pope went to work for a nightclub in Houston. I went to work for Patsy Goss and her husband at the Riverside Inn in Channelview, a small town on the outskirts of Houston. Constance was working as a cocktail waitress for another Houston nightclub. We continued to visit one another, and we continued to read metaphysics and practice meditation.

When the spring semester at San Jacinto Jr. College ended, Patsy Goss and her husband offered me the manager's job at work. Patsy suggested I consider whether work or higher education was more important to me at that point in my life. I accepted the manager's job.

As business increased, I eventually offered Pope and Constance jobs as head bartender and head waitress for the club. Since the club was located in East Houston, considered a redneck side of town to us, Pope and Constance were not exactly excited about the offer. Also, they complained about the distance they would have to drive. As an incentive, I offered Pope and Constance the large, furnished mobile home (located on the nightclub property) that had been given to me to use by the owners. They finally agreed. I moved to an apartment.

During meditation one morning that summer, I felt a warm stream of energy moving up my spinal column. It entered my head and caused it to fill with light. A general feeling of extreme well-being filled me. It didn't last.

One Saturday night, late in the summer of 1971, our riverside nightclub was raided by the Harris County Sheriff's Department, the Texas Department of Public Safety and the Channelview Police Department. They were looking for drugs. It turned out the conservative-minded residents of East Houston were offended by the presence of long-haired hippies. My hair was now long, too, and our clientele was comprised of many long-haired types, attracted by the rock music being played on some evenings. Someone had reported that drugs were for sale there.

After a long search of the nightclub, the frustrated police officers, having found nothing, entered the mobile home being used by Pope and Constance. Their search warrant covered the entire property, they said, and the mobile home was on the property. Here they discovered marijuana, hashish and the paraphernalia - rolling papers and pipes - used to smoke them. Pope, Constance and I were arrested on three felony counts: two for possession of drugs and one for possession of narcotics paraphernalia. The possession charges were felonies, and the paraphernalia was a separate felony. We were booked and placed in detention in the Harris County Jail pending trial. Bail bond was set at $100,000 per charge, per individual. That was $300,000 for each one of us. To put this in perspective, individuals charged with murder are often released on lower bonds.

Pope and I were placed in the same tank. He was frightened. I was enraged. I wasn't guilty, and my righteous indignation grew by the hour. I attempted to extract a promise from Pope that he would plead guilty, if necessary, in order to clear me of the charges. Since he had never been arrested, I told him, he would almost certainly receive a probated sentence. I, on the other hand, had a criminal record and would probably be returned to prison, perhaps for a lengthy term if I weren't cleared of the charges.

"Besides," I pressured him, "you are guilty, and I am not."

Pope and Constance were from well-to-do families and had no trouble obtaining counsel. Their attorney quickly filed a motion to lower their bonds to a more reasonable amount, and within days they were out. I was alone, in jail, and charged with crimes I didn't commit. Eventually, I was assigned a court-appointed attorney, but the court refused to lower my bond because of my long record of prior arrests. The district attorney notified my lawyer that the district attorney's office intended to make an example of me. They were cracking down on drugs. There would be no bargaining in my case. The prosecuting attorney was certain of my guilt and intended to ask the jury to give me a life sentence.

All this news served to further fire my righteous indignation. I told my lawyer to get in touch with Patsy Goss and her husband. They would certainly explain to the court that I was not living in the mobile home. My lawyer reported that they had closed the club. The bad publicity had destroyed their business. They couldn't be found to comment.

I told my lawyer to get in touch with Pope and Constance. Weren't they willing to admit their guilt to keep me from going to prison for life for something they did? My attorney told me that their attorney had advised them to plead not guilty. The fear, frustration and rage mounted. Constance came to see me at first, but I'm sure my attitude discouraged further visits. I was livid. I tried to convince her that they should be willing to take the rap off of me.

My attitude was growing more and more negative. My court-appointed attorney seemed incompetent and appeared to offer no hope. He wasn't able to find anyone willing to testify in my defense. Eventually, the attorney representing Pope and Constance came to see me. He said Pope and Constance were concerned for me. He knew I wasn't guilty. But, he explained, his job was to protect his clients. He couldn't ask them to jeopardize themselves to save me. Confidentially, he agreed that my court-appointed attorney might not be up to the task and he offered to represent me. I was grateful and accepted. He warned me, however, that thus far he had nothing to work with in my defense.

Some three months into this jailhouse experience, I picked up a small book entitled *As a Man Thinketh* by an eighteenth century mystic named James Allen. To paraphrase this book, it said:

"If you are in the gaol (jailhouse) or almshouse (poorhouse) right now, you are there by virtue of the thought seeds you have planted and nourished in the garden of your mind; and you are the Master

27

Gardener. The good news is, since your experience is the result of attitudes developed over time, you can also change your experience by changing your attitudes. As any gardener knows, there is no need to become angry with weeds (negative attitudes). Just pluck them out and set them aside. Cease giving them nourishment (attention). Nourish only that which you want." Mr. Allen further suggested that blame, resentment and anger were among the most destructive thoughts and feelings we can harbor, for they inevitably result in experiences of lack, limitation and bondage. "Love," suggested Mr. Allen, "is the most liberating state of consciousness."

For the first time since leaving prison, I began to remember what Michael Lewis had told me in the penitentiary. The recollection was shocking. I was living out the same pattern he had described. I was innocent, and the world appeared to be unjust. Yet Michael had said the lesson is to undergo such experiences without resentment. And here, in this tiny book, was hope and a reminder of the applicable spiritual principles. Also, if what Mr. Allen was saying was true - if I was responsible, if my attitudes were causative - then I held the key to changing things. Once I recovered from the shock, I decided to take a mental inventory of my attitudes. I was further shocked into humility to discover I resented nearly everyone I knew. I had been living my whole life with thoughts and feelings of blame and resentment. I realized I saw myself as a victim.

Following Mr. Allen's advice, in the best way I could imagine, I began a practice of mental and emotional forgiveness. I began to visualize all the people I had known thus far and hold them in the mind's eye. I would apologize to them for having blamed and resented them. I would say things like, "I am sorry I have hated you and blamed you. You are just a human being like me, and you were probably doing the best you could. I am really sorry, and I hope you are able to forgive me. But no matter what, I can't afford to blame you anymore because it is hurting me."

I was highly motivated to practice these spiritual disciplines. If it were true, as Michael Lewis and James Allen had suggested, that we could change our experience through changing our attitudes, then there was everything to gain and nothing to lose, particularly when facing a life sentence. I practiced steadily and consistently, day in and day out. Before long, I began to feel the fear and anger subsiding. I wasn't in a state of tranquility, but I was no longer filled with negative emotion either.

The first manifestation to follow this inner practice of forgiveness occurred while engaging in my daily pastime - playing poker. We played for script. Script was our currency and represented the money that one had on the books or that a visitor had left for you. With it, one bought envelopes, stamps, candy, cigarettes and the like. While playing poker, I was privately practicing my discipline, attempting to forgive others. My attention was on the poker game only minimally.

I began to win more than usual. The more I practiced my discipline, the more I won. After three to four weeks, I began to win in phenomenal fashion. After six weeks, I opened a loan shop, loaning script for short periods at what, I now realize, were exorbitant rates of interest. Under my bunk, I had cardboard boxes filled with cigarettes, candy and everything else that could be purchased in jail. Within the jailhouse community, I had become exceedingly wealthy.

Approximately four and a half months into my stay, as I awaited the slowly grinding wheels of justice, I was transferred to another cell block or tank. In this tank, I found a copy of *Be Here Now* by Ram Dass. In the book, I read about fasting. It reminded me that fasting not only gives the digestive system a rest, it also frees energy and may lead to expanded states of consciousness (shades of Michael Lewis again). I was already meditating privately while lying on my bunk. This, of course, is not the correct posture. Yet it was the only way I knew of practicing meditation without revealing that fact to everyone around me. And I can say, unequivocally, it would not have been popular, in those days, to reveal such practices in the Harris County jail. It is an understatement to say attitudes would not have been receptive.

I embarked upon a fasting experience. After the third or fourth day, even though feeling weak, the hunger left me just as Michael had said. I hid the fact that I was fasting from fellow inmates as well. On the tenth day of the fast, as I lay on my bed meditating, I noticed a body lying on a bunk directly below me. Then I noticed that "I" seemed to be somewhere near the ceiling of the cell, looking down. It slowly dawned on me that the body I was looking down upon was my own, and this other "I" was not located in a body. Two realizations occurred. These realizations occurred without thought. However, in order to convey them, I have translated them into words as best I can.

First, I realized that I am not my body. I have a body, but the body is a vehicle in which "I" live. I did not, at the time, identify myself as spirit or anything else because there was no thought. I only knew I was not the body. Secondly, I realized that I am not my conscious mind. I have a conscious mind, and its nature is to think, but I am not that mind. I saw my body lying there in a jailhouse cell, and I saw my mind was attempting to forgive as best it could, and yet it was still having thoughts of fear.

I felt a sense of indescribable compassion in relation to my body and my conscious mind, as if these were attributes of mine, which needed my acknowledgment from this elevated or transcendental perspective. Here, words become even more inadequate.

I became aware that, until this moment, I had lived with the underlying, unconscious belief that I was fundamentally flawed. Because of this, I believed I deserved the pain and difficulty I had experienced. Now, as I watched the body and the thoughts flowing through the mind, I saw that the person was not so much flawed as confused, helpless, and perhaps, well-intentioned. Then, in the blink of an eye, I was back in my body looking up at the area of the ceiling from which I had, only moments ago, garnered this nearly incredible new perspective. I felt I had somehow awakened from a dream - a nightmare. I ended my fast.

Not long after this, my attorney visited me. He told me we were scheduled for trial the following month. On all previous visits by him, I had been filled with anxiety and fear. This time, however, I told him that I appreciated all he was doing. I said I knew he was doing the best he could to help me. I told him I was aware that the predicament I was in was not his fault, and I just wanted him to know, no matter what happened, I wouldn't blame him. I said somehow, I felt now that everything would be okay.

He responded with surprise. He said he still had no hopeful news. He asked if something had happened to me. I just said I had had a change of heart. Although I couldn't explain it, inwardly, I felt, no matter what happened to me, I could bear it now; that by resolving to give up blame, I was getting my self back. Or, in other words, I was returning to integrity by giving up the victim role.

After six months in jail, the trial date finally arrived. I was transferred to a holdover cell just outside the courtroom. I could hear the courtroom proceedings, but only barely. After about an hour, I heard a gavel bang and saw my lawyer come walking around the corner and up to my cell. He asked me, "Are you ready to go home, Mark?"

I looked at him in complete surprise.

He explained, "All three cases against you have been dropped on the basis of illegal search and seizure. One night about a month ago, I opened a law book to a case involving search warrants. The judge had ruled a search warrant to be illegal when not naming the address, city, county and state of the property to be searched. I then took out a copy of the search warrant in your case and noticed that it named an address on River Road, Harris County, Texas. There was no city named.

"The judge realized that any conviction obtained would eventually be overturned in the appellate courts, so he decided to save the taxpayers' money. He has found the search warrant to be illegal. Therefore, any evidence obtained by the search warrant cannot be introduced in court. The state now has no evidence against any of you, and all cases have been dismissed. You are free!"

I was stunned. Was this the result of my inner work? I knew I had changed. Yet I hadn't been prepared for such a dramatic result. I felt lifted by something I could not name. Again, I was filled with gratitude and wonder. Yes, I was free again. And this time, I walked out of locked doors, never to be locked up again.

Regarding his spiritual awakening, Eckhart Tolle says in *The Power of Now,* "the intense pressure of suffering that night must have forced my consciousness to withdraw from its identification with the unhappy and deeply fearful self… this withdrawal must have been so complete that this false, suffering self immediately collapsed, just as if a plug had been pulled out of an inflatable toy."

In my case, there seems only to have been a partial and temporary withdrawal of consciousness from such identification with the suffering self. For, I returned not only to the body, but also to identification with the *little me*. I would continue to undergo inflations and deflations time and time again, without understanding why.

Nonetheless, I now knew there to be a spiritual dimension to life. I had re-entered my body with this awareness. Through this experience, I had been given access to new transcendental resources. I would now begin to experience expanded or heightened states of consciousness and glimpses into spiritual awakening on a more and more regular basis.

# Chapter 4
## Psychotherapy: A New Point of Reference

My miraculous release, after six months in jail facing a life sentence, left me stunned for weeks, unsure what to do or how to adjust to having been introduced to another dimension to life. Although still very mixed and confused with the ego of the criminal, another kind of motive - a movement that was coming from the spiritual or transcendental dimension - began to operate through me. There would still be a great deal of suffering and lapses into complete unconsciousness. Nonetheless, I would now be driven by a longing for more spiritual understanding and experience. This desire was fueled by a deep passion. In retrospect, it seems that life was living me and guiding me into and through a sacred curriculum.

Although I have rarely made decisions according to a grounded sense of practicality, I understood that I needed to learn to take care of myself and provide for myself in ways that fit the conventions of the world and its values. So I returned to the one way I had learned to earn a living; I took a job as a bartender. At first, I had to take any job I could get and didn't earn much. Within a short time, however, I gained a reputation in the nightclub business in Houston for being friendly, honest and hardworking. I had taken the internal stance I first learned from Michael and later practiced in jail. I was trying to develop constructive attitudes and treat people with respect, in the belief that these kinds of motives and actions tended to produce positive results. My attempts in this direction seemed to bear fruit. Within a year, I was offered a position as bar manager.

In late 1972, I bought a 1965 Mercedes Benz 190. It may have been the least expensive model and several years old. Yet for me, it was an important symbol of a new and better life. Also, I had my own home - a little garage apartment behind a large, two-story Victorian house in the Montrose District of Houston.

In 1973, I was hired as the manager of Smuggler's Notch, a nightclub on Richmond Avenue. It was my first opportunity to assume the full responsibility of management. The nightclub was owned by a large consortium and had been neglected for some time. Business was all but dead. I had asked for and received a small budget with which to restructure and rebuild the business, according to an idea I had for creating a new kind of disco.

First, I hired Ronnie West, who was a part of my life again. He too, was intent upon staying free by living differently. I taught Ronnie to tend bar and told him about my sense that one important key to success was to create a good feeling in the environment, and I knew that "good vibes" had mostly to do with people. Ronnie and I purchased a sophisticated sound system, complete with dual turntables, concert quality speakers and echoplex. We built a stage and enclosed it in royal blue curtains. I hired another friend to spin records and dressed him to look like Merlin the Magician. The music of Santana, the Doobie Brothers, Van Morrison, the Beatles and the Moody Blues exploded as the curtains opened to Merlin amid clouds of simulated smoke.

Our small advertising budget was used to make and distribute fliers throughout the neighborhood. Within sixty days, we had achieved success. We were open six days a week and packed every night. On weekends, we charged a small cover charge, and still had a line waiting for admittance throughout the evening. We now employed five bartenders and as many cocktail waitresses.

I applied for admission to the University of Houston and was accepted. In the daytime, I pursued my undergraduate studies, with an emphasis on philosophy and psychology, and managed the nightclub in the evenings.

One evening, on a night off from the nightclub, while reading an essay by philosopher, David Hume, I experienced a shift in consciousness. One moment I was sitting in my little garage apartment. The next moment my little garage apartment was sitting inside of me. Once again, I had somehow been moved into a transcendental experience. I had no point of reference for this experience, and yet I knew it was real - far more real than the world of words and thoughts I had just been reading. Somehow my sense of self had expanded; the boundaries of the *little me* had partially dissolved. As quickly as this expanded awareness arrived, it receded. I glanced down at the textbook I had been reading and smiled. I had glimpsed the limitations of the intellect. In the blink of an eye I realized there would be no satisfying answers for me in the philosophical realm.

In my studies of psychology, I did find a point of reference for my mystical experiences, however. Abraham Maslow described what he called "peak experiences" as elevated or expanded states of consciousness. "That's it," I thought. And he verified my conclusion. These experiences were not the result of intellectual pursuit. According to Maslow, they arose spontaneously from a transcendental Source.

Larry Ford, one of my college classmates, introduced me to a little book on the mystical life entitled *The Practice of the Presence of God* by Brother Lawrence. He also recommended other books on the pioneering work being done in the field of psychology. These so-called *humanistic* and *transpersonal* approaches took into account a transcendental realm. I decided that I would be more likely to find what I was looking for in psychotherapy than in a college classroom.

I dropped out of college and joined a gestalt therapy group. It proved to be a rich experience. In group, I began to discover that it was possible to remove my mask; go below my persona, and talk about my feelings. For the first time in over a decade, I cried... and I was able to do so openly. Something magical began to happen. The more I revealed myself, the more I was willing to be vulnerable, the better I felt about myself. I had found a place where I could tell the truth about my fears, my sadness, my insecurities, my wild past and my peculiar spiritual experiences - all of it. And I was not simply accepted for my willingness to be transparent, I was appreciated for it.

Occasionally, I had private sessions with my therapist. In one session, Dr. Androse explained to me that I had an internal guidance system, which I could learn to rely upon. He said we all have a kind of visceral reaction to other people. He said that if we paid attention to this feeling-level response to others, it would reveal to us which people would be most helpful, most nurturing and, therefore, most valuable to us. These he termed *nutritious*. "That is," he said, "these people will naturally support you in unfolding and in being authentic. Relationships with those who are nutritious are characterized by a feeling of trust."

"On the other hand," said Dr. Androse, "certain individuals can be *poisonous* and hamper your growth. These individuals," he hastened to add, "are not bad or evil. They simply do not serve your unfoldment at this time. When you feel uncomfortable, or when you feel the need to pretend in the presence of others, Mark, you can know that these relationships are not healthy for you. At another stage of development," said Dr. Androse, "these same individuals may not cause you any discomfort at all. In a nutshell, you can learn to listen to and trust your feelings about others."

I learned this lesson slowly at first. More often, I ignored it and paid the price. One case of applying the lesson would soon prove its value in a somewhat dramatic fashion. This time, it wouldn't entail any pain at all.

# Chapter 5
## Mrs. Wells and the Golden Pyramid

"Astrology is a pseudo science!" Such was the teaching, as expressed in my high school sociology textbook, and so I informed my mother whenever she would speak to me about the subject. For the last two years, she had been repeatedly suggesting I consult with Mrs. Wells, an astrological reader. In the summer of 1973, Mother made the suggestion again. This time, however, it was different. Instead of attempting to convince or otherwise persuade me, she simply seemed to be delivering a message, "Mark, I went to see Mrs. Wells the other day. She told me to tell you it's time for you to come see her. She said I should let you know. She has some things she wants to tell you."

Since Dr. Androse had recently taught me to trust my gut feelings, it occurred to me I should at least be open to the possibility this woman might be someone I could trust. I noticed that I didn't feel any resistance to or uneasiness about the idea. It seemed somehow provocative. Even logic seemed to suggest I not judge this person I had never met. "I'll go see her and trust myself by listening to her and to my own inner responses to what she has to say," I thought. So I called her, made an appointment and proceeded toward my first experience of being "read."

When I arrived at her address at the appointed time, the first thing I noticed was that no sign was visible. In fact, there never had been signs, I learned. I had associated astrologers and psychic readers with large, hokey signs advertising their skills and abilities. Mrs. Wells worked by referral only and declined many referrals. I would guess she was well beyond seventy years old when I met her. She explained that she only worked a few hours a day now, because she needed more time for rest and meditation.

I arrived at Mrs. Wells' modest little white clapboard home in Pasadena, Texas. It wasn't far from where I had grown up in South Houston. As I entered her home, she seated me in an old, easy chair and herself on a sofa across a coffee table in her living room. She took up an old deck of standard playing cards and began to shuffle them, laying out three and four cards at a time while she talked. She actually never mentioned anything about astrology, even though she had asked for my birth date, time and place in advance of my visit. Nor did she pay much attention to the cards she was laying out. She would close her eyes each time she began to address another subject. I watched her carefully, and it seemed as if her eyeballs were rolling upward behind her closed eyelids.

She began, "I've known about you for quite a long time. I know your life has been difficult. Things will begin to improve for you now, though. You will find a man teaching in a golden pyramid-shaped building. He will prove very helpful. I believe you will find his teachings very comfortable.

"Son, you have a spiritual work of your own to do eventually. You must begin to prepare yourself now. You are very receptive," she said, "and that will help. Just continue to follow the path you feel most right about." I was struck by the similarity between her suggestion that I follow the path I felt most right about and Dr. Androse's recent teaching about learning to trust my feelings about others.

"I see much good for you in the future. Many people will be helped by your work. But there are difficulties along the way. It has been given to me to help you. It is my honor and privilege to do all I can for you. You may come to see me anytime you want. Don't worry about money. If I can help you, that's enough."

I had been involved in all kinds of hustles in my life, and I had never seen one where money wasn't of utmost interest. Of course, Mrs. Wells was no charlatan. Following along the lines of listening and trusting my inner responses to others, I drew the following conclusions: I liked her; she seemed sincerely interested in my well being; I felt good being with her. Much of what she told me was too vague to be called definite advice. However, the man and the golden pyramid seemed concrete. I decided to remain open to this idea, peculiar as it sounded. It was good, too, to hear her reinforce the idea of trusting myself.

As I took my leave, I thanked her and tried to pay her. She declined. "No," she said, "I've been receiving spiritual guidance for several years to try to assist you. I've seen that, with some help, you will eventually accomplish an important spiritual work. Just call me, and come when you feel guided to do so." I did return to see Mrs. Wells, and she never accepted payment. She was always helpful, and I always felt gifted by her.

Several months later, my mother called and told me she had found a church that she thought I would like. A few weeks later she mentioned it again. The third time she mentioned this church, she said, "Mark, you really ought to come and listen to this man. He is not like any other minister I've ever heard. They just finished building a new building, and it's really wonderful," she said. "It's in the shape of a pyramid - a golden pyramid." I caught my breath….

All attempts to logically explain or understand such events are destined to failure. The noted psychologist, Carl Jung, coined the term "synchronicity" to describe those events that do not follow the law of cause and effect. He defined this term as the "acausal connecting principle," by which he almost certainly intended to convey that there are events and circumstances that are mysterious to the surface consciousness, but which reveal much deeper connections than can be seen or explained. This term, *synchronicity,* and another, *grace,* seem to best characterize much of my life experience.

The man teaching in this golden pyramid was Dr. John Rankin. The church was the Unity Church of Christianity. To say I found his church comfortable would be an understatement. I felt I had come home. There were hundreds in attendance listening to his words of love and wisdom. The teachings were simple and easy to understand, and the resonance within me was unmistakable.

I had never been comfortable with religion as I had known it. I felt there was something deeply wrong about a God that would create men and women, cast them into a world filled with temptation, and then condemn them to eternal hell for succumbing. Dr. Rankin had something very different to say about all this. "God is Love, and we have each been created in the image and likeness of this Creator, which," said Dr. Rankin, "implies that our true nature is unconditional love. At no time does God condemn us. We do, however, out of ignorance, condemn ourselves and others, thereby creating a hell on earth. We also have the ability to resurrect ourselves from this hell, at any point along the way. We only need to change our attitudes - and keep them changed. Ultimately, we are to realize ourselves to be one with God or Love; therefore, individual expressions of this Love."

I definitely felt a resonance with Dr. Rankin. At the heart of his teaching was Love and Undeviating Presence as the Ground of our Being. Beneath the words about Love, I could also feel what I would eventually recognize as the frequency to which I would be in spiritual service... the awakening of the spiritual heart, which is the experience of Grace or Divine Love. John Rankin would be my first spiritual mentor and a life-long friend.

I had no idea what I was setting myself up for in my pursuit of spiritual awakening. Perhaps it is best I didn't. My attitudes had been negative for years and the roots of my ignorance were still far below the surface. Thank God for naivete. The gargantuan ordeal of individual transformation is a slow, evolving process for most, and, in my case, did not lead immediately to any Godhead. Neither, though, was I to draw any more go-to-jail cards in the game of life.

# Chapter 6
# Theodore's 19th Century Fox:
# A Career Move

"Do you see that guy sitting at the end of the bar? He's one of the best bartenders in Houston." These comments were made by James Benford, who, at the moment, was tending bar at Theodore's 19th Century Fox, a new nightclub in the Montrose District of Houston. He was talking to John Moss, the manager, about me. I was hunched over a beer, wearing jeans, a T-shirt and sporting several days' growth of beard.

I had been involved in an auto accident in which my back had been injured. I had been rear-ended by a petroleum company truck while sitting at a stop light in my little Mercedes. I had been hospitalized for several days, and unable to work for some two months. As a result of the accident, I had received an insurance settlement of several thousand dollars. Thus far, I had not felt moved to seek further employment.

To this day, I still have to wonder what caused James Benford to recommend me. Yes, I was a skilled and honest bartender. James, however, was not. In fact, I had fired him after only four days at Smuggler's Notch for stealing. As I sat at the bar in Theodore's, I observed him at it again. He was using the "olive method." That is, every time he placed money for a cocktail in the register without ringing it up, he would transfer an olive from one section of the fruit tray to another. Then, at the end of the night, he would simply count the olives in the second section, multiply the number of olives times the price of a cocktail, and pocket that amount while reconciling his cash drawer.

James had been pointing me out to John Moss because John was apparently looking for another bartender. John came around the bar, introduced himself, and asked if we could sit down and talk. He and Ted Scruggs, the owner, had great plans for Theodore's, he said. He knew he needed good help to build the business. He looked right past my tawdry appearance and asked me about my experience. Within only a few minutes, he offered me a job. I told him I didn't think it was the right place for me. John persisted though. He knew he had offered me a decent wage. "Why not?" he asked. "What would it take to change your mind?"

"Well," I said, "I can see some problems here that need to be corrected before you could be successful. I'm not sure you really want to hear about it from me. But," I said, "if you really want to hire me, I would accept the job with two stipulations. First, I'm very involved in some spiritual studies and practices, and I don't really want a full-time job. I'd only be willing to pull four shifts a week. Secondly, I'd ask you to give strong consideration to my recommendations on the hiring and firing of bartenders. If I were going to work here, I would want to help build the right atmosphere. That begins with the right kind of help."

"So you want to be a part time bar manager?" he asked.

"No," I answered. "It's that I know some good people, and I want to work with people I like. I'm sure it will help your business, too. The right people will put out the right vibes," I said.

John looked at me carefully for a few seconds. Then, without checking a single reference, without even asking me to fill out an application, he agreed. "Well," he said, "I don't know why, but I have a good feeling about you. When can you start?"

"As soon as you fire James Benford," I replied. "He's stealing from you right now. In fact, I couldn't fathom why he would recommend me. I just fired him last summer from Smuggler's Notch for stealing from us there. Maybe he thinks I need a job and will keep my mouth shut if he helps me get one. I don't really know. But I know we can't trust him, and I can't work with him. It wouldn't be right for me. You see, John, I used to be a thief. In fact, I've done a lot of time. I don't want any part of that world anymore. Even being around it is not healthy for me."

John sat back in his chair looking contemplative. Then he broke out in a huge grin. "Can you start tomorrow and work through the weekend? And do you have anyone in mind to hire, because we're going to need help right away?"

"Yes," I said, "I can start, and don't worry about these whiskers - they'll be gone. I'll make some calls before I come and see who we can get."

This career move led to one of the most enriching periods of my life. I would work for Theodore's for nearly four years, off and on. The flexibility I was given by John allowed me to travel pretty much at will in my pursuit of spiritual interests. I would also gain a model for the successful turnaround of a business that would serve me throughout my career in food and beverage, and later as a consultant specializing in the rebuilding of failing businesses.

Theodore's evolved into a kind of spiritual community. The staff was comprised of eclectic and highly educated bartenders such as Larry Ford, who was also attending the University of Houston; a convicted felon, Ronnie West, whose life was being altered spiritually like my own; a student of microbiology working on his doctorate; a professor of history, and many others with eclectic spiritual interests. The customers loved the place. They were made to feel a part of us. The live music eventually became the best in the city. Local musicians clamored for gigs at Theodore's. As business grew, Ted, the owner, and John, the manager, built an additional bar upstairs and another on a huge courtyard in the rear.

I believe spiritual values were at the heart of our success. That was the upside. For me, there was another side. I was so filled with enthusiasm about spiritual matters that, at times, I know it turned some people off. For many, doing the right thing came naturally. For me, it was new and, as I saw it, remarkable. In fact, fewer remarks may have been wiser. There are those who become so excited about a degree of spiritual awakening that they seemed compelled to talk about it. To a degree, I had become one of those. I was so zealous, I suspect some people were ducking for cover when they saw me coming.

I would suffer, time and again, for this tendency to inflate, a term used by Swiss psychologist, Carl Jung, to describe the tendency of the ego to appropriate the transcendental experience, to claim it for itself.

I was also completely unconscious of my tendency to project my need to learn, or my need to substantiate what I had already learned, and then proceed to tell or teach others what I most needed to learn myself. I would only learn about these unconscious tendencies slowly, through many years of suffering the always attendant deflations. That understanding wasn't mine yet, though. For now, I was just excited about what I viewed as nearly unlimited spiritual potential. A certain grace was at work in my life.

## Chapter 7
## The Neighborhood:
## Sex, Substances, Spiritual Teachers
## and a Meeting with Swami Muktananda

The Montrose District of Houston, in the 1970s, was the epicenter of diversity. For those not living there, for those looking in from the outside, Montrose was seen and described variously as crazy or kooky, immoral, liberal, outrageous, drug-oriented, a hippie-haven, interesting to drive through, a fun place to eat out, or scary as hell to be alone in at night.

In the minds and hearts of those of us who did live there in this era, something very different was going on. There was one common denominator - in Montrose, it was acceptable to be different. The only hard and fast rule was, "Do your own thing as long as it doesn't harm others." Individualism was worshiped with reverence. It was a neighborhood where "neighborhood" was practiced. We helped each other. We conferred visits upon one another, often unannounced. We fed each other without ceremony. One would often spend the night with friends by nonverbal invitation. We shared our homes, cars, food and philosophies of life.

Sexuality found free expression as well. This was the height of the sexual revolution, and I took full advantage. I was living in a sexual paradise. Along with reverence for individuality also came reverence for freedom. Commitments were rare. Long-term commitments were nearly non-existent. If one happened to express a degree of commitment, an escape clause was assumed to be implicit.

For the first time, I was able to move easily between the extremes that had, until now, torn me apart emotionally. The conflict between my need for closeness and my fear of engulfment found a semblance of balance. My relationships with women during these years were warm, sincere and emotionally honest, inasmuch as this was possible for me at the time. Today, I view intimate relationship as a powerful spiritual path for those so inclined. As a spiritual path, however, it is not for the immature or developing psyche. And I was, in many ways, still quite immature.

The Montrose community was devoted to the unfettered exploration of consciousness. All models, methods, tools and perceived gateways to this exploration were appreciated and tested. This definitely included consciousness-altering substances. Yes, these experimentations were illegal. Nevertheless, during this time and in this place, these laws were routinely treated as unnecessarily restrictive at the least, or more extremely, as part of an established but unenlightened societal structure.

At any rate, these substances were in ready supply. Marijuana, psilocybin, mescaline, peyote and LSD all offered temporary glimpses into the expanded states of consciousness that had already begun to visit me. In comparison, meditation seemed like the proverbial slow boat to China. On the other hand, substance-induced states seemed always to dissipate rapidly, and were often followed by a disappointing let-down.

We were a culture devoted to the achievement of higher states of consciousness. We did not recognize the value of ordinary states of consciousness or the need for balance. Life, however, being the true Master Teacher, always insists on balance. Coming back down, crashing was inevitable. The higher we flew, the harder we fell. Equilibrium as a spiritual principle, though unappreciated at the time, nevertheless asserted itself, again and again and again. Not that this wisdom was unavailable to us. Most of us just weren't ready to hear it.

Spiritually speaking, the Montrose neighborhood was a veritable marketplace of paths, disciplines, teachings and teachers. Metaphysics and mysticism flourished, and nearly everyone ran their own independent taste test. I was re-birthed, rolfed, regressed, had my aura cleansed, my chakras balanced, my chart read and listened to psychic channels and instruments galore. More forms of yoga were taught in Montrose in the '70s than Patanjali could imagine. Montrose was a must for most all of those on the metaphysical circuit. Every would-be master, guru and spiritual teacher in America and from abroad seemed to make an appearance.

Early 1974, however, brought rumors of the first truly realized being coming to our neighborhood. *Who is Swami Muktananda?* The word went out. A yogi of the Siddha lineage. A realized being from India is coming! *What does he do?* He awakens the activity of the *kundalini*, the spiritual life-force in sincere seekers. *How?* He brushes you with his peacock feathers.

Really, I was told, the feathers were a symbol. It is said that the male peacock can impregnate the female with a glance. In like manner, it is said that a siddha yogi transmits power to you and awakens this kundalini, this spiritual life-force, that otherwise lies dormant at the base of the spine. Once awakened, this life-force begins its ascent upward along the spinal column, awakening the spiritual centers or chakras along the way. Just to be in the presence of a realized being brings manifold blessings, I was told.

This was all a bit new to me. I'd read about chakras and kundalini in the teachings of other Eastern mystical traditions. But, to be blessed just by being there? Well, what could I lose? I certainly knew I could stand a blessing. Besides, even though I didn't exactly understand, I was getting that *yes* feeling inside.

The night arrived, and I was in attendance. Swami Muktananda was a small, very dark-skinned man, sitting upon a throne-like chair. He was dressed in orange robes and wore a funny little orange hat that resembled a nightcap. He was wearing sunglasses, at night, inside the building. Halloween came to mind. The question looming was, "Trick or treat?"

Every last bit of my Montrose do-your-own-thing training was called into play to support my ability to remain open. "What should a realized being look like?" I wondered. "Who knows? Not me," I thought. At least he looked happy. Indeed, he seemed to be having a great time. After a period of meditation, Muktananda entertained questions from the floor. When he answered, someone would interpret for him. I thought, "If this guy is so enlightened, why can't he speak English? Oh well," I concluded, "What do we, the unenlightened, really know?"

We were meeting in the enormous great room of an old Victorian mansion. There were perhaps three hundred of us packed into the room. Toward the end of the evening, we were invited to come forward and bow down in front of Muktananda, to receive his transmission of spiritual power. No discipleship was necessary we were told. The blessing was freely given. My girlfriend and I both went forward to receive this invisible blessing. Swami Muktananda administered the blessing or transmission by brushing our heads with peacock feathers.

Upon our return to the back of the room, my girlfriend asked me, "Did you feel anything?"

"No, but I'm not sure you're supposed to feel anything right away," I replied.

My companion decided that maybe she had missed "it" somehow. She said, "I don't think I got it. I'm going back up, just to make sure." When she reached the feet of Muktananda for the second time, this little perfected being began to beat her with his peacock feathers. He was laughing and speaking again, in what I can only guess was Hindi.

The translator interpreted, "Muktananada wants to know - did you get it this time?"

Hmmmm...

# Chapter 8
## Unity Village and More Unity Village:
## The Emergence of a Teacher

I cried and cried. I cried in public and I didn't care. I wiped the tears from my eyes and continued to read, and I wept even more.

St. Thomas University is located smack in the middle of the Montrose area, and I was lying on a towel beside the University swimming pool. I had spent about an hour meditating in the Mark Rothko Chapel. This chapel is adorned with the extremely dark works of the artist for whom it is named. I had left the chapel with its reflections of the darkness - an intermingling of blacks, deep purples and occasional touches of red. As I stepped out into the light of a brilliant sunshiny day, I instantly felt a stirring, a sense of being lifted into a supernal realm. An ecstasy arose within me as I was carried swiftly into an awareness of the sacred nature of all life.

I walked across the street to the pool and lay down on the towel I had been carrying and began to read Pearl S. Buck's *Story Bible: New Testament*. The book is not a metaphysical or mystical document. It is the author's attempt to compile the gospels into a single narrative that unfolds in chronological order. As I lay reading, I began to experience the unfolding story, not as that of Jesus but an unfolding within me. As the story moved toward and through a crucifixion, I felt the power of an Unconditional Love capable of facing abandonment and death. My tears felt like the result of an opening into that Love, as well as a cleansing of my perception. It was as if the Christ, as a living interior pattern, was awakening within me. Jesus seemed more like a forerunner, a model for this pattern as potential in us all, than an external savior.

As I reached the story of the resurrection, I was lifted into an even more profound sense of love. As I completed the book and set it aside, tears still streaming down my face, I heard an inner voice say, "Go to Unity Village for Easter."

I arose from the grass, gathered my things and left, contemplating the meaning of my experience and the meaning of the words of the inner voice. As always, the transcendental experience waned. At the time, I had never heard of Unity Village. This was early spring of 1974, and I had only been attending the Unity Church for a few months. At the Golden Pyramid Sunday, I asked about Unity Village and discovered it indeed existed. It was located just south of Kansas City, Missouri.

Unity Village was exactly what the words implied: a small village incorporating a school that trained teachers and ministers; a publication department that distributed the popular *Daily Word* and other works; a retreat department that organized programs for students and members of field churches to attend for spiritual renewal; motels and cottages to accommodate visiting students; a cafeteria that featured standard fare, and, being far ahead of the trend, had served vegetarian cuisine as an option for many years. More specifically, I noted that a retreat was being held at Easter.

One evening, the following week, I was working the bar at Theodore's when an attractive, red-haired woman approached the bar and asked, "Are you Mark?" I answered in the affirmative. She then handed me a yellow, legal-sized sheet of paper with the words *Message to Mark* written across the top of the page. I still hold the majority of this message in the privacy of consciousness since its full meaning is still unfolding. It seemed to prophesy certain events that would come to pass. Two thirds of the way down the page, I read the words, "This retreat will prove to be a turning point in your life."

The wheels of my mind seemed to stop. Was this *the* Easter retreat? If so, how could anyone know about it? I had not mentioned it to anyone. Later, I would become close friends with Lucretia Marcano, or Luke, as we called her. She said she had channeled this message through a method she called "automatic handwriting." She later explained to me that she had not even known my name until it came in the message. Personally, she had no conception of what the message might mean to me.

I had no idea how to fund an excursion to Unity Village on my four-night a week bartender's wages. I was still in a daze from reading Luke's *Message to Mark*, when, moments later, John Moss walked by. I turned slowly toward him and said, "John, I have to go to Missouri for Easter. I need to have the whole week off."

"No problem, Mark. Thanks for letting me know."

I felt as if I was being guided by a mysterious force, and all I could do was acquiesce.

That following Sunday after services, as I loitered in the fellowship hall next door to the Pyramid, my mother and Ann, my former wife, approached me saying, "Mark, we have decided to give you a birthday present. We have to tell you about it now because it will take some planning." (My birthday is in July, and this was still early spring.) "We are giving you a trip to Unity Village, all expenses paid. You can either go to a retreat, or you can attend one of the teacher training sessions this summer. It's up to you."

A sense of Providence and nearly incredible synchronicity gripped me. "Since I am already planning to attend the Easter retreat, I can only say thank you. I felt I was being guided to go, and have already arranged the time off. I just had no idea where the money would come from."

I remember, I was reading Muktananda's autobiography, *A Play of Consciousness*, on the flight to Kansas City en route to Unity Village that Easter. At the time, I was being made privy to an elevated state of consciousness revealing life to be a kind of magical mystery tour; a sacred unfolding of event after event; indeed, a play of consciousness. After deplaning, I was greeted by hosts for the retreat. I found myself riding in a van with a number of other arriving retreatants A powerful sense of expectancy was growing within me.

Upon arriving at Unity Village, I couldn't help but be even further impressed. The grounds were exquisite and perfectly maintained. The architecture was old-world Spanish with red tile on the roofs. And the feeling - it seemed as if the place was enveloped in an otherworldly aura. I noticed that I was the youngest person there. I was also the only male with shoulder length hair and wire-rimmed glasses. I suppose I stood out. No one seemed in the least bit judgmental about my appearance, though.

In fact, many people took an immediate and sincere interest in me.

"Why are you here? Are you going to become a Unity minister?" Or, if they didn't know I was there on retreat, "Are you a ministerial student?"

Some gave me spontaneous readings, "I feel something wonderful is going to happen to you here." And, "You are here for a special purpose."

My response was nearly always the same. "I don't know why I'm here. I just followed my guidance." Most importantly, I kept telling myself over and over again, "I'm open."

During that week at Unity Village, a feeling of grace was growing within me. Everything seemed connected, meaningful, and so purposeful and yet, still quite mysterious. I really didn't know why I had come. I only felt that something important would be revealed. I continued to affirm to myself, "I am open."

We attended classes, meditations, and a variety of events throughout the week. I kept looking for some kind of sign, some sense of what it was I had come to discover. Toward the end of the week, I decided to consult with one of the teachers. We had been told we could call on members of the teaching staff for counseling. I just didn't have any sense of which one to talk to.

Finally, I decided to speak with Gwen Norment. During my time with her, I told Gwen the entire story of what had been happening to me, beginning with the experience at the St. Thomas swimming pool. In fact, I showed her the *Message for Mark*, which Luke had written.

Gwen proved to be the perfect one for me to trust. After hearing my story, she read the message. As she read, tears began to flow down her cheeks. "Mark," she said, "I feel this message is very sacred. Above all else, I would counsel you to keep it private. It is for you only. Don't get me wrong," she continued, "I am honored that you have trusted me. I have learned through the years, however, that these things have a substance to them, and the substance can be diminished if revealed without discrimination. At least wait until you feel a strong sense of guidance before sharing it with others.

"I am not given to know why you are here either. I do think the attitude you have come with is the right one. Just remain open and receptive, and trust the process. Whatever needs to reveal itself to you will do so at the right time."

As we closed the session, I walked outside into heavily falling snow and across a little bridge, which I would later learn is called the Bridge of Faith. In the middle of this bridge, I stopped and stood staring upward at the snowflakes swirling down. In that instant, the inner voice spoke again, saying, "You will return to school here this summer."

Unity Institute for Continuing Education, or U.I.C.E. as it was called, would hold three two-week sessions that summer. These sessions were a part of the preparation required for licensed teachers. Each two-week session included all food and lodging for a set fee. Although very reasonable, it was still beyond my humble earnings. On the one hand, this appeared to be a practical barrier to fulfilling my latest guidance. On the other hand, I was in a state of consciousness such that there was little doubt that the power guiding me would also supply me.

A few hours later, I was in the main hall. An energetic, elderly lady approached me. "Mark, did you figure out why you came here?"

"Yes," I answered. "I'm to return for U.I.C.E. this summer."

"Good," she said. "That's what I thought." With that, she opened her purse, took out a checkbook, tore out a check which had already been made out to me in the amount of $200, and handed it to me. "This should help you with the cost," she said. Before I could respond, she quickly departed.

Minutes later, another woman approached me, a gestalt therapist from Del Rio, Texas. "Mark, have you found out why you came here?"

"Yes," I answered. "I'm to return for U.I.C.E. this summer."

"Good," she said, "That's what I thought." She opened her purse, took out a checkbook and tore out a check already made out to me in the amount of $100, and handed it to me. "This should go toward the school, Mark. Take it with my blessings," she said. She too, turned and departed before I could say more than a quick thank you.

All this, and the sense of expectancy had not subsided. In fact, it was increasing. I felt something else was yet to happen. Now, a new thought had entered my mind. I was to *do* something. I had no idea what that might be.

I lay on my bed in one of the cottages awaiting the final function of the week, a banquet. Perspiration was rolling down my sides. My hands were clammy and my insides quivering. The banquet. I had to do something at the banquet. What was it? And why had this feeling of expectancy grown to resemble fear so much?

I procrastinated until the last minute. Finally, I arose from my bed and walked slowly to the cafeteria. I remember the taste of fear in my mouth. It was metallic. The banquet had been carefully planned. The seating only allowed for the exact number of retreatants registered and the staff. Since I was the last to arrive, there was only one chair unoccupied. It was, coincidentally, beside Gwen Norment, with whom I had consulted just prior to my revelation. She noticed I wasn't eating and asked if I was alright. I confided the reason for my distress.

"I feel like I'm supposed to do something here at the banquet." Then, just as the idea was occurring to me, I added, "I'm not sure, but I think I'm supposed to stand up and speak to the people here." As these words passed my lips, the tension I was feeling increased again. I had a deadly fear of public speaking, dating back to an extremely embarrassing experience in the sixth grade.

"Let me tell you a story about myself, Mark," offered Gwen. "Before I entered the ministry, I worked in theater. One of the things I learned about actors is that some have a feeling that the performance actually comes through them; that something other than their personality is at work. Although they may feel some nervous energy, just prior to going on stage, they have learned to trust that "something else" will come through.

"Other actors actually believe they are, personally, the ones who do the work. I am even aware of one actor who becomes so nervous that he vomits before every performance. He believes he is doing it all. Don't worry," she counseled. "You are fortunate. It is the Christ at work within you. Just let go, and trust that."

At that exact moment, Foster McLeland, the Director of Retreats, was walking past me. I stopped him and asked what the program would be for the night. Among other things, he informed me that Virgil Woodside would be leading us in singing.

"Then there is a microphone available?" I asked.

"Yes," answered Foster.

"I have something I'd like to share. Would that be possible?" I asked.

"Of course," he said. "I'll call you up a little later in the evening."

I entered a state of shock. What was I talking about? I had no idea what I would say, no conscious plan. The request had simply leapt out of my mouth. Nevertheless, I felt committed. "I must go through with it," I thought. Minutes began to feel like centuries as I waited, in a state of consciousness somewhere between utter terror and slight confidence in something unknown.

Finally, Foster McLeland spoke. "In a moment, Virgil Woodside is going to lead us in some singing, but first, one of our fellow retreatants wants to share a few words. Mark?" And with those words, I began the longest walk I had ever taken. As I write these words, I recall it vividly - the fear, the nervous tension, the abject terror that gripped me. I was not certain I would even make it to the podium.

I did make it. As I lifted my leg to step up, I thought I might faint. Then, as I stepped behind the microphone, all fear magically lifted. The slight sense of confidence that had been mine just minutes before became a deep sense of peace, and a conviction of the presence of something transcendental. I spoke. As I spoke, it was as if I were a witness to myself. I could see and hear the words, and yet, once a thought was clothed in voice and left my mouth, it would disappear. I couldn't remember what I'd just said and I still do not recall exactly what was said. In part, I spoke about my profound gratitude to God and to the people who had been the instruments of grace for me. And I expressed the conviction I was feeling at that moment... of the imminent presence of God.

As I finished speaking, I began to return to a different state of consciousness. I became aware that the room was filled with thundering applause. The room seemed to be swirling with movement. People were standing and a few moved toward me and claimed to have been healed as I spoke. Some were laying money at my place-setting. In particular, I noticed one man who was completely still. He seemed to be studying me carefully. It was as if he was the calm at the center of the storm. This man was J. Sig Paulson. Years later, he would become a mentor and, even later, a friend.

I can tell you, it wasn't so much what I said that evening, as it was the power and love with which the words were expressed. Something new emerged in me that night.... It was a teacher.

Back in my room, I counted the money that had come to me in the last twenty-four hours. After counting, I checked in the school catalog. It was within pennies of the amount needed to pay for all three of the two-week sessions that summer.

# Chapter 9
# New Orleans:
# Mad Moses, King Tut and Plans

The following summer, I returned to Unity Village and completed all three sessions of school. The power with which the "teacher" had emerged and expressed itself at Unity Village was not to repeat itself anytime soon. In the meantime, however, the experience did bestow upon me the courage to teach. Over the next three years, I began to do field work toward a teacher's license by teaching adult classes and Sunday school at the Unity Church of Christianity - the Golden Pyramid. I would return to Unity Village on several occasions to take additional courses for credit.

I would also marry and divorce again in a matter of months. Lynn and I never stood a chance. I still failed to appreciate the depth of the opposing forces operating unconsciously within me. On the one hand, I sought relationship out of a need for the sense of security and containment the relationship appeared to offer. On the other hand, my fear of engulfment and my defenses were even stronger. As has been said, "The problem with the unconscious is that it is unconscious."

I continued to work for Theodore's when I was in Houston. But I traveled extensively. During this period, I would visit and/or live for short periods in over a dozen cities, from South Padre Island to the Teton Mountains in Wyoming and from Long Island, New York to change Puerto Escondido, Mexico.

My closest friend, Ronnie West, who had accompanied me in crime and into prison and had assisted me with the success of nightclubs in Montrose, experienced a particularly dramatic spiritual awakening during this period. During a meditation one evening with Luke, our psychic friend, and me, he felt an energy moving up his spinal column that exploded into an experience of white light. He would not enter any formal priesthood. He would pursue his spiritual development by joining me on an eclectic journey. Over time, we shared a number of these obviously divinely guided adventures as the light of spiritual awareness continued to break through to us. One of the experiences we shared follows:

At first glance, I saw a hobo beside the road with his thumb out, begging a ride. A second glance revealed a perceptible twinkle in the eye of a well-worn fellow sojourner. So I stopped. Ronnie and I were on our way to New Orleans. In lieu of any real point to the trip, we had decided upon a visit to the King Tut exhibit there. Really, we had no idea who King Tut was. We just had a feeling about visiting New Orleans. Someone had told us the night before we left that we should go see the King Tut exhibit there.

Our newest travel companion, we learned, had lived for many years in the mountains outside Missoula, Montana, in prayer, meditation and regular communion with the saints. He told of occasional dialogue with the archangels, as well. The university students in Missoula, having been similarly informed during his visits to town for supplies, had nicknamed him Mad Moses, he told us. Mad Moses was not mad. His stories, though far out, were laced with love, goodwill and humor. Our little 1961 Plymouth Valiant fairly shook with laughter for the next 100 miles.

Ronnie and I decided upon lunch at a truck stop near Lafayette, Louisiana. At the table, our conversation centered on ancient advice: Live in the *here and now*; the past is gone and the future yet to be. Here and now is all that's real. Referencing this sage advice with humor, Mad Moses finished another story with the line, "No point in crying over spilled milk." Whereupon, at the very instant he spoke the words, a five-gallon bag of milk, intended to replenish the milk dispenser in the truck stop, burst and emptied its contents on the floor. Spilled milk was instantly everywhere evident. A burst of laughter rose in waves from the three of us.

The other truck stop guests and employees were less appreciative. At first, they stared daggers at us. "What is so damned funny?" their looks seemed to be asking. Then, slowly the thought, "No point in crying over spilled milk" seemed to be telepathically received. Within seconds, everyone in the entire restaurant was roaring with laughter.

God's mad messenger of mirth left us in Baton Rouge, and we continued on into New Orleans' French Quarter. Food for the stomach and nourishment for the mind were next on our unstated agenda. While munching hot dogs on a street corner in this festive atmosphere, we chatted with a bearded young man accompanied by a girl friend and a German shepherd dog. He leaned on crutches while we talked. One leg was lost in a motorcycle accident in Malaysia, he volunteered, as we exchanged road stories. He said his name was Alan.

"Where are you headed next?" he queried.

"I don't know. We don't make plans; we just go with the flow," I answered rather smugly, intending to convey our greater freedom to move as the spirit moved us.

"Why not?" He looked me straight in the eye. "They're your plans. You could change them anytime you like."

If further conversation followed, I wouldn't remember it. His words sank to the marrow of my bones. Such a simple truth, and yet it had never occurred to me. Thus far in life, goals, plans and commitments had felt like prisons and forms of bondage. I had not yet fully accepted what was obvious to others. I was free. Nonetheless, Alan had only begun to teach me.

We left Alan. We had decided to follow our open-ended plan to visit the King Tut exhibit. Having asked for and received directions, we left the car parked and walked. The distance proved greater than anticipated. Pouring with perspiration and hungry, we spotted a Hare Krishna Temple and opted to stop for rest and meditation. Upon entering the grounds, we were warmly greeted. Yes, there were facilities for meditation, but we should be fed and allowed to bathe first, our host told us. Welcoming this advice, we gratefully accepted.

Later, while sitting in meditation, a face appeared upon the screen of my awareness. It was a young face with no hair and almond eyes. The face seemed to be radiating light from every pore. Simultaneously, a deep wave of peace engulfed me. All tension and fatigue were instantly lifted from my being. As quickly as it appeared, this beatific face disappeared. I continued to wait in meditation (or rather, what I would later learn to recognize as "spiritual greed"), but no additional visions or blessings were conferred.

As we continued on toward our visit with King Tut, we wondered aloud about what to expect. Neither of us had seen nor read any literature about the exhibit. Our friend had only said King Tut was an Egyptian Pharaoh who had lived long ago. His tomb had been discovered, and its contents were being displayed. Arriving at the museum, we purchased our tickets and waited in line. Upon entering the building, I saw a small bust. My view was of the profile. Upon reaching the bust, I turned and looked full-face into a perfect, statuette version of the young, almond eyed, hairless face in my vision.

King Tut, we learned, was a child Pharaoh, worshiped as the Sun God incarnate. Perhaps, realizing the essential unity of all life, King Tut had easy access to the open minds of young pilgrims like me, seeking that same realization.

In Austin, Texas, two weeks later, Ronnie and I stood on a street corner, enveloped in a festive atmosphere reminiscent of the French Quarter. The undefeated University of Texas football team had won its ninth straight game. The entire city seemed caught up in the celebration. I glanced to my left and saw a bearded young man on crutches headed my way. There was no girl friend, but there was a German shepherd dog following along behind him. I approached him, nearly incredulous over his coincidental reappearance. I said, "Hey, Alan, you remember us, from New Orleans? What you said to me about plans - that really was important to me...."

"Oh yeah, man, cool," said my guru of plans, and he continued to move on down the street, clearly unimpressed with me or any lesson he may have imparted.

Here, I will jump forward in time from the mid '70s to Albuquerque, New Mexico, in 1985. I was working at the Regent International Hotel as a bar manager. I worked in a tuxedo. Standing behind the bar, I happened to glance up and see another fellow standing there, dressed in a tuxedo. He had a beard, and as my eyes moved downward, I noticed that one leg of the tuxedo was tucked up and pinned. He was leaning on crutches.

I said, "Hey, man, have you ever been to New Orleans?"

"Uh, yeah, a long time ago, why?"

"Yeah. You were traveling with a dog and a girl friend, and you lost your leg in a motorcycle accident in Malaysia, right? Your name is Alan, isn't it?" I queried.

"Wow, man, what are you, psychic?"

"No," I explained. "But you said something that day that really made a difference to me. In fact, it's still a lesson I'm learning!"

But Alan didn't really care. He was just glad to get a job at the Regent as a part of a three-piece jazz trio playing during happy hour five days a week. It wasn't his lesson. It was mine.

Fast forward again to 1990. I was in a Cajun restaurant on the north side of Albuquerque, again reminiscent of the French Quarter. I was eating and looked up to see two fellows with their musical instruments standing beside our table. One had a beard and was on crutches. I said, "Hi, Alan!"

He said, "Hi, Mark!" By now, we let it go at that.

# Chapter 10
## Hollywood: You Light Up My Life

In Austin, Ronnie and I met up with Larry Ford, who had turned me on to gestalt therapy and had joined the staff of Theodore's early in the building stage. Larry and Ronnie were suddenly interested in making money. They had entered what sounded to me like a shady deal which would require them to go to Hollywood. I felt guided to return to go to the southwestern United States. In particular, I felt inspired to go to Phoenix, Arizona. "Let's just go do our deal in Hollywood first," said Larry, "and then we'll check out Phoenix."

We would be taking Larry's car, and he would buy the gas. I would, as a result, be dependent on him for transportation. I hadn't admitted it to myself, but I secretly wished, shady or not, they would be able to successfully consummate their deal. Having some extra money was an experience I hadn't had much of lately. I was constantly stepping out on faith, and even though the needed supply seemed always to arrive just in the nick of time, I still often felt financially limited.

In Hollywood, the deal wasn't coming down. But Larry and Ronnie were in entirely new personas. They were wearing sunglasses and had been wheeling and dealing for days. I was feeling very uncomfortable. A sense of irritation was building. "Stop the car, and let me out right here!" I demanded. As we drew to a halt, I bounded out of the car telling them I'd talk to them later.

My sudden exit from their company on the streets of Los Angeles placed me directly in front of a movie house. I glanced up at the marquee which read, "You Light Up My Life." Altogether lacking any new plan, I purchased a ticket and entered the theater. The movie appeared to have been filmed in Hollywood and told of a young lady's disappointments, her break from dependency on others, and her discovery that she had talents and inner resources of her own that could be relied upon. Following this discovery, she had left California for New York, alone, and ultimately achieved success as a singer. Her hit recording was entitled, "You Light Up My Life."

As I left the theater, I pondered the similarities between the young lady's initial predicament and my own. I realized I had ignored my guidance to visit Phoenix, secretly hoping my friends would make some money and that I would share in their ill-earned loot. As I walked back to Hollywood, I stopped at a bar and had a beer. I glanced around the bar and noticed it bore a striking similarity to a scene from the movie where the young lady had met the man who would break her heart, which would ultimately lead to her finding inner strength. As I sipped my beer judiciously, I thought, "Perhaps God speaks twice."

I left the bar and returned to our temporary habitat in Hollywood and went to bed. Early the following morning, I packed my bag. I asked Larry and Ronnie to drive me to the outskirts of L.A., where I could more easily hitch a ride to Phoenix. Without argument, they accommodated me. When they dropped me at a freeway exit heading out of town, I noticed this particular point on the freeway bore a remarkable resemblance to the final scene in the movie from the previous evening. This scene simply showed the young lady driving on the freeway, presumably leaving L.A. and following her heart. "Sometimes God speaks three times!" I thought.

As I hitchhiked through southern California, the title song, "You Light Up My Life" played, time and time again, on the car radios of those blessed couriers who deigned to lift me from false design. Among my many shortcomings is a tendency toward almost endless waves of oral expression. It occurred to me, regarding God, as I'm sure it has my acquaintances regarding me, "Doesn't He ever stop talking?"

# Chapter 11
## Phoenix: Carny, Psychic or Mystic?

On the road to Phoenix, I met Lefty. Lefty was a "carny," a carnival worker headed to Phoenix to work the Arizona State Fair. The fair was due to open the very next day. Lefty was my age, late 20s, about 5' 3" tall, intelligent and good-natured. He had grown up an orphan with no clue about his roots. He had worked his entire life for the carnival. The carnies were his family. The life of the carny entailed much travel, as they moved from town to town to work the games or the rides.

Lefty introduced me to another strange and different world. Carnies are a closed little culture. Their favorite description of themselves is "freaks." Rather than consider this an insult, it is the primary qualification for carny-hood. Being rejected by society for one's looks, physical features, skin color, sexual orientation or unique handicap was a virtual endorsement in the world of the carny.

One is either a carny or a "mark." A mark is considered the gullible target of all carnies. Everyone except a fellow carny is viewed as a mark. This presented us with a major problem. Lefty intended to introduce me to people he knew who would hire me to work the state fair.

"But," he told me, "your name just won't do."

As we traveled along together, though, I convinced him that we could present me as a kind of novelty; that my name could become an inside joke. He liked it. So, I became the only Mark in any carny's memory to work the inside of a game. They put me on the Pepsi toss, a game where the player would attempt to toss rings over the necks of Pepsi bottles. The bottles were arranged so that it was nearly impossible to accomplish. We would attempt to "help" the mark by pointing out the best bottles to try for or the best position from which to toss, as if we wanted to help them win. And, we attempted to "hook" the mark by engaging his ego in any number of schemes.

The best marks were generally considered to be young men. They needed to be old enough to have money. They needed to be accompanied by a girlfriend, adding to the possibility that he could be hooked by the desire to prove his skill to her.

"Shills," carnies skilled in acting, would move into the game, attempting to help "place the hook" in marks. They would attempt to keep them engaged in the game by successfully ringing the bottles and winning big prizes that were really impossible feats for any mark. The shills were given rings that looked exactly like the ones the marks were given, but were heavier and would more easily land and remain over the necks of the bottles.

Every game in the carnival had a similar twist or con to it. There were professional pickpockets who worked the lines at the rides. The operators of the rides created occasional jerks and quick stops. These abrupt changes in speed were designed to cause loose change or even an occasional wallet to fly free to the ground below where "watchers" stood. The watcher would quickly gather the booty. If a mark happened to notice his loss, there would still be no recourse. The watcher would disappear into the crowd before the mark could exit the ride.

My acceptance into this world was not altogether smooth. For one thing, I am generally considered handsome, a rare characteristic for any carny. And my name was not always seen as the comical irony I had hoped. A few flat-out rejected me. Lefty, however, had strong ties and used his influence. Little by little, most of the carnies warmed up to me.

Eventually, however, I realized that my presence was a difficulty for Lefty. One night he engaged in a fistfight in defense of his decision to support me. I felt badly and told him I probably wasn't cut out to be a carny anyway. I think he was partly grateful that I had decided to leave. I was touched, however, when I noticed he had a tear in his eye as we said our good-byes.

It was not my destiny to be a carny. It seems to have been my destiny, however, to be allowed to peer into other worlds and cultures and, in many instances, to be allowed to experience them firsthand. I was named for Mark Twain, the author of tales of adventure and travel. Also, I was nicknamed Marco Polo, after an adventurer and explorer of new worlds. It seems, my consciousness has been expanded by these experiences.

Leaving the fairgrounds, I slipped into my bartender's garb and cleaned up in a public restroom. I stashed my duffel bag under an orange tree in a park in downtown Phoenix. I was seeking employment. Having saved almost nothing from my carnival earnings, I was again nearly broke.

I entered a small neighborhood bar on Central Avenue. I seated myself at the bar, two stools down from the only other customer, a tall, lanky, somewhat homely woman. I asked the bartender about any shifts that might be open and quickly learned there were none. He had no leads to offer, either. I had not intended to order anything, but the lanky woman said, "Have one on me, why don't you?"

"Thanks," I said, and ordered a cold beer.

As I glanced toward my most recent benefactor, I noticed the insides of both her wrists had stitches. She wasn't happy. I attempted to cheer her up, but she wasn't having any of it. Or so she said. Something I said must have been comforting to her, though, because she invited me to stay on her sofa for a few days while I looked for work.

The following morning, she also volunteered to transport me in my search to find a job. Meanwhile, I decided I should be looking for work in a spiritual environment, if possible. I made a list of health food restaurants, religious bookstores and other spiritual organizations, and we embarked. In late afternoon, still unsuccessful, I noticed a growing heaviness on the part of my companion. I intuited she was beginning to view me as an added burden in her already burdensome trek through life.

At the next stop, I said to her, "You can just leave me here. This is going to be the right place."

"How do you know?" she asked.

"I just know," I said. "I told you last night there are powers you don't know about. They always take care of me. Really, don't worry. I'll call you when I get settled. I'll be fine."

"OK," she said, in a weak voice, and she left, looking as if she felt doubtful but relieved.

I had only too recently suffered the lesson of attachment. I needed something that would allow me to earn my own way, not someone to hang on to. As I glanced toward my newest destination, I saw what looked like an old church. I would discover that it was, indeed, an old Mormon church, now housing an organization calling itself the University of Life, just off midtown Phoenix. I set my bag down outside the door and entered.

"I'm hungry," I informed the Rev. Lin Martin. "Would you have some work I could do for a meal?" I asked.

Looking me over carefully, Rev. Martin responded, "You should eat first, then you can buff the floor of the auditorium, if that sounds alright to you."

While I ate, Rev. Martin engaged me in no short conversation on the merits of the spiritual life, metaphysics, the Unity Church, psychic abilities and other related topics. At the end of our discussion, he politely offered me the job of caretaker for the University of Life. Pay would be only $50 per week, but the job also included a private room, formerly monks' quarters, with a telephone extension of my own. And, he added, I could take my meals from a communal refrigerator. In addition, Rev. Martin - "Just call me Lin," he had said - told me all classes offered through the University would be included as well, should I care to attend them. Duties, he informed me, would require only two to three hours a day and I would be free to seek additional employment if I so desired. Lin closed his offer, saying he believed my presence there would be a positive influence, should I choose to accept.

I did.

That evening I called my overburdened friend, to relieve her of any possible weight I may have added to her mind. I informed her I was calling from my place of employment; more specifically, from my private room on my own telephone line. She was surprised and grateful for my good fortune.

The University of Life was devoted to the development of psychic gifts and served as a training ground for beginning "readers" and "channels." My training through both the Unity School and in other Eastern teachings warned the student of Truth not to become enmeshed in the phenomenal world of the psychic. There were gifts and powers which came with the territory, I already knew, but the student should not lose sight of the goal - Self-Realization.

My understanding of what Self-Realization meant was still far from complete. I did know, through my experiences of heightened states of consciousness, that, in part, it meant the realization that all life is a part of a whole; that all life is sacred. And I had seen many psychics who seemed more concerned with their gifts than with this goal.

I did attend many classes, readings and trance channeling sessions. I conversed regularly with the so-called disincarnate beings, who offered their guidance and instruction through the mouths and bodies of the clearly incarnate channels. For the most part, I found the disincarnate both wise and delightful. I grew especially fond of Dr. Durant and Flying Eagle, an English doctor and a Native American medicine man, respectively. These two unique characters taught me to see the value of psychic abilities in a new way.

I had taken a very strong position about my relationship to these possibilities. I watched as the "channels" entered into a trance state of consciousness, which rendered them unconscious of the proceedings that followed. I would never relinquish my conscious awareness in order to allow channeling to occur through me, I promised.

Both my friends without bodies honored my decision. However, they reminded me I was unusual and fortunate, in that I had been blessed with many spiritual experiences. Others, they said, often needed help to open their minds to the spiritual dimension. Realizing there were powers beyond the rational through being impressed by psychic phenomena, often met that need. The psychic, my disincarnate buddies told me, is often a gateway for such as these.

"We are helping them to step onto the spiritual path and begin their quest for true knowledge," said Flying Eagle.

Trina Martin, Lin's wife, who channeled these two particular invisible friends, often "sat" or entered trance for me, so that I might have these conversations. I was never charged a fee for these sessions. In fact, on occasion, she would tell me one or the other of them, Dr. Durant or Flying Eagle, wanted to talk to me. During one such session, Flying Eagle told me that Trina, who was very gifted, lacked the confidence to take her show on the road and suggested I accompany her and support her on her first road trip. I agreed.

We were to visit a ranch on Swan Road in Tucson, where a small, spiritual community was developing. The primary residents of this ranch were three young women who had begun to publish one of the early guides to spiritual organizations. They called themselves the Aquarian Angels, and the publication was *The Aquarian Age Almanac*. Trina and I arrived on a cold afternoon in winter. A group gathered in the living room of one of the residences. I made myself at home immediately by helping to wash the dishes. Pretty soon, we were all feeling very comfortable, Trina included.

I sat in a rocking chair as we gathered for the trance session. There were thirteen of us, all told. As we began, I felt a subtle and easy flow of energy move up my spinal column. By now, I knew some kind of expanded state of consciousness was imminent. As the energy entered my head, I felt my eyeballs roll upward involuntarily and lock in a position, pointing directly at the third eye or sixth chakra. Immediately, I entered a state that I would privately think of later as a "mini-samadhi."

My consciousness expanded in the most substantial way to date. I entered a state of ecstasy. A profound sense of gratitude, beyond anything I had ever dreamed possible, filled my heart. Trina entered the trance state and began to speak. It was Dr. Durant. It was the most unusual trance channeling session I had ever experienced. Dr. Durant, who usually spent most of his time giving medical advice and answering health questions, began this session by describing a scene in ancient Egypt.

My experience was one of imagining that this particular group of individuals gathered in this room had been together before, during the time being described. Dr. Durant went on to say just that. We had come together, he said, because the particular energies we carried would tend to awaken us all to spiritual abilities and potentials we had not yet rediscovered in this lifetime. He would hear no argument from me. My eyes were open now, and I was experiencing everything I saw and heard as being within me. Even the desert landscape I saw out the window was now a part of my larger Self.

Other participants were moved, as well. Tears were rolling down many cheeks, including my own. After the session, I kept quiet about the depth of my experience. It was a rare choice for me to keep quiet. This time the expanded state didn't immediately pass. It diminished, and yet the general feeling of connectedness, the sense that all I saw was a part of my larger Self, remained.

Trina returned to Phoenix. I stayed in Tucson with one of the Aquarian Angels. I remained in an expanded state of consciousness for several days. My new lover was as reluctant as I to make commitments, and I began to sense my time to go was fast approaching. I said my good-byes and hitchhiked back to Phoenix.

I vividly recall the moment this expanded state of consciousness receded. I was at an intersection on the south end of Phoenix, climbing out of the car that had delivered me from Tucson. I saw a roadside stand selling velvet paintings. Specifically, my eyes landed on one painting of a Bengal tiger. In that instant, my world contracted painfully. I gasped as I suddenly felt myself again enclosed in only a physical body. This contraction left me in a mild state of depression for several days.

One of the other residents of the University of Life was Daniel. Daniel was a little like I had been, in the first months after my awakening. Zealous. Especially about food. Vegetarianism was his religion. He would capture anyone he could find to convert. Someone kept a large box of wieners in the fridge, and I occasionally ate one. My mischievous side picked wieners to eat on purpose when Daniel was in the kitchen. He would launch into his little sermonette, and I would laugh and eat a wiener. Most other students at the University were less entertained by Daniel's professed beliefs and his insistence upon sharing them. Some became downright irritated.

One evening during a session with Dr. Durant, Daniel, who tended to dominate these sessions with questions on health issues, received a surprise. He had asked a question. Dr. Durant answered it by saying that Daniel had followed too rigid a diet lately and had depleted himself of certain necessary nutrients. Daniel wanted to know what supplements he should use to counter this deficiency.

"No supplements. You need liver. At least a pound a day for the next five days will do it." exclaimed Dr. Durant.

Daniel nearly came out of his chair voicing his resistance.

"Daniel," Dr. Durant continued, "you have to understand that every person's body is unique; therefore, each person's needs are unique. Further," said Dr. Durant, "every person's body evolves through time; therefore, any one person's body may require any number of dietary measures at different stages of development. The liver I am prescribing for you now is simply the best way to restore a certain imbalance I am perceiving."

"How long did you say I need to eat the liver, Dr. Durant?" asked Daniel.

"About five days," answered the good Dr. "I realize you don't like the taste of liver, Daniel, but the results you will achieve in only five days will be greater than any you could achieve with supplements, over many months."

The transformation in Daniel was quite dramatic. As he ate his liver in the communal kitchen, he continued his sermons. The contents of these sermons had been drastically altered, however.

"Everyone's body is unique," he would begin, "and our dietary needs are unique, too. Not only is this so, but our needs are constantly changing. We have to be open to whatever need may arise. Dr. Durant told me that by just eating this liver for five days, I can accomplish more than I could by taking supplements for months. I figure it'll be worth it."

Exactly five nights later, as we met again for a trance session, Daniel was eagerly awaiting his chance to ask Dr. Durant if he could now quit ingesting the liver, which he obviously despised.

"How am I doing now, Dr. Durant? I sure hope I've had enough of that liver."

"Yes," said Dr. Durant. "You've had quite enough. The balance has been restored."

That might have been the end of it if Daniel hadn't asked the next question. But he was ever the gatherer of information, most of which I suspect he gathered more for the purpose of dispensing to others than applying to himself.

"What exactly was it that was out of balance, Dr. Durant?

"It was primarily your attitude, Daniel. You had developed the belief that your dietary preferences were right for everyone. It was only an error in judgment. You may now rest assured, the balance has been restored."

Another psychic channel in attendance at the time re-entered my life years later, via the television screen. Kevin Ryerson was playing himself in Shirley MacLaine's popular mini-series *Out on a Limb*. John and Tom, the entities speaking through Kevin for all the world to see, were teaching small classes in Phoenix in the '70s. Now I could see that psychic demonstrations were serving to open the minds of millions of television viewers.

About six months later, near the end of my time at the University of Life, my tall, lanky friend with scarred wrists showed up at the University, saying she had met someone she thought I would like. His name was Wolfgang Krauss. Wolfgang claimed to have achieved a degree of Self-Realization. She had been joining him on a nightly basis, at a large circular booth in a coffee shop where he held court.

"He will answer questions until dawn," she said, "if people stick around that long. And he doesn't charge anything. It's free."

I was intrigued. Claims of Self-Realization are more likely made by the unenlightened, I thought. But I was curious, nonetheless. My friend picked me up that night, around midnight. We made our way to the coffee shop.

There sat Wolfgang.

His audience was comprised of the rejected, the downcast, the cast-outs, the street people. They appeared to be enchanted. No wonder. As I listened, I heard a voice of love, a voice of reassurance. I heard no claims of mastery. His attention was on those he was serving. He was reminding each one of his or her inherent value as a spiritual being. He explained that poverty and suffering were a part of life and that certain lessons were learned through these experiences that couldn't be learned any other way.

I asked him where he came by this wisdom. He said he had asked; that an inner voice, God's voice, was accessible by all, if one learned to listen.

He said he had asked God, "Why is there so much suffering?"

The answer that came was, "I permit suffering, that humanity may know compassion."

That answer alone was worth more than the price of admission. I thought Wolfgang was a jewel amidst the rough world of the outcasts. My friend with the scarred wrists, whose mind had clearly opened, had begun to find a spiritual meaning to her existence.

I still do not seek the path of the psychic. I have obviously been gifted with certain intuitive abilities. These are helpful and valuable, and yet I do not think of myself any more as a psychic than I do as a carny. If anything, I was following the path of the mystic. I had glimpsed the sacred nature of all life. And it was the natural and ready access to this awareness I was seeking.

## Chapter 12
## Aspen: Little Werners Everywhere

I returned to Houston from Phoenix, via Unity Village where I had taken another session of U.I.C.E. John Moss, the former manager of Theodore's, had opened another nightclub in the downtown area called the Green Room. I had been offered and accepted a bartender's job on the day shift. One afternoon, Clint Williams, an attorney friend that had frequented Theodore's, entered the bar. Judging by his appearance, it was about to rain.

"Why do you look so depressed?" I asked.

"My only friend at the firm just quit. He's going to Aspen to ski all winter. He said he didn't give a damn if he had to wash dishes for a living. He says he has to give up the rat-race. I just wish I had the courage to do the same."

At that precise instant, John Moss walked by.

"John," I said, "I have to go to Aspen next week. I'm not sure when I'll be back, so I'll have to give you notice. I think I know someone who'll take my shifts."

"OK, Mark," he replied, without batting an eye.

Clint's face was a picture of incredulity.

"Are you joking?"

"No, Clint. I know it's strange, but the minute you said the word Aspen, something inside me jumped. I instantly knew I should go to Aspen as soon as possible."

Clint had shared his feelings with me for years, about practicing law in a huge firm where he felt like a cog in a wheel. But, for various reasons, he felt trapped. Just the sight of others choosing to extricate themselves seemed only to remind him of his own sense of bondage. Clint departed, still shaking his head in disbelief.

The next morning, I lay in my bathtub, wondering why I was being prompted to Aspen. The only possibility I could imagine was the result of a conversation I'd had while attending U.I.C.E at Unity Village. A friend had told me about a particular training called EST, Erhardt Seminars Training. She was quite enthusiastic about the transformative effect it had on her life. I remembered thinking, "I'll do that somewhere along the line."

As I lay there pondering, it occurred to me that the friend she had said she had attended the seminar in Aspen. After bathing and dressing, I walked across the street to another friend's house. Kathy King, a former cocktail waitress from Theodore's, and I had the habit of taking our coffee together on her back porch.

"It's really strange," I said. "I've only been back from U.I.C.E. a few weeks, and here I go again. I can't figure out why Aspen. I've never found the idea of skiing particularly attractive, and I don't much care for cold weather."

"I know why Aspen." Kathy responded. "Did you know I used to live in Aspen? There are lots of spiritual activities there. It's one of the main training locations for EST."

Kathy continued to tell me about the spiritual virtues of Aspen, but I could not hear her. I had received confirmation of my guidance. The inner voice was verified through Kathy's words. Again, I felt that resonance that had been my guide for so long. As I rode a taxi to work at the Green Room that day, tears fell. What grace was this that moved my life in such magical ways? There were many names for it, but no name had ever captured the wonder of it for me.

The following week, my girlfriend at the time gave me a pair of wool socks for my journey into the cold. It was late October and it would no doubt be snowing in Aspen. As usual, I had little money and decided to travel again by thumb. In Denver, it was snowing, so I splurged on a bus ticket for the remainder of the trip.

This last leg of the journey was punctuated by the reading of a small paperback book I had picked up at the Pyramid in Houston. *Contemplation: The Activity of Mystical Consciousness,* by Helen Brungardt impacted me greatly. Just how greatly will have to wait for another chapter. At this point, I was simply moved by the power and simplicity of the message. Here was a teacher who minced no words. She would win no popularity contests with this work. To those committed to spiritual awakening, she was reinforcement of eternal principle; to the uncommitted, a relentless confrontation. Here are a few words from the book:

The key to understanding is: There is only One Reality, period. Why don't we want to accept it?.... When we do adopt this principle of Oneness, it is only a mental concept at first. But, as we move the principle to the Heart Center, the Truth behind the principle reveals Itself to us.... This One Presence is the Truth that unites all things.

Oneness. Almost every book we read in the field of metaphysics teaches this same basic principle. You'll no doubt agree that the principle of Oneness is fairly simple, but our ego doesn't like that. There is only one conclusion to be drawn from the principle of One Presence. Regardless of all apparent duality, there really is only One. The presence of your body, mind and soul, the room where you are right now, the city where you are, are all of this same One Presence. Even the worst enemy you have ever had is still of this same One Presence. There is only One Presence, and you and I are It. We cannot change the reality of this Truth, in any way.

In my opinion, one of the major contributions Helen made was placing emphasis on the Heart Center (Sacred Heart in the West, or Heart Chakra in the East). She somehow knew this Center to be significant. She pointed to our need to bring attention to the Heart, and she proposed we learn to live from this Center, rather than from the intellect. I didn't grasp this at all in the beginning. Although I would follow her advice and work with the Heart Center, it would be another twenty years before I would begin to realize the profound value of an awakened Heart.

I arrived in Aspen. The jobs were all taken for the winter. Even the dishwashing jobs. EST was being held only once all winter, and the date was two weeks away. Once again, the cost was out of reach. I had rented a small but private attic room in a dormitory style ski house called the Mouse House. I had paid a week in advance, and the week was almost up. Answering a knock on the door, I opened it to the presence of a young lady. She was one of two ladies who owned the Mouse House, she informed me. She and her partner had decided they liked me and thought I would make a good manager for them. The pay was nominal but included room and board.

"Would you like the job?" she asked.

"By all means, yes," I answered.

Two days before the EST seminar was to begin, I was still far short of the needed registration fee. A heavy snowstorm had arisen. In the evening, I received a phone call from Ann, my first wife. Incredibly, she was still attempting to help me. Upon learning that the seminar would be held in two days, she had decided to call and wish me luck.

"Oh, by the way," she added. "I noticed the training is rather expensive. Do you need any money?"

I confessed my situation, and she offered to wire the money through Western Union.

I was in another state of wonderment. How life could unfold so magically. Yes, there were transcendental forces at work. There were also individual human beings, acting in accord with those forces, to manifest the many, many blessings that were poured out on me. There is a little story that makes this point quite clear.

A man had cultivated quite a beautiful garden. He had worked for months and continued to devote many hours to the care and upkeep of his garden. This man had a neighbor who would pass his house each evening on the way home. Whenever this neighbor would see the man out tending his garden, he would exclaim, "Oh, what a beautiful garden you have. God has blessed you indeed."

The man would nod his head and continue his work. Again and again, this neighbor stopped on his way home to admire the garden, and again and again, he would remark, "Oh, yes, what a beautiful garden you have. Yes, God has been good to you. You are certainly blessed."

One day, as the neighbor passed his house again, remarking, as always, on the beauty of the garden, how blessed he was, and how good God had been to him, the man stood up in the midst of his garden and looked his neighbor square in the eye and replied, "Yes," he said, "it is true I am blessed. And yes, God has been good to me, but you should have seen this garden, when God had it alone!"

During this period of my life, I was the recipient of an almost continuous flow of grace. This grace required the participation of others, often in very practical ways. I was only beginning to appreciate the value of the practical, however. Eventually, life would require this understanding of me. I would first resist, struggle and suffer, and finally begin to accept the lessons.

The following afternoon, I went to the Western Union office to pick up the check. It had not arrived. A snowstorm was underway and expected to build in intensity that night. The single operator of the Western Union office told me he had to close to make it home.

"We are closed for the weekend," he informed me.

This was Friday afternoon. The training would begin the next morning. After some discussion, I persuaded the operator to return the next morning if the snowstorm subsided, and give me my check, provided it was there. I then called Ann, who checked on her end and discovered a mistake had been made. She was promised by Western Union that the funds would now arrive in Aspen by the next morning.

I arrived at the Western Union office at 6:00 a.m. the following morning. The snowstorm had died. The operator arrived a few minutes later and let me in. My check was coming over the wire at that moment. Thanking the operator, and silently thanking Providence, I proceeded on to the Aspen Institute where the training would be held.

"I'm sorry. We do not accept checks on the day of the training," I was told.

"It's a Western Union moneygram," I said. "It's as good as a cashier's check."

"I'm really sorry. We just do not accept checks on the day of the seminar," said the polite young man at the registration table.

"I'm sorry, you don't understand," I said. "I'm supposed to be in this training."

"No, you don't understand. You see, we have a policy. We don't accept checks on the day of the training," said the assistant firmly.

"I don't think you understand. I'm supposed to be in this training."

A supervisor was called in. "You see," said the supervisor, "we really do have a policy. It's a rule. We do not accept checks on the day of the training."

"I understand," I replied. "Only you don't understand. I am supposed to be in this training," I calmly asserted.

The trainer was called in. "You see," he explained. "We don't accept checks on the day of the training. It's a policy."

"I understand your policy, sir," I replied. "The thing is, I am supposed to be in this training."

"I got it," he said. "You are supposed to be in this training."

He turned to the assistants and instructed them, "Please make an exception. Accept this check. You see," he explained, "he's supposed to be in this training."

I attended the basic EST training twice, as well as a number of post graduate seminars the organization offered. The encounter I had at this first training became more and more humorous to me as I took their courses. Without realizing it, I had exercised and demonstrated the use of a basic EST teaching, referred to as "persistence in intention." The thing is, I wasn't consciously practicing any principle. I just knew I was supposed to be in the training.

I wasn't at all shocked or surprised by the techniques of EST, which became somewhat controversial over the years for, among other things, its stringent structure. Its primary message of the individual being the cause of his or her experiences was already a part of my consciousness. I just enjoyed the training.

One great benefit I received from EST involved a fuller appreciation for my father. I called him from Aspen that winter to wish him a Merry Christmas. I told him how sorry I was for all the anger I had directed toward him over the years. I now understood that I was the one responsible for all my difficulties. There was a long pause at the other end of the line; then I heard something I had never heard. My father's voice was cracking with emotion when he said, with a barely detectable sniffle, "Son, that's about the best Christmas present I've ever gotten."

I am grateful to EST for the opportunities to grow, which I experienced through their organization. Ultimately, however, it was my observation that most who became deeply involved in EST began to take on the appearance and mannerisms of its founder, Werner Erhardt. "Little Werners everywhere" was not my idea of the evolution of the species.

## Chapter 13
## Montana is Cold; Texas is Warm:
## One Door Closes and Another One Opens

While in Aspen, I received a telephone call from a Unity minister living in Montana. I had met her at the Unity School where she was in the ministerial education program and I was in the licensed teacher's program. She explained that she was nearly overwhelmed with the duties of ministry and was looking for help. She was serving two churches, one in Bozeman and another in Missoula. She was providing Sunday services and midweek classes, as well as all the administrative details, board meetings and counseling. She asked me if I could come and help serve there.

I felt inspired to go.

A friend from the Mouse House agreed to drive me to Montana. It was February. We could easily have encountered inclement weather. Instead, although quite cold, the drive was an easy one. It was sunset as we crossed the border into Montana; and the sky, the entire sky, filled with cumulus clouds turned into molten gold. It was breathtaking and felt like a wonderful sign that I was headed in the right direction.

As is so often the case, circumstances would afford me life lessons in Montana that were not what I might have imagined. There were challenges from the beginning. Not that I wasn't well received. I was. In fact, that was part of the problem. I was quite popular with both churches, and my popularity didn't please my minister friend. She began to find fault with nearly everything I did. I was still quite naive, though. I just didn't get it.

The upside of my Montana experience was the re-emergence of the inner teacher. It wasn't nearly as dramatic as the Unity Village experience. I just began to know that something in me would shift when I stood up to speak. The most rewarding experience occurred in Billings, Montana. They had their own minister, but for some reason I no longer recall, he or she was unexpectedly unable to be there one particular Sunday. One of the board members called us in Missoula, late on a Saturday night, and asked if one of us could come to fill in. It was determined I would do it.

It would be a very long drive. If I left before sunup, I could make it in time for the service at 11:00 a.m. I had almost no time to prepare and had not spoken publicly, without preparation, since the Unity experience. I made a pie-shaped diagram, listing the key ideas from a book by Stella Terrill Mann entitled *How to Live in the Circle of Prayer and Make Your Dreams Come True*. It was my finest hour in Montana. Something seemed to take hold and speak through me again. Afterward, I couldn't remember exactly what had been said. I only knew I had been well received.

I didn't last long in Montana, though. I was fired soon after. No reason was given. I believe my minister friend felt threatened by my growing popularity. I probably failed to appreciate her feelings about this. I only knew I had given it my best effort. Knowing this gave me a sense of faith that, if this door was closing, it only meant another would open.

I didn't loiter. I left the day I was fired. It was April, still very cold and snowing heavily as I stepped out onto the highway. Even though my destination was Texas, I had decided to travel west toward the coast, where it would be somewhat warmer; then down through California, back across the Southwest and on through Texas to Houston.

I was beside the road all of five minutes when a new Mercedes Benz pulled over, picked me up and carried me to Portland. I no more than got out of the Mercedes when I was picked up again. It was now about 2:00 a.m., and this time, surprisingly, it was a woman. Even more surprisingly, she invited me to spend the night on her sofa. The next morning, this trusting lady took me to the south end of town, where I was picked up within minutes by a large, luxurious recreational vehicle. The driver informed me that he was headed for

Los Angeles and said he would welcome my company, especially if I were willing to help drive.

In L.A., I was again picked up quickly by another Mercedes going to Tucson. In Tucson, the pattern broke. My ride came in the form of a fellow about forty years old, with long hair and a beard, driving a VW bug. He was headed to Las Cruces, New Mexico. In Las Cruces, the pattern resumed. I was picked up in another recreational vehicle and transported to San Antonio. Outside of San Antonio, I stood and basked in the warm, spring sunshine of Texas. Within minutes, I was offered a ride by a fellow about my own age, driving a van. As we drove, he asked me where I was coming from.

"Most recently, I was in Montana, but I spent most of the winter in Aspen, taking some spiritual seminars."

"Really," he replied. "I was just in Steamboat Springs, Colorado, myself. I'm an electrician, and I was doing some work with a friend of mine from Boerne, Texas."

Suddenly, I felt that funny feeling again. Larry Ford was from Boerne and was, among other things, a skilled electrician. I had also heard him speak of Steamboat Springs, Colorado.

"I'll bet his name is Larry Ford, isn't it?" I asked.

He glanced at me and turned back to driving.

"Yeah," he answered. "And I'll bet you're Mark Pope, aren't you?"

It was my turn to be surprised.

"Yes, how'd you know?"

"Larry talks about you all the time. He said he'd heard you were in Aspen, and he always said you were pretty wild, but very spiritual." He continued, "You'll never guess where I'm headed right now. I'm headed for the Green Room to meet Larry and Ronnie West and Lee Campbell (one of my other good friends, who had been a bartender in the early days at Smuggler's Notch). We're supposed to meet and listen to some music for a while. Then we're going to the grand opening of a new restaurant in Montrose, called T. E. Scruggs. It's owned by Ted Scruggs (who also owned Theodore's 19th Century Fox)."

The synchronicity was mind-boggling.

In Houston, Ronnie West, Larry Ford, Lee Campbell and I gathered and celebrated our reunion. Later, as we entered the doors of the T. E. Scruggs restaurant, Ted called out my name, "Mark, when did you get back in town? What perfect timing. I need a bartender in the worst way. Please tell me you're going to be around awhile."

One door closes - another opens.

## Chapter 14
## Encinitas:
## In the Footsteps of Paramahansa Yogananda

Sometime in the '70s, I read *Autobiography of a Yogi* by Paramahansa Yogananda. Yogananda brought his message of Self-Realization through Kriya Yoga to the United States in 1920. His autobiography documents an extraordinary life, including his training under and relationship to his teacher, Sri Yukteshwar. Yukteshwar was the disciple of Lahiri Mahasaya, whose teacher was Mahavatar Babaji, the Himalayan master, who revived the ancient science of Kriya Yoga.

Babaji is said to have great interest in the Western World. According to Yogananda's autobiography, he was appointed by Babaji and trained by Yukteshwar specifically for the purpose of bringing this *spiritual science* to America. Upon reading this autobiography, I resolved to learn the science, reputed to accelerate (not shortcut) the soul's evolution toward Self-Realization.

In one chapter of the autobiography entitled, *Two Penniless Boys in Brindaban,* Yogananda tells of visiting Brindaban (Vrindaban today), the birthplace of Krishna, under a peculiar set of circumstances. During a debate over spiritual priorities with his elder brother, Ananta, Yogananda accepted the challenge to visit Brindaban with his friend, under the following agreement: He must take no money; he must not beg for food or money; he must not reveal his predicament to anyone; he must not go without his meals; and he must not be stranded in Brindaban. His brother would supply him with a one-way ticket. Yogananda's position was that an ever-present, all powerful, all knowing God of love would supply the every need of his faithful devotees.

During this pilgrimage to the holy birthplace of Krishna, Yogananda fulfilled all conditions of the challenge. Along the road, he is fed, guided and transported in wondrous fashion. His companion on the trip, Jitendra, is less faith-filled and worries at every turn, even in the face of constant supply. At one point, the two pilgrims are invited to attend a lavish banquet, where they enjoyed many delicious courses of Indian delicacies. They returned to Ananta's home in Agra with money to spare, never having once begged or revealed their predicament to anyone.

In 1978, I was living with Mary and her prodigious young daughter, Annette. We were inspired to read this chapter from *Autobiography of a Yogi* together. I proposed a similar test of faith for us. We were to visit Encinitas, California, under all the same conditions. Encinitas was our choice for one particular reason. It was there Yogananda had founded the Self-Realization Fellowship, devoted to the continuing education of its students of Kriya Yoga. We went, hoping to receive initiation in the practice of Kriya Yoga.

We arrived in Encinitas without incident, having left Houston two days earlier. We were offered meals and rides without asking or begging. We were given overnight shelter in El Paso. Annette, who was about sixteen years old at the time, and quite mature spiritually, found the trip exciting. Her mother, although adventurous, also played out the role of Jitendra, worrying from time to time. Annette's boyfriend, a young truck driver about twenty-five years old, who had no idea we would be out on the road, just happened to see us, some six hundred miles from home, and picked us up in El Paso in his 18-wheeler. He took us all the way to California. We had revealed our predicament to no one. Even Annette's boyfriend remained in the dark.

We proceeded to the Self-Realization Fellowship and asked for Kriya initiation. We were told we would be required to take a year-long correspondence course to qualify. Having been declined this gift, we continued into the city proper to a Self-Realization temple. As we sat on the steps of the temple, Mary began to be discouraged. It was afternoon, and we hadn't eaten. I urged her to concentrate on the everywhere-present, all-sufficiency of God. Within minutes, an elderly lady appeared before us.

"What do you need?" she asked.

"Nothing," I answered. "We're just fine, thank you."

Mary was nudging me, in an attempt to remind me of our need.

"You must need something," she said. "I was just meditating at home, and I had a vision of you sitting here. I was directed from within to come after you. You are to come with me," she said, authoritatively. "At least I will feed you."

So, we all piled into her car and proceeded to a beautiful beachfront home. There we were fed several courses of fruits, vegetables, rice, juices and sweets. She was a student of Kriya Yoga, she explained. And, she added, her son was a monk and her daughter a nun in the Self-Realization Order.

She explained further that she would have to enter the hospital for a week's stay, beginning the following day. Would we drop her off at the hospital in her car? If so, we could use the car and stay at her home. "Also," she added, the next day on the way to the hospital, "my purse is in the kitchen. There should be approximately $200 in it. Use it for whatever you need."

I was filled with a boundless gratitude to God and to this stranger of extraordinary vision and faith. Mary and Annette were similarly impressed. Although my initiation into Kriya Yoga would have to wait, our return to Houston the following week was no less miracle-laden.

Later that year, I visited with Helen Brungardt in Albuquerque, New Mexico. During that visit, I noticed an altar in her church, The Symphony of Life. Upon the altar were pictures of Babaji, Lahiri Mahasaya, Sri Yukteshwar, Paramahansa Yogananda and Roy Eugene Davis, a disciple of Yogananda's, who would eventually initiate me into Kriya Yoga. Also, there were pictures of Swami Muktananda and J. Sig Paulson, whose calm and studied face had caught my attention amid the swirl of activity during that Easter retreat at Unity Village.

I could not fully realize it at the time, but the major spiritual influences that would impact my life over the next twenty years, from both East and West, had come together.

# Chapter 15
## Texas Instruments:
## The Kingdom of Heaven Arrives and Departs

While I was looking for work in the late '70s, my mother told me she had heard that George Perez, another of the old staff at Smuggler's Notch, was working as a supervisor for a company doing contract work for Texas Instruments. George hired both Ronnie West and me to take down, move and reconstruct office furniture. The job paid extremely well and included all the overtime one wanted. The overtime paid time-and-a-half, up to sixty hours a week and double time after that.

Our little crew of about ten workers was on the clock twelve to fifteen hours every day. We were working at least six days a week and raking it in. About a week into this new job, I entered another expanded state of consciousness. This time, the expanded state was less dramatic. This time, it lasted for weeks. It was characterized, as usual, by the sense that all things are connected. There was also the general feeling that everything was unfolding effortlessly, by grace.

In fact, the job was unbelievably easy. We were simply taking down and putting up modular furniture. Although each member of the crew carried a toolbox, we rarely used anything more than an Allen wrench.

Ronnie was in an inspired state, too. We began a little running joke about being in the Kingdom of Heaven. I explained it to the crew. "The Kingdom of Heaven is here and now," I said. "We are in it, and what it is, is the awareness that everything is connected to everything else. In the Kingdom, we know that everything is happening just as it should, every second," I said. "Of course, most of the other workers here don't realize this. That's why they aren't smiling so much," I told our fellow workers. "Also, we can't try to tell them. They'll know when it's time for them to know. That's not our business. We're here to just enjoy this awareness. If we just remain aware, we get to stay in the Kingdom, and others will be positively affected by us."

As you may imagine, the other workers just smiled at these comments in the beginning. Then, little by little, our whole crew caught on. When they saw Ronnie and I were constantly enjoying ourselves, they began to ask more about what I had been saying. I continued to swear them to secrecy and repeated what I thought, at the time, was the essence of this state of consciousness.

"We're all connected. Everything is a part of God, and everything, in every moment, is purposeful. It's all a divine unfolding."

This experience stands as one of the longest periods of sustained higher consciousness I have known. It lasted several weeks and was followed by a long period of a sense of loss and depression. I never knew what caused these states to come, how long they might stay or when they would leave. I was often fooled into thinking I had arrived at some elevated state that would now be mine. I had no idea that, by identifying these altered states as *mine*, ego was inflating. I just innocently assumed they had been given to me to keep. I was mistaken.

Balance is a universal law. Inflation always constellates deflationary forces. Until I learned to recognize these heightened states as gifts flowing from a transcendental Source, and until I learned to see that ego was attempting to appropriate and identify with these forces, I was destined for hard landings. I, however, had developed an attachment to these heightened states. I never just released them. I never wanted to lose them. So Life, the ever-present Master Teacher, showed me again and again, by withdrawing the gifts.

Now, feeling invulnerable (that is, grossly inflated), Ronnie and I flew to Las Vegas where we proceeded to gamble. We would lose the heightened state and almost everything we had earned. We plummeted to the ground. The loss of the money and the loss of the heightened state were simultaneous. I would return home feeling confused and broken. The Kingdom had arrived and departed. You would think I would learn. But it wasn't time.

# Chapter 16
## The Tetons: Living and Dying and Living

*I was riding through the Teton Mountains on horseback, a pack mule bringing up my rear. I had left St. Louis by horseback late in the summer, in a state of despair. I had broken off a relationship with the daughter of an affluent store owner there. I was a trapper and unaccustomed to civilization. I couldn't adjust to the St. Louis city life. She had only known the city and wanted no part of my rugged outdoor existence.*

The preceding is a part of a vision I had late one night, while working with Lin Martin in Phoenix. At the time, I thought of it as a past life recall. Today, I no longer concern myself with ideas of reincarnation, one way or another. It may have been a past life, and yet, no matter how I contextualize it, the vision presented me with a little more understanding of my present life difficulties.

*I had left home at an early age, perhaps thirteen or fourteen years old. My mother, the foundation of our home, had died. Father had gone crazy with grief and begun to drink. Native Americans found me and took me in. They taught me their spiritual values.*

*The medicine wheel was life and its constantly changing experiences. The turning of the wheel is life's teaching. To meet life, without losing one's balance or equilibrium, is the spiritual goal of every person. The Great Spirit guides us, but its means of communication is often subtle. A medicine man is one ordained by the Great Spirit to interpret these communications for the people. Dreamed events were considered as real and often more significant than events in the waking world.*

*I was taught to trap. Every man and every animal has an appointment with death. The trapper doesn't seek to kill. He lays his traps and trusts the laws of nature. Certain animals will surrender to these traps at their appointed time. They are giving their lives and their pelts to the trapper. These gifts are to be honored.*

*I lived mostly alone in the wilderness country of Wyoming in my last years. I never received any formal education, nor did I embrace civilization. I made occasional trips to San Francisco and St. Louis, to sell my pelts and buy supplies. While there, I generally drank more whiskey than I needed and played poker. I viewed civilized white men with self-righteous indignation. They were weak and foolishly lacking any understanding of life, in my opinion.*

*I had visions of my late mother during this period. While leaving San Francisco, her face would appear and warn me to remember that humility and gratitude were essential to real understanding. I failed to accept and practice these teachings. I was extremely pained and angry at her for abandoning me by dying.*

*My refusal to accept the opportunity to learn civilized living in St. Louis cost me, first, companionship with a woman I loved deeply, and my life, soon after. Having spent that life in the wilderness, I knew better than most how early winter might arrive in the mountains of Wyoming.*

*But I attempted the crossing anyway. Subconsciously, I knew it was my turn to surrender. I had an appointment with death. I had refused the opportunity to grow. The medicine wheel, in the form of a heavy snow storm, arrived with me in the Tetons Mountains. It was over, and I knew it. I built a small lean-to, shot my horse and mule (as an act of mercy since I knew we were doomed) and settled in to smoke the peace pipe. I left my body, experiencing no physical pain.*

This vision reflects the important lessons I was learning in this lifetime. I have obviously had great difficulty accepting the rules and values of civilization. My mother's advice in the vision, to develop gratitude and humility, has been central throughout this lifetime. The sense of life being a sacred unfoldment and the feeling that experiences work together for spiritual purposes have been recurrent themes during my transcendent experiences. Last but not least, the lesson about balance and equilibrium is, from my present perspective, one way of expressing the heart of the matter.

In the present lifetime, I have visited the Tetons on a number of occasions to attend spiritual retreats sponsored by the Unity Church of Houston, Helen Brungardt and others. I was now attending a retreat again. The miraculous guidance, the synchronicities and the ready supply I had received and have documented in previous chapters had ended rather abruptly nearly two years before, and had not returned. I no longer knew which way to go or what to do. I received no inner promptings from Spirit or outer guidance from people or situations, at least none I could discern. Nothing was clicking anymore. I was living in a state of despair.

The Teton Retreat (now called the Big Sky Retreat and Meeting in Montana) is a joyous occasion for most people. Just being there in my present state of despair was torture. Being depressed, while those around me were celebrating their good fortune, seemed to accent my suffering. I wanted to hide, yet I was there hoping to find some help. I survived the week. At the end of the retreat, I approached Helen Brungardt.

"Helen?"

"Yes, Mark?"

"You know I've been studying these teachings for a long time, but something has gone wrong. I no longer know what to do. Nothing seems to be working for me any more. I have a feeling that you could say something that would make a difference."

"No, Mark. You know the truth. There's nothing I can say to you." And she turned her back on me.

I tapped her shoulder. "Helen!"

"Yes, Mark?"

"That's not true. I know there is something you could say."

She turned to face me, squarely. I still remember the incongruity of the scene. She held a glass of scotch in one hand and a cigarette in the other, destroying forever my preconceptions of how a spiritually evolved person might appear.

"OK, Mark. You are in what I call the 'dark night of the soul.' You know the truth. There are no more guides and teachers for you, at this point. You are your own teacher. It's time for you to create your own structure."

Without consciously knowing why, I felt the weight of despair lift. A deep thrill coursed through my being. Once again, I felt the light touch of Spirit awakening deep within me. On the road home, a simple idea broke through into my awareness.

The answer to the eternal quest is one-and-the-same as the answer to the question, "What do I *really* want?" - a question, I would discover, which is infinitely easier to ask than to answer. I still lacked much understanding. I had new, unanswered questions. But this much I knew. Spiritually, I had been dead - and now I was alive again.

## Chapter 17
## Corpus Christi: Is all the World a Stage?

What do I really want? And what exactly does it mean to "create my own structure?" Helen Brungardt's comments had certainly stimulated something within me. However, Buffalo Springfield lyrics came to mind, "...just what it is, ain't exactly clear."

I had spent the previous months in various levels of food and beverage service; waiting tables at Harvey's on Richmond Avenue, bartending at Captain John's on West Gray and managing the upstairs jazz club at Las Brisas Mexican Restaurant on Fairview, all in and around the Montrose District of Houston. Now I felt that something new was trying to happen. Something new wanted to be born.

I left Houston for the hill country of central Texas. I took a job as a laborer for a builder constructing a geodesic dome outside of La Grange. Only one carpenter and I were contracted by the builder to complete the project. My skills in carpentry can be expressed as "barely able to drive a nail." Fortunately, the dome came in a kit that required mostly bolts, and nailing was done with a nail gun. Knowing what to do wasn't important. Freddie, the carpenter, knew what to do. I just followed his directions. Freddie was no talker, so we spent a lot of time in silence. I was still pondering the meaning of those questions, "What do I really want?" and "What does it mean to create your own structure?"

Out of this contemplative period arose the memory of a childhood dream. In watching films as a young boy, I remember thinking, as I watched actors express a wide range of emotions portraying a variety of characters convincingly, "I could do that." And, "I'd like to do that."

Also, I had a sense at this time that I wanted to connect again with my father. He was living in Mathis, Texas, just north of Corpus Christi. He had entered the life insurance field, having retired from the Air Force after twenty years. Now he owned a small Ford dealership in Mathis. He told me he bought the dealership, partly with the hope that my younger brother, Neal, would follow him into the business. Neal had shown a great deal of technical and mechanical aptitude. Yet he had also begun to use heroin at an early age. My father says he felt, at the time, that Neal was his last chance. In his words, with Maralyn lost to schizophrenia and me lost, first to crime then to religious zeal, he hoped to salvage Neal. This was not to be, however.

When I arrived in Mathis, Neal was working for the dealership and, I suspected, still using heroin. He had been arrested on numerous occasions for possession and had stolen from my father, time and time again. My father and I both worked hard to reconcile our differences. He seemed to know Neal might be lost now. I think he hoped I might achieve some semblance of balance and maturity, and he wanted to help me.

So, my father hired me and began to train me in the sales department. He tried to teach me what he knew. He bought a brand new 1981 Thunderbird for my birthday. The agreement was that he would make the down payment and one-half of each monthly payment. I was to make the other half. This, from the person I had resented most throughout my life.

I had arrived in Mathis just before my 33rd birthday. I had accumulated nothing of material substance. I was still unsuccessful in auto sales, though the lessons learned would serve me much later. My father and I agreed that I would move on and try to "create my own structure." I had the idea that I would go to Corpus Christi, buy a lawnmower and start my own lawn maintenance business. The resources I carried into this little business were mostly interior. I had built a set of values related to work, which gave me a sense of confidence. I was honest. I kept my word. And I always tried to do more than was expected, rather than less. In my career, however humble, it had become obvious to me that many people missed these basics.

I had learned to communicate these values, also. In an endeavor to make myself stand out, when interviewing for a job, I would express this. "Just so you know," I would say, "I can be counted on to be here on time every day. I am honest, and I always keep my word. You will also see that I have a positive effect on others, because I understand I am here to solve your problems, not add to them."

I felt if I did the job right, it wouldn't be hard to build a business in this way. I had made up my mind. It would require one more lesson, however, before I would have success. For a change, I learned it quickly, from the person with whom I had experienced the most difficulty learning - my father.

After several weeks, I had plenty of work. But I wasn't getting ahead. I was working hard every day and barely surviving. When my father asked me about the business, I told him the truth. I had plenty of work, but I was barely making it. He said, "You're not charging enough, Mark."

"But," I objected, "I have tried to charge more. They won't pay it."

"What area of town are you working in?" he asked.

When I told him which neighborhoods I was concentrating my work in, he responded quickly, "That's the problem. You are in the wrong part of town. You are trying to serve people who cannot afford to pay you properly for your services. Go to the better neighborhoods, Mark. Your customers need to be those who can afford to pay you. I can promise you, if you keep your word and you do the job right, as you say you do, they will be happy to pay you adequately. Be sure to call on the businesses in the better areas, too. Successful businesses generally place a high value on the maintenance of their property."

This lesson was a missing key for me. Over the next few weeks, I established relationships with a number of successful businesses and prosperous homeowners. I eventually discontinued working for anyone who could not pay me enough to maintain my equipment and earn a profit. My clients, who were pleased with my dependability, began to inquire about my ability to do more than just maintenance. They needed trees trimmed and gardens weeded. Some needed landscaping done. I knew little about landscaping, but I could see the potential. I started looking for a subcontractor who did these things, and I decided to try to learn more about landscaping myself. Eventually, I hoped I would be able to bid on these jobs.

While looking for someone with whom to subcontract, I rediscovered Wendell, who had befriended me in high school and whose mother had allowed me to live with them during my final year of high school. He was in the landscaping business in Corpus Christi. He taught me much about the business and partnered with me on contracts while I learned about landscaping.

I named my business Miracle Maintenance and Landscaping. I now owned a pickup truck, many lawnmowers, edgers, weed-eaters, pruning shears, saws, ladders, spades and other tools. I had two employees and now spent as much time coordinating them as I did at physical labor. I was making more and doing less of the hard, physical labor.

The missing key had been learning to be more selective about who I was willing to serve. It was the old "beggars can't be choosers" lesson, reversed. By choosing my clients, I had lifted myself out of the beggar category. My dad was right. The majority of my clients were much more concerned with the quality of my work and my dependability than with the fact that I charged a little more than others. I had created my own structure. Most of the principles I followed had actually been learned from my father. Although, to be honest, it is only as I look back, that I am able to appreciate this fact.

I was also still contemplating the answer to the question that had emerged from within me, "What do you really want?" I still wanted to try my hand at acting. I knew a girl who was part of a small community theater and asked her if she could arrange for me to audition for the next play they were doing - William Saroyan's *Time of Your Life*. The director asked me to read for the part of Blick, a cop on the waterfront beat in San Francisco, described parenthetically in the script as "oily." The character was one who abused his authority and took advantage of weakness in others. This was to be a stretch for me. Blick was everything I had rejected. He was an authority figure, and the worst kind.

When I first read his lines, the director screamed at me, "That's not oily... *give me oily!*"

Something in me responded to the director's harsh words, and I discovered Blick within me. I suddenly became everything I had hated. I read the lines with a natural contempt.

"That's it. That's oily!" said the director. "That's what we want. Exactly! Don't you agree?" He looked to his assistant director, who was nodding affirmatively. "We've got our Blick." Turning again to me, he said, "You've got the part."

I was shaking inside. The discovery of this hated potential inside me had rattled me badly.

However, as we rehearsed the play, I found that my ability to relate to authority figures began to change. Some of my fear and judgment about those in authority began to dissolve. At one point, I found myself calling the police for assistance. After the phone call, I sat stunned...as I realized I had never seen law enforcement officers as servants. It had certainly never occurred to me to call them for help before.

On stage, I was hated and hissed at by the audience. For the antagonist, being hated is the sure sign you are believable in the role. In the final scene, when Blick, my character, is killed, the audience invariably applauded.

Through this experience as an actor I was undergoing a degree of transformation or healing. Later, I would come to understand this as a form of "shadow work." By bringing the hated and repressed patterns and potentials inside me out of the unconscious and into awareness, I had redeemed them. Without realizing how it worked, I had, to some extent, ended the need to project these patterns onto others. I would learn more about this later. For now, I only recognized that something had shifted within me. I had changed.

Next, I was cast as Beauregard Jackson Pickette Burnside, the wealthy Georgian courting Auntie Mame in the play by the same name. Again, I was to discover the magic of spiritual transformation taking place for me on the larger stage of life, as a result of playing a role on the small stage of theater. The role of Beauregard called for me to express a consciousness of great wealth and a certain humility. At least, that is how I interpreted the role.

"It was luck that caused me to smell oil, when I was walkin' across that soybean patch Cousin Marvin left me, and it was pure, damn Georgia luck that roller skated us together last Christmas," my character, Beauregard, says to Auntie Mame, about his good fortune in finance and in meeting her.

Again, as he walks in the door, after searching for Auntie Mame, he says, "You know, I've been lookin' all over this town for you. I was even in that place over thar, they call Brooklyn.... I'm so happy to find you. Will you excuse me for a second, Ma'am, while I skittle out and pay my taxi driver, so he can go home to his family?"

"You mean you left a taxi meter running in the middle of the depression?" asks Auntie Mame.

"Ma'am," says Beauregard, "when yar in oil, a stock market crash is... well, it's just somebody else's noise."

At the time I began to act, I also began to study Constantin Stanislavski, the father of what is commonly referred to as "method acting." I found little difference between his ideas for building a character for the purpose of portraying the role on stage, and many of the metaphysical teachings for transforming one's overall character on the larger stage of life. However, Stanislavski, at one point, warns that the actor should create the character or build the character out of only a portion of the psyche, like an inner suit of clothes, which the actor can then step into and out of at will. Just as a painter confines himself to a canvas and does not paint up and down the walls, floor and ceiling of his studio, the actor should similarly limit the character to be played.

Also, Stanislavski taught the use of creative imagination in the building of the character. That is, the actor should imagine the emotional life and the details of the character's life, far beyond anything contained in the script. This helps to access one's rich emotional potential and brings it to the role. Proper preparation enables the player to trust the instincts of this inner character while on stage. True acting is not acting in the common sense of the word. It is tapping one's inner resources, allowing them to emerge and, hopefully, bringing truth and believability to the role.

These were the techniques I was attempting to employ, as I prepared for the role of Beauregard. The qualities - prosperous and humble - that I considered most important to the role were actually attitudes and characteristics that I wanted to develop personally. So, I decided to break the rules, again. I conducted an experiment in consciousness. I decided to paint, not just on the canvas, but to allow these traits to spill over, as much as possible, onto the whole of my consciousness.

"What would happen," I wondered, "if I just adopted these attitudes for my own?" As I considered these possibilities, another question occurred to me, "Is all the world a stage?"

## Chapter 18
## Austin: Being Rich; Being Poor

During the run of Auntie Mame, the results of my experiment in consciousness appeared to be positive. My client base for Miracle Maintenance and Landscaping expanded. I began to find myself moving in a wealthier social circle. One encounter would present me with another painful life lesson.

I was attending a class on A Course in Miracles. It was held outside, during the afternoon. I wasn't paying much attention to the proceedings in the class and fell asleep in the grass. As I awoke, I heard two of the other students at the class discussing their need to find transportation to Houston. They were musicians and were scheduled to play at the Unity Church, the Pyramid. I kept my eyes closed and pretended sleep, while I considered whether or not I wanted to make a trip to Houston. I had been contemplating such a trip. I was also undecided about whether or not I would want traveling companions along the way. I decided to go and to offer them a ride.

They accepted and asked me if we might make a quick stop at a friend's house on the way out of town. I agreed, and they directed me to an upper middle class ranch style home. We were let in by a housekeeper, and I took a seat on the sofa. I was wearing blue jean shorts and a Superman T-shirt. I crossed my legs and waited. From of the back of the house emerged three very attractive women. I could feel a kind of electricity in the air as they entered. I had met one of them at the ranch on Swan Road in Tucson while traveling with Trina Martin on her first road trip. Another of them, in particular, was a wild-eyed blonde. I remember the first thought that entered my mind when I saw her - "LSD." Not that I used drugs in those days. Nor was she under the influence of any psychedelic drugs. But later, she would tell me she had been "on the bus" with the Merry Pranksters and Ken Kesey for a time. (This story of the LSD generation is chronicled as *The Electric Kool-Aid Acid Test* by Tom Wolfe.)

We fell in love, instantly. The connection was overwhelmingly powerful. The attraction was intense. The home we were in was the home of Jennifer Sugerman, whose parents were, in the words of Beauregard, "in oil." The wild-eyed blonde was Susan Zahdah - and she would rock my life to the extreme. She was quite well-to-do. I'm not sure I ever knew just how well-to-do. She had several homes and a ton of money. She began to talk to me about it. She issued a warning, too. She said her wealth had proven too much of an adjustment for previous men in her life.

After a brief trip to Houston, I returned to Corpus Christi. Over the following weeks, Susan also began to speak of the money as *ours*. "If we're going to be together," she said, "then you have to adjust and understand now that *we* have plenty. And really, you can do anything you want. If it's acting you really want to do, then we should probably go where some real opportunity exists. We might start in Austin," she continued. "The creative and performing arts are flourishing there, and I have a townhouse there I've hardly even used. It's a fully furnished investment property and will soon be vacant. You don't really have to continue this landscaping business, unless you want to."

I thought I had really hit the jackpot in life. I believed it had been the character-building experiment that caused this dramatic manifestation. As within; so without. The prosperous characteristics of Beauregard seemed to have affected my personal consciousness and were making me wealthy on the larger stage of life, I thought. I was in love. The sex was otherworldly. Now I had discovered that *we* were rich.

As Auntie Mame completed its run, Susan and I planned our move to Austin. I gave Miracle Maintenance and Landscaping, along with the pickup and all the tools, to my primary employee. I had been blessed beyond belief, I thought, so why not pass the blessings on. Susan seemed to share my interest in spiritual matters. On one occasion, she and a friend were planning a trip to Albuquerque, New Mexico, to attend the annual balloon festival there. I told her that one of my favorite spiritual teachers, Helen Brungardt, lived there.

While in Albuquerque, Susan attended services at Helen's church, The Symphony of Life. Later, I learned that Susan and her friend had shown up, after an early morning balloon ride, still soaked with the champagne that had been a part of their ballooning ritual. Nevertheless, Susan and Helen hit it off big time. They got together and decided to fly me out to join them. During our time in Albuquerque, we visited with Helen and her youngest daughter, at great length. We sang at Helen's piano. We drank scotch and discussed spiritual principles till the wee hours.

Susan had a rental car and wanted to visit Santa Fe, too, while we were in New Mexico. She was looking to purchase some art for *our* townhouse. On the way to Santa Fe, I entered an elevated state of consciousness. Suddenly, everything I saw seemed a part of the landscape of my consciousness. As I glanced out of the window of the rental car, I noticed some words printed on the rear view mirror, "Objects in mirror are closer than they appear." That tickled me to no end. "What an understatement!" I thought. In my present state of consciousness, that of experiencing life as one's larger Self, it was indeed an understatement.

I was once again inflated. On top of the world this day, I would soon fall harder than ever - and faster, too. While still in Santa Fe, I began to feel inadequate. Maybe *we* had money, but *she* controlled it, and I didn't have any. Little by little, I began to feel uneasy. I didn't know what to say to fix it. I figured if *we* had money, she would give me access, in some gracious way. However, that was not to be. By the time we got back to Austin, I was in a depression. Feelings of inadequacy and worthlessness had overtaken me.

For a few days, I floundered around Austin, attempting to find some work. If she wasn't going to share anything right away, I thought I had better find an income stream of my own. I was now in a depressed state, however, and I am certain I wasn't a very attractive candidate for employment to anyone. Susan told me she was going away for a few days to think. When she returned, she informed me she had decided it wasn't going to work, after all. "You'll have to go," she said. "And really, Mark, I think the sooner, the better."

As I packed my Thunderbird, I realized I had no money. I didn't even have enough for the gas to get to Houston. I was shocked by the realization. "Surely, she'll be conscious and considerate enough to ask and to offer something," I thought. She didn't, though. I would have to *ask* - and that was the most painful moment of all. She wrote me a check for $25, handed it to me and said, "Good luck." I had been reduced again to a beggar. I had lost everything in less than two months.

In Houston, I met an old friend I had known from the Teton retreat. Sylvia had undergone chemotherapy for a form of brain cancer. She drove an old, ragged, purple VW beetle, and was living in her car with a huge dog when I'd last seen her. Now she was living in an old, vacant house in Montrose. An absentee owner had given her permission to sleep there, and she had managed to get the electricity turned on. She invited me to stay there, while I attempted to recover from my loss. I slept on the floor on a piece of foam rubber.

A spiritual birth was on the way, but it wouldn't arrive in time for Christmas. That Christmas, our decorations consisted of a single branch of an oak tree in the window. On Christmas Eve, I ate beans from the can. I wasn't that hungry, though. I was attempting to digest an enormous slice of humble pie. I still missed the principle of equilibrium and could not see the patterns of ego inflation, which, of course, always lead to deflation. It would be a long, tough lesson. I only knew that, where I had been rich, I was now poor.

## Chapter 19
## A Return to Corpus Christi:
## A Star is Almost Born

As I sat looking out the window on Christmas Eve, the city lights obscured the stars. Turning back to the room, I picked up a book. I believe it was written by Hugh Prather. I cannot recall which one. I only read a quote given at the very beginning of the book. I seem to recall it was from a Hemingway novel. It went something like the following:

The mother's voice could be heard screaming.

The father asked the son, "Do you know why your mother is screaming?"

"She's having a baby," the boy answered.

"No," the father said. "It's called labor. What's happening is, everything your mother has, every ounce of energy in her is laboring to give birth to a child."

As I read these words, a tiny bit of life stirred within me. I sensed that, perhaps, I was laboring to give birth to something. In the vacant house, I had found an old poster from the movie, *A Star Is Born*. Without knowing why, I propped the poster against the wall, picked up a pen and began to write:

*I am my own director today,*
*And it's up to me to write the play,*
*Then direct myself each step of the way.*
*Now a step-by-step order, I pray*
*Will become so clear that I'll not stray.*
*Begin at the beginning, the Creator would say,*
*From where you are this very day,*

*Then add to, rewrite and edit your play.*
*Adjust and adjust away the gray,*
*Till it's black and white as night and day,*
*That you've done all you can to plan this play.*
*Then follow the steps, one-by-one,*
*Forgetting not to enjoy the fun.*
*Don't wait for some projected date, when you're done,*
*Or you'll find yourself in a frantic run,*
*Feeling as if your plan weighed a ton,*
*And your goal is chasing you with a loaded gun.*
*And the fun?*
*Well, there won't be none.*
*So, if you're thinking ahead,*
*To looking back, having won,*
*And being proud of or admired for what you've done,*
*Let me remind you, you are your Creator's son.*
*It is the Creator's plan, or play, if I may.*
*So to the Creator, let's remember to pay*
*The credit due each and every day,*
*Enjoying each scene within the play,*
*Even when it doesn't seem to go our way.*
*For the Creator will always have the last say.*
*Whatever our role, we always portray*
*A part written for us, we can never betray.*
*Now, don't miss the point, we do have a choice,*
*What thoughts we think, what words we voice.*
*We can hitchhike or drive a Rolls Royce.*
*But whatever we choose is on lend or lease,*
*Except when we choose for love or peace.*
*For these things, time and space cannot crease,*
*But are changeless and will never cease.*
*So, let's plan first for the things we can keep.*
*By sowing love and peace, we'll surely reap*
*That same love and peace, rooted deeper than deep,*
*And never again fall into sleep.*
*All the rest will be added us then,*
*And we won't take personal credit again.*

*We'll accept our good fortune as women or men,*
*And we'll remember, of ourselves, we can't lose or win.*
*We leave that for the next of kin,*
*Our Creator, that is, whom we all live within,*
*And who lives in us and guides us in*
*Ways that return to our faces a grin,*
*Wiping away all the pain that's been.*
*So that now it's no nightmare*
*But a cartoon, we live in.*

Well, I wasn't laughing yet...

I spent Christmas day attempting to write a plan for my life. That plan is long lost now. I can only remember that it began with finding employment again. The next week, as I moved from place to place, looking for work, I ran into Rico Cedeno. Rico had done some time in prison earlier in life but was now a successful businessman. He had originally earned a great deal of money in the oilfields, then invested it in real estate, and was now starting a new business in Houston - convenience stores that cashed payroll checks. I don't know how successful he was. I do know check cashing centers now flourish in almost every major city in the country.

Rico made me laugh at my predicament. He said, "You know, people like you and me have to always keep one foot in the gutter, so we won't forget where we came from." In other words, he was reminding me again, in a kind of street language he knew I'd understand, of the need for humility. He then told me to call him the next day and come by his apartment. He said he had an idea.

When I arrived the next day, Rico gave me a large, illustrated book that explained the oil business from the ground up. He said, "Mark, you're intelligent. If you'll take this book home, study it carefully, and memorize all of the common terms, you'll be able to speak the language of the oil field well enough to convince someone you have experience. Once you're out there," he continued, "no one will give a damn how much experience you have. It's really just hard work, and you'll learn the rest, while you're doing it. The upside is that the work pays very well. Call me when you think you have the book down, and I'll give you a lead for a job with a company I know. You can use my name," he said. "Just tell them that you worked with me on rigs in Mexico. I know they're hiring, and I'm sure my name will be all you need."

Two weeks later, I was hired by Weatherford Lamb. The personnel director told me Rico had already called him about me, and if I was okay with Rico, I was okay with him.

"Can you start right away?" he asked.

"Absolutely," I said.

"Can you be in Corpus Christi by next week?"

"I can be there tomorrow, if you want."

"Really? Well, I'll call down right now, then." He gave me an address and the name of a supervisor to whom I should report. "By the way, Rico told me you don't really have experience. So don't feel any pressure. The supervisor on this job is an old friend of mine, and he'll know, too. Rico says you're smart, and you'll work hard. You'll catch on in no time."

There is a good reason that roughnecking pays so well. It was some of the hardest work I've ever done. And it is dangerous. One's life is in the hands of others, off and on, every day. If anyone were to make a mistake or fail to pay attention to what he was doing, it could cost someone else a finger, hand or even their life. Indeed, many workers silently testify to this danger with missing fingers.

When I was in the oil field, roughnecks were working very long hours. I worked as many as eighteen hours a day, day in and day out. I didn't enjoy the work. The world of the oilfield worker was one of the few cultures in which I was never really at ease. Also, I had not really regained my emotional footing. I was still experiencing, in the words of Van Morrison, an "underlying depression."

My brother, Neal, and I connected during this time, and after some discussion, he admitted to me that he was strung out on heroin. I wanted to help but knew there was little I could do, unless Neal wanted to kick the habit. He told me he would like to try. He asked me if I would stay with him, and help him make it through the hard part.

I was not altogether naive about this process. During my years in county jails, I had seen any number of addicts be forced into kicking the habit, cold turkey. Typically, there were about four or five days, during which the user would be very sick, experiencing chills and/or fever and an aching body. I had seen them wrap themselves in a blanket and shiver. I didn't really know what it was like, though. Only the heroin addict can know that.

I agreed to help Neal. I took a week off from work, and the two of us moved into a vacant mobile home that someone had given him permission to use for this purpose. Neal seemed fine for about a day and a half. I didn't know exactly what to expect. He wasn't telling me much. On the evening of the second day, I was sitting in the living room, listening to the radio. Neal had gone into the bathroom to take a bath. I suddenly realized that he had been gone awhile. I turned the radio down and called his name. No answer. It was deathly silent.

I had to jimmy the bathroom door open to get in. Neal was lying on his back in the tub. On the floor beside the tub were the remains of a plastic, disposable razor. He had broken it open and used the blade to cut both of his wrists open. The water in the tub was dark red and warm. The blood was flowing freely from both wrists. In the center of Neal's chest was a tiny, porcelain rose. He had read Helen's book and was relating to the concept of the Heart Center.

I shook him, and he came to consciousness for a few moments. "Please, Mark. Just let me go. Please," he begged me. "It's okay, I'm ready. I just can't do it. I can't make it in this world," he continued. "I'll be okay. I've made my peace, Mark. Just remember, I love you - but please, let me go."

You may think I was nuts to consider it, but he was so sincere, I actually hesitated to disrupt his attempted suicide. Part of me felt I should honor his choice, and another part rationalized that it was just the heroin talking. At this point, the Ice Man in me took over and shut down my feeling nature. Since Neal was still somewhat conscious, I felt that he wasn't that far gone. I decided I could afford to take the time to call Helen Brungardt in Albuquerque. She took the call in the middle of the night and listened, as I described the situation and my dilemma.

"Mark, I cannot tell you what to do. It is a very difficult circumstance. The only thing I can say to you is that this is not the best way for one to depart. No one is ever lost, Mark, but the consequences of leaving in this way can be dark. You will have to decide for yourself. I will hold you in my prayers, however."

I still consider Helen's response to me that night to have been an expression of wisdom. I decided to intercede. I called in a medical emergency and was told to wrap his wrists as tightly as possible, in order to stop the flow of blood. I did, and an emergency medical vehicle arrived almost immediately. Within minutes, they had picked Neal up and were gone.

I was now alone in this vacant mobile home. I started to gather our few belongings into a suitcase. I glanced into the bathroom and considered cleaning it. The only way I have of expressing what came next is to say I felt a powerful sense of foreboding. My mind began to imagine dark forces attempting to overwhelm me. I could almost hear gnashing teeth, as if entities were furious with me for having interfered and interceded in Neal's suicide attempt.

I ran from the mobile home, as fast as I could. As I ran, I continued to feel as if, or perhaps imagine, there were dark entities flying just above me. I was terrified. I got behind the wheel of my Thunderbird and drove back to the room I had rented in Corpus Christi. This feeling waned to some degree, but did not leave me for many days. Neal survived, and I visited him at Memorial Hospital, once. I then returned to the oilfield. The strange dark feeling, however, continued to haunt me.

One evening, after a long double shift, I went to bed. I was scheduled to return to work early the next morning, and I needed to get some sleep. Finally, I dozed for about an hour and awoke with a dream. The image of the dream was simple. I was receiving several shots in my arm with a hypodermic needle. When I awoke, my arm actually ached, physically. As I lay there, I again felt a sense of foreboding. I couldn't go back to sleep. With only a few hours until I was due to work another double shift, I was worried. One part of me thought, "I should go out and have a couple of shots of scotch... maybe that will allow me to catch a little sleep." Another sense I had was more cautionary... a sense of danger was in the air.

My rational mind won over the intuitive. I was too unclear to recognize the intuition. I left and drove to a bar. After a couple of stiff drinks, I drove back home. A thick fog had settled into the late evening. As I drove down a major residential thoroughfare, I suddenly saw a pair of headlights coming around a bend in the road. They appeared to be headed directly toward me. I swerved the wheel of my Thunderbird to the right to avoid the oncoming vehicle. In swerving, however, I lost control of my car on the fog-dampened street. I remember having a sense of time being suspended... as I watched the car sliding sideways toward the trunk of a huge tree. Realizing I could not regain control of the car, I reached across the car, attempting to grab the right front door handle to try to pull my body away from the anticipated point of impact. The centrifugal force was too great, though. The impact sent me into shock.

I have a vague recall of the resident of the house, where the large tree was located, coming out to help. Then I must have passed out. Though unconscious most of the time, I was now in a medical emergency vehicle myself, heading toward Memorial Hospital, the hospital that had released my brother the day before.

The next thing I knew, someone was giving me a shot in the arm with a hypodermic needle. In the emergency room, I was again administered a shot in the arm. When I awoke from orthopedic surgery, hours later, my arm felt sore from shots, just as in the dream. The socket of my left leg was fractured. My leg was in traction. There was a large screw in the socket and a silver bar sticking all the way through my leg just above the knee, through which ropes extended to weights and pulleys.

My doctor, whom I would later learn was reputed to be one of the best orthopedic surgeons in South Texas, had apparently done an excellent job. But, he warned me, there were no guarantees. He said he felt the prognosis was that I would probably have a slight limp. I should not even be thinking about running again (I had done a great deal of long-distance running in the '70s.) He also suggested that I begin to consider other work. I probably would not be able to work on my feet for long hours anymore, he told me.

Interestingly, the day he shared this prognosis with me was the day after I had received a visit from a friend, who had brought me a copy of a new book she thought I might like. The book was entitled *Joy's Way* by W. Brugh Joy, M.D. While expressing his prognosis, my surgeon glanced down at this book as if he recognized it, and added, "Remember, this is a conservative view I am presenting. There are often positive surprises in the healing process. And, in my opinion, those surprises are more likely to occur for those with the right attitude or those exposed to the kind of material you are reading." He gestured toward the book.

Over the next several weeks, I watched as my leg withered. The rate at which it atrophied was amazing. It was the experience of "use it or lose it" made personal and visible. While reading *Joy's Way* by Dr. Brugh Joy, which is about spiritual transformation and healing, I actually felt energy running through my injured leg and hip. This book also mentioned the Heart Center or Heart Chakra. I had no idea at the time, but I had just come into contact with the teacher who would eventually facilitate my moving to another stage of spiritual development. However, this was still almost two decades away.

I also wrote Helen Brungardt and told her what had transpired since our telephone conversation on the night of Neal's attempted suicide. I was re-reading her book and noticing the emphasis on the Heart Center. She wrote back and said she was sorry to hear about my accident. I remember smiling when I received her note. I thought, "She knows there are no accidents, and since there is purpose in everything, she isn't really conveying regret, either. This is just her way of expressing compassion and being appropriate in the situation." I don't really know this. I just share it to show what my state of mind was at the time. I was no longer depressed.

Upon release from the hospital, I began the slow and painful process of stretching the muscles that had atrophied. I signed up for food stamps and housing aid, through the welfare department. Talk about being humbled.... The Thunderbird had been totaled, and my father gave me a little, used Ford Pinto to drive. Again, despite all my seeming errors and despite my harsh judgments of him earlier in life, he was still doing whatever he could to help me.

I drove back to the scene of the accident in Corpus Christi. The cross street at the intersection was named Pope Street. I had collided with a tree on Pope Street in Corpus Christi - which means "body of Christ." Coincidence? Synchronicity? Clearly, something beyond the linear was at work here.

Still in Corpus Christi, I began to visit the Unity church there. It was a small church and empty most mornings. So I would just sit and read. The minister, Ron Barringer, visited with me, from time to time, and was supportive toward me during my healing process. One day, I read an article in a magazine about an acting school in Jupiter, Florida, which had been founded by Burt Reynolds. I grew excited. I decided I would head east, stop in Houston a while, continue to work on healing my leg some more, then head to Florida for acting school.

On the way to Houston, while listening to a cassette tape of Neal Diamond singing *Heart Light*, a song inspired by the movie, *E. T.,* I was moved so deeply, I threw my crutches away. "I *will* heal. I *will* walk again," I thought.

The day I arrived in Houston, I picked up a newspaper. Quite coincidentally, it contained another article about Burt Reynolds' acting school. Toward the end of the article, I discovered the school was associated with one of Florida's major universities, and entrance was limited to residents of the state of Florida. The school was apparently not my destiny after all. The movie poster from *A Star Is Born* flashed back to mind. "More like... A Star is *Almost* Born," I mused.

## Chapter 20
## The Theater of Prosperity:
## A Rising and Falling Star

In Houston, my mother offered her couch for me to sleep on while I attempted to work on healing and strengthening my leg. I was still limping badly. I could barely place weight on the injured leg. Little by little, though, it began to stabilize. I took a part time job and enrolled in some acting workshops. I auditioned for another play, *The Odd Couple*, at a small dinner theater. My part was small. I would play Roy, one of the poker players. My leg would not pose a problem, as the role called for me to sit at a poker table almost the entire time on-stage.

One Sunday, I went to services at the Unity Church, the Golden Pyramid. The audience that day was enormous. The guest speaker was addressing the spiritual principles of prosperity. The church had overflowed into the fellowship hall, where we were forced to watch the service on a closed circuit television screen. As I watched the speaker, I sensed she was somehow familiar.

Finally, I recognized Edwene Gaines as a ministerial student I had known at Unity Village in the '70s. When I had known her, she had been a modest, young school teacher from Conroe, Texas, who didn't have two extra dimes to rub together. At that time, it would have been hard to imagine her as a powerful speaker, much less a prosperity teacher. Yet here she was, speaking to a standing-room-only audience with enormous power and a refreshing, self-deprecating humor.

Edwene was telling her story of being stranded, broke and pregnant in a foreign country, and how she had decided it was time to apply the spiritual principles of prosperity. If God is the Source of our supply, and if that Source is unlimited, she reasoned, we ought to be

112

able to access this supply. Among other things, she suggested the use of a tool she called A Prayer Treatment for Unexpected Income. I was impressed. I could see that some kind of significant transformation of consciousness had taken place within her. She was changed. So I decided to work on my prosperity consciousness. At the same time I continued working on healing my leg.

As usual, however, I wanted to perform this next experiment in consciousness by creatively combining a number of disciplines. First, I would use Helen's idea of bringing spiritual concepts out of the head and into the Heart Center. I would use the Prayer Treatment for Unexpected Income from Edwene Gaines' recent presentation. I would also use the tools of theater to add depth to the process. If an actor, through memorizing lines and through disciplined attention and creative imagination, could create a sense of conviction that translates as *believability* on the small stage, I hypothesized, I should be able to alter the nature of my own consciousness by exercising an even greater discipline in preparation for the role of being prosperous on this larger stage we call life.

Spiritual law says, "as within, so without," or "as ye sow, so shall ye reap." I determined to put it to a rigorous test. I would focus my attention in the Heart Center, twenty-four hours a day. I would memorize the words of the Prayer Treatment for Unexpected Income as if they were a script. I would bring these ideas to the Heart Center, hold them there, and wait for the deeper spiritual forces to move through me, and bring the results into manifestation. I would move the body, expressing a sense of prosperity and a belief in good fortune through my physical body. This, I imagined, should help heal my leg, as well.

I began this new practice by spending my days walking around the track at Memorial Park in Houston. It was a place I liked and which had been the scene of other transformations for me. I had spent many hours here in my running days, and I hoped I would eventually run again. I remember realizing that my sense of commitment was almost as strong as when I had begun to practice spiritual discipline while facing a life sentence. It was obvious to me that the motivation was also similar. My life had fallen apart again, and this time, the depression had been almost more than I could bear. I had to change, and I hoped that greater commitment would do the trick. My father's words drifted into awareness again, "That boy can do anything, when he makes up his mind."

Over the next few weeks, I walked dozens of miles. I held the words of the Prayer Treatment in the Heart Center consistently. I imagined that I had nostrils in the center of my chest. Every breath I took was drawn into the Heart Center. Within three weeks, I began to experience a subtle current of energy moving in the area of the Heart Center. My leg began to strengthen. One day, as I was walking around Memorial Park, I thought about the fact that I had gone from Memorial Hospital to Memorial Park. Was there something I needed to remember?

I considered the two points that had arisen within me through my encounter with Helen Brungardt. One was that the answer to the eternal quest is one and the same as the answer to the question, "What do I *really* want?" I thought I knew. I really wanted to be an actor. At least, that was true for now. The other point was, "You need to create your own structure." Then I saw my mistake. What I had failed to fully appreciate was the fact that all my good fortune in Corpus Christi in business and acting had been predicated upon the fact that I had created my own structure. I had created a successful business. I had been serving others. I had been contributing to life. And as we give, so shall we receive. That structure had been the source of my confidence and self-esteem, and that was what had made me attractive to Susan.

Yes, the spilling over effect of the prosperous attitude of Beauregard had also helped. But, I had cut away the very foundation of the new consciousness I had been trying to build. In giving away my business, it seemed I had unconsciously destroyed the foundation of my prosperity consciousness. I determined not to forget again.

An unusual experience took place one evening while I was still staying on my mother's sofa. I was watching the movie *Cool Hand Luke*. A scene unfolds in which Luke, played by Paul Newman, receives a letter. Luke reads the letter, drops it on a table and quietly walks off. The Swede, another central character, picks up the letter and reads it. He looks up and says to the other inmates, "His mother died."

The instant Swede said those words, I felt a powerful intuition. I called my mother, who was working late that evening. I asked her how long it had been since she had visited Grandma. My maternal grandmother, who had taught me to read and write and who had an interest in mysticism, was now in a nursing home. My mother said, "Not for a couple of weeks. Why?"

"If you want to say good-bye to her, you'd better go soon. I think she's getting ready to leave."

"Mark, don't say that," my mother responded.

"Mother, I'm not trying to be negative. I just got a very strong feeling, and I'm telling you so you will have a chance to say good-bye."

"Well, all right, I'll go by on my way home," she replied.

Late that night, my mother came home and said, "Well, she was okay when I was there, but to tell you the truth, I had a feeling, too, that she might go soon." That night the phone rang about 2:30 a.m. It was the nursing home, calling to inform my mother that Grandma had passed on.

About that time, I met Dell Gibson, an actor and acting teacher, who was also a media consultant for the Unity Church. As I talked with Dell about my ideas for The Theater of Prosperity, he became enthusiastic. He invited me to come and live with him and his girlfriend. He said he had an extra bedroom, and he wanted to help me. He also invited me to attend some workshops he was giving.

My sense of self-esteem was growing. Good things began to happen again. Several people, who knew what I was attempting and were attracted to the ideas, began to tithe to me. I had a new place to live rent-free and an income. It certainly seemed the principles were working. The energy in my Heart Center began to feel like a kind of grace.

Suddenly, the thought dawned on me that I had the makings for another creative structure. I would teach the metaphysical principles of prosperity, combined with the disciplines of acting. Yes, the entire world is a stage, I thought. We can choose to lift ourselves into a greater consciousness. I must use what I now understood to serve others. I would call the combination of focusing on the Heart Center, the prosperity principles and the disciplines of acting, as taught by Stanislavski, The Theater of Prosperity.

I created a brochure and presented my idea to the new ministers of the Unity Church. Sig Paulson and his wife Janie had recently accepted the ministerial post in Houston. I presented my proposal to teach what I now called The Theater of Prosperity. I remember feeling inspired. I had no doubt my project would be approved. Sig listened attentively and tentatively approved the project, saying, "I don't see why not. You'll have to take this to Janie for final approval, though. She's in charge of the education department. I think she's in her office." He then called her and sent me to her office. Janie gave final approval and scheduled a date for my first public lecture.

The Theater of Prosperity ideas were well received and well attended from the very beginning. In my lectures and workshops, I was suggesting the use of basic spiritual principles and practices, such as identifying our true desires (answering the question, "What do we *really* want?"), setting goals and making plans (we always teach what we need to learn), prayer and meditation, love and forgiveness, positive attitudes, creative imagination, and so on. The idea was to use these tools in a much more disciplined way, as if each of us was an actor, preparing to play a new role.

I suggested to students that we use the same period of time that actors typically use to prepare for a role on the small stage - six weeks. We were to adopt these new attitudes and practice as many hours a day as possible. Without really understanding why, I taught the students to focus on the Heart Center throughout. All I knew was that Helen Brungardt had taught this idea in her book, *Contemplation: The Activity of Mystical Consciousness.* I knew I felt something in that area of my chest, which seemed to be associated with the heightened state of consciousness I was experiencing.

Within weeks, I had invitations to teach these ideas at a number of Unity churches in Texas. I was flying from Houston to Corpus Christi to Dallas each week. I also began to receive invitations from other groups and Religious Science churches. At one point, I received a phone call from a Religious Science church in the Clear Lake area, just south of Houston. The minister wanted to know if the stories he had heard were true; that I had spent time incarcerated in my past. In particular, this minister wanted to know if I had been in Gatesville. When I affirmed that I had, he announced his identity to me. He said, "I don't know if you'll remember me or not, but my name is Mark Sills, and I knew you in Gatesville. I was the superintendent of the Gatesville State School when you were there. I am now a Religious

Science minister and have been writing a book about my experiences in Gatesville."

Synchronicity strikes again! "Yes," I replied, "of course, I remember you."

He then went on to explain that he felt he was still undergoing his own healing related to having been a part of Gatesville State School and its brutal practices. He seemed quite regretful to have been associated with it. I do not recall even a rumor of his having been personally involved in doling out any of the harsh punishments. I guess he had to know about it, though. Nonetheless, I had to honor his being so forthcoming.

Mark Sills was calling for another reason, too, he said. He had heard about my prosperity workshops and seminars and wanted me to present one at his church. I had no ill feelings at all about him. In my opinion, I was responsible for my experiences, and holding grudges was not an option. When I visited his church, we talked more about the old days. I still remember that he was the only minister that refused to accept any part of the love offerings received for the workshop. The generally accepted arrangement between churches and guest presenters was that we would split the proceeds 50-50, since the church provides the space and promotes such programs within the membership. But he would have none of it.

During this period, I also did volunteer work at the Unity Church in Houston, one day a week. I had been doing this volunteer work even before I received the inspiration to launch The Theater of Prosperity. I had understood for some time that a part of prosperity consciousness required giving, and I almost always did volunteer work as a part of attempting to stay in tune with this spiritual principle. I was particularly interested, during this period, in finding ways to give. I was still working on healing my leg, and I was recovering from some enormous losses. About all I knew to do was practice these principles.

I began to have conversations with Sig Paulson from time to time. I knew he was somehow important to my spiritual development. He was affluent, and I could sense he was very balanced. He was not only the one calm center during my Unity Village experience; he was also represented by a picture on Helen Brungardt's altar in Albuquerque. She considered him her mentor. One day, I was talking to Sig about giving, and he quipped, "Yes, Mark, in reality, if we can't share it, it isn't really ours." The depths to which this single comment pointed continue to serve me today. One revelation I have had about what he meant is that our attachments actually possess and control us. Another is that we can never fully enjoy anything unless and until we share it.

In another conversation, I asked Sig to share his view on tithing. Before I share his response, let me offer some historical information on tithing and some understanding of its purpose as a tool for spiritual growth and development:

The word "tithe" literally means "tenth." To tithe is to give the first ten percent of everything we receive to the person, place or institution that reflects or brings into awareness our highest spiritual nourishment. Where one should tithe is, therefore, entirely up to the discernment of the giver.

The practice is ancient. At one point, it was established among the tribes of Israel, in order to support the priesthood, so that the spiritual leaders could devote their time to seeking and providing spiritual inspiration and guidance to the larger community. This was extremely important, since Israel was a theocracy; that is, Israel looked to God (theos) to govern them. Tithing to a priesthood that devoted their time to staying connected to God in prayer and meditation was seen as the means of keeping the entire society and the government in tune with God.

Tithing has nothing to do with giving to the needy or to charity. Although charity is wonderful, it does not fulfill the basic principle of tithing, which has its basis in scripture, saying, "Bring ye all the tithes into the storehouse... and prove me now, herewith, if I will not open ye up the windows of heaven, and pour you out a blessing...that there will not be room enough to receive it."

This principle has to do with giving to God or, in lieu of God, giving to the person, place or institution that gives one the greatest spiritual nourishment or reflects the Truth best to us. Do we get our highest spiritual nourishment from the needy? Usually, our answer to this question is "no." In fact, when we give our tithe to the "needy," we impoverish ourselves, for "we become that to which we give our attention." It is fine to help the less fortunate, but that is not a tithe.

The more important question may be why not tithe? And if we look closely, we may find fear of scarcity beneath our arguments against tithing. And fear impoverishes. Period.

Now, back to Sig.

"Mark, tithing is a tool we use to heal our sense of separation from God. It's like using training wheels on a bicycle, though," Sig added. "In the long run, our lives become the tithe."

Sig had the ability to simplify the truth; to reveal its essence. He knew that any degree of real spiritual awakening reveals that we are the expression of the Divine; that our lives were never ours to begin with. He saw that giving ten percent back to the Source of our being was a minimal gesture and only the beginning of what we will eventually be called to see, as we mature in our spiritual development.

These understandings became only partly mine, by the same grace that was continuing to awaken me spiritually. This grace still required a more complete surrender than was yet possible. Looking back from 2011, on this earlier developmental period, I see both the extraordinary light that was coming into the story, and I see the immaturity and unconsciousness that were yet to be exposed to that light. I almost want to shout back through time, and say to myself, "Mark, in all thy getting, get understanding." Of course, that is happening and will happen exactly as Life wants it to happen.

Another of Helen's mentors visited the Unity Church during this period. Roy Eugene Davis is one of the few living disciples of Yogananda and was authorized to administer the Kriya initiation. His picture, too, had been displayed on the altar of Helen's independent ministry in Albuquerque, NM. I volunteered to pick him up from his hotel and drop him off after his lecture. On the way back to his hotel room after the lecture, I asked him for the initiation.

"Mark, I used to give initiation pretty much upon request. As you know, it was Babaji's wish that Kriya be given to all sincere devotees. I now feel a greater responsibility, however, to offer some instruction with the initiation. That just cannot be done on the spur of the moment. I would ask that you make an appointment with me, come to Georgia, and spend at least a couple of days. If you'll do that, I will give you the initiation."

This resonated. A few weeks later, I called and talked with one of Roy's assistants and made an appointment to visit him in at his headquarters, CSA, the Center for Spiritual Awareness, in Lakemont, Georgia. In the meantime, I received two offers to affiliate myself with Unity Churches in Dallas and Corpus Christi. Frank and Margaret Pounders, the ministers in Dallas, were gracious. Yet, I didn't feel the guidance.

The church in Corpus Christi had been supportive of my work and had sponsored my presentations on a number of occasions. I felt conflicted about that offer, too. I felt a sense of obligation to help them, but I didn't really believe the place would bear much fruit. It was too small, and the church seemed something less than dynamic.

In Georgia, Roy asked me a number of questions about what I was doing with my life and what my plans were. When I told him I was teaching prosperity, he perked up and made several recommendations of prosperity teachers he thought might assist in my development. At one point, I mentioned my offer from the Corpus Christi Church. He looked up and reacted quickly, "Oh, Corpus Christi. That's a dead place!"

I nearly fell out of my chair laughing. He had, in that cursory comment, revealed the essence of my inner conflict to me. In so doing, he had released me from my unconscious conflict about affiliating myself there. His words, in my opinion, were not a condemnation of the church. They were simply an objective observation of the facts. He had only said what I had sensed all along. It is quite likely I was saved another hard lesson by the grace of this encounter.

I am not at liberty to share specific information about the practice of Kriya Yoga. The initiation and the instruction are carefully guarded and dispensed only by those who have been authorized to do so. I suspect this policy is intended to protect the gift from being diluted by those with mixed motives. I will say that its effect is supposed to accelerate awakening in a balanced way. Well, balance was certainly called for in me. Some balance would begin to develop for me, at this point. Since I didn't even know that balance was what was needed, it would still be a slow development, however.

One evening, at Dell Gibson's house, I met Dorothea. I had just come off the road from doing some workshops and was feeling very uplifted (in danger of inflation). Dorothea and I fell in love. The relationship rapidly became intimate, and we married.

Dorothea was a grounded woman, one who had a balancing effect on me. She helped me to establish The Theater of Prosperity as a non-profit organization and to form a board of directors. She and her family did everything possible to support us and my work. They were wonderful people.

Professionally, my star was rising. My work was popular and seemed to be of service to others. Dorothea and I had begun an ongoing class at our house, comprised of some of the most committed students and board members. One evening, our group was meditating. We were using a chant made popular by Swami Muktananda, *Om Namah Shivaya*. At the end of the chant, one of the students asked me what I had meant by the comment I had made during meditation. I had no idea what the student was talking about. I hadn't made any comment, I thought. And I said so.

"Yes, you did," the rest of the class chimed in. "You said, 'It won't work, Joe.'"

"What are you talking about?" I asked. "I didn't say that. I didn't say anything."

"Yes, you did," said the entire class again, in unison. "You said, 'It won't work, Joe.'"

I was flabbergasted. I had no awareness of these strange words coming out of my mouth. Yet the evidence was overwhelming. The whole class was there to testify. I overcame my sense of confusion about the strange event long enough to finish the class, but any inspiration I had felt was now gone. Over the next days, I prayed about it. I called John Rankin and talked to him. He said he felt it had arisen from the unconscious depths of my being and was telling me that something about my approach to teaching wasn't going to work. He said he felt it might be the particular combination of disciplines I was attempting to integrate.

As usual, my relationship with Dorothea began to deteriorate in only a matter of months. It wasn't that we fought or argued. It was that something within me began to withdraw from relationship. I was still years from being able to see the unconscious patterns moving me in and out of relationship. There is a teaching that declares, "Everything is always in divine order, regardless of appearances." The realization of this teaching is a far deeper matter than affirmations or declarations might suggest, however.

A few days later, I heard an inner voice say, "Stop teaching." I felt this message was definitely related to what John had said; that something I was doing in the teaching wasn't right. I knew, too, the message meant exactly what it said - to stop teaching. No new guidance came. This message coincided with the building sense that I needed to leave Dorothea.

Dorothea's father, aware of the disintegration of our marriage, offered to help me in any way he could. He thought I might need some further financial support and told me, if money was a problem, he would be happy to help. He was sincerely opening his fairly deep pocketbook to me. I remember sitting there, thinking it was one of the most generous gestures anyone had ever made to me. I also knew he loved his daughter. He wanted her life and her love to work out. I knew, too, if I were to accept his offer, I would lose all integrity, because money was not the problem. I told him the truth. It wasn't money, and it wasn't Dorothea. It was me and my inability be in a marriage.

The problem was one of my being unable to see much of what was living through me. I was out of balance, both in my relationship and in my approach to teaching. Grace was allowing me to consciously participate in the reestablishment of equilibrium this time, though. If I would cooperate, life was going to let me down a little more gently, for a change. Nevertheless, my rising star was once again falling.

# Chapter 21
# Albuquerque:
# Going Underground for Understanding

I left Houston for South Padre Island, at the southernmost tip of Texas. It was summer, and I had decided to work out on the beaches in an attempt to complete the healing of my leg. I sold the little Ford Pinto my father had given me. I needed cash and was now without transportation. Although I did some work answering the phone and paying the bills for a friend in the interior decorating business on South Padre Island, I earned very little, and my funds dried up pretty quickly again.

Meanwhile, I walked and walked and finally was able to run again on the beaches. The muscles of my left leg were only slightly less developed than those of my right leg now. While I walked and ran, I again worked with Helen's little book, *Contemplation: The Activity of Mystical Consciousness*. This called for keeping attention focused in the Heart Center. I had been directed to stop teaching others, but I felt strongly that I needed to continue to work on myself.

As the summer drew to a close in South Padre, I determined to visit Helen Brungardt again in the Teton Mountains. I had written her, and in her response she said she planned to attend the annual retreat there. I was physically strong again, but I was also nearly broke. I chose to hitchhike to Wyoming. I was now thirty-seven years old. Only months before, I had been flying from town to town, teaching prosperity. The irony wasn't lost on me. I felt humbled and, to some extent, humiliated. Still, I had chosen to focus on my body and my spiritual work, rather than on earning money or anything else of a practical nature. Nevertheless, my failure to embrace the practical would soon be addressed. I was headed for a rather rude awakening.

This time, however, I would at least begin the task of coming into balance. That yo-yo I stole in the third grade continued to be an apt metaphor for the ups and downs that had unfolded and were still to come. Now I would still be yo-yoing along. I just wouldn't fall as far again.

The trip from Texas to the Tetons in Wyoming was the dark side of the trip from Montana to Texas. I started the trip four days before the retreat was scheduled to begin. It was early September. I spent hour after lonely hour standing on the side of the road and night after night in my sleeping bag. It wasn't as if I looked like a pariah. Having begun to discover the value of image in the theater, I no longer wore my hair long, and I did everything I could to stay well-groomed. Life just wasn't cooperating. I thought of quitting and going back. But no, there was nowhere else to go. I felt I should go see Helen. I had in mind asking her to be my teacher. I couldn't understand why it was so hard, if I was following my guidance.

Four days later, on the side of the road in Albuquerque, I remember thinking, "At this rate, I won't arrive at the Tetons until the retreat is over." I pushed on, though, and arrived in Wyoming two days before the retreat would end, still many miles from my destination. That night, I slept beside the Wind River on the Shoshone Reservation. When I awoke, I shaved and bathed in the river, put on clean clothes and began again. Once more, I stood for hours. The traffic was sparse, and what little there was seemed unaware of my presence. No one even waved.

That night, I slept again beside the river. And I prayed. My plan to go to the retreat now seemed absurd. It would be ending the next day. On the other hand, where else was there to go? As the sun rose the next morning, I felt moved to drop to my knees and kiss the ground. I felt as if I might need to acknowledge that this place was sacred, and until I accepted that, I wouldn't be allowed to move on. This thought would later prove to be an insight, upon which Helen would build. As I lifted my eyes from the ground, I saw, through my tears, an eighteen-wheeler pulling over.

The last miles to Jackson Lake Lodge were covered rapidly, and I walked out onto a deck at the lodge to find Helen still there. The retreat had ended, just minutes before. I shared my story with Helen, saying that I didn't understand why the journey had been so difficult.

She said, "Mark, there is a commandment in the Bible that says, 'Thou shalt not tempt the Lord thy God.' You have some lessons to learn about the practical side of life. Perhaps you are ready to learn them now. What are your plans from here?"

"I would like to come to Albuquerque and study with you. My guidance is to stop teaching. I believe I am supposed to be more of a student again. It's been my idea that I have been missing something essential and that you are the one to show me. Would you be my teacher?"

"Of course," Helen replied. "But you will have to make a commitment to the work. And I'll warn you, it won't always be easy. You have missed some very fundamental lessons, and I agree, it is time for you to learn them now."

After lunch, Helen asked me if I had learned to weed a flower bed in my landscaping business. I told her I had. So, she offered to buy me a plane ticket to Albuquerque, suggesting I could work off the price of the ticket by doing yard work. "There are no free lunches from here on," she told me.

In Albuquerque, I slept on the floor of the Institute for the Emerging Self (IES), and I worked in Helen's flower beds. I was paid slightly more than minimum wage. She had large flower beds that had been neglected for some time. The work was very hard, and I felt more and more deflated by the experience. At one point, I was attempting to find some sense of the spiritual in what I was doing. I started thinking that maybe this was symbolic of finding the roots of my issues and weeding them out.

When I said that to Helen, one day, she replied, "A friend of mine, Alan Watts, was visiting here at my home once. I think I can tell you what he would say, 'No, you're just digging in the dirt.'" There would be no chance to inflate again anytime soon. Life intended me to stay "grounded."

My next move, after paying off the plane ticket, was to be the caretaker for the Institute for the Emerging Self. I was living there and had to earn my rent. I was to do the janitorial duties. Also, Helen asked me to help solicit works of art for a benefit art auction she was planning as a fundraiser for the Institute. Since I had no car, I was to work with another of Helen's students. Pat, my coworker, was a former bookkeeper and, from my point of view, very picky with details. I was experiencing sharp resistance to working with her.

Finally, I brought my problem to Helen. She said, "Mark, as I indicated before, you are here to learn some very fundamental lessons. Without Pat, whose car is needed to call on artists, you have no way to succeed at acquiring art for the auction. Pat is a very practical woman. Unlike you, she is concerned with the details. That is one of the lessons you need to learn. Underneath it all, you are here to learn humility and gratitude. Until you learn to be grateful for what you have, no more will be given. I suggest you take a little time, and consider what I'm saying. You said you wanted to study with me. These are your first and most fundamental lessons. The only question is - are you really ready to learn them?"

I was stunned by what I would later learn was one of Helen's essential teaching methods. Her other students had a name for it. It was called "blasting" or "being blasted." No one who came to study with her had managed to avoid it. I stepped from her office, or I should say I stumbled from her office. Talk about feeling off balance.

I walked outside for a few minutes. As I walked, I considered the teaching technique Sri Yukteshwar had used to help Yogananda grow, as recorded in *Autobiography of a Yogi*. Yukteshwar's way was not popular, but it was deeply effective for those students who could bear it. At one point, Yukteshwar told Yogananda he knew that his way of pointing out the deficiencies in the student was very hard on the ego. On the other hand, Yukteshwar had said, "It is my way. I only seek your best interests, and should it prove too difficult, you are free to go, anytime you wish."

It seemed to me that Helen's comments were made in this same vein. It was also a little like my father saying, "Unless you are willing to follow the rules of the house, you can head on out that door." I was still reeling and in emotional pain when, a few minutes later, Helen appeared again.

I said, "I want to stay and learn, but I don't know how to move through this pain."

"Yes, you do," Helen replied - and walked off.

Although I would know Helen for fifteen years, I never knew what it was she thought I knew about moving out of the pain I was feeling. I can only say that I walked back outside, stood looking at the ground and remembered a sentence in her book, "We must learn to live this way, as we go through the routine of our daily lives - Heart Centered; Heart Centered and consciously knowing the truth, no matter what is occurring, until we come to be habitually at home at the Center of our being, with both feet on the ground."

The ground...digging in the ground...kissing the ground...and now, as I stood looking at the ground, I shifted my attention to the Heart Center. Amazingly, I felt an immediate lifting of the painful emotions; I felt a sense of balance return. I felt "grounded," and I returned to work.

Helen's next assignment for me was to have a home and a car of my own. These, she explained were practical matters, I could no longer afford to ignore. Did I say *practical?* She was relentless on the subject. I took a second job, washing dishes at night; then a waiter's job and another bartender's job. It was the bartender's job at the Regent International Hotel, where I would encounter Alan, my guru of plans, again.

About this time, Helen asked Tyrone Campbell if he would consider allowing me to stay with him, while I was getting on my feet. Tyrone was, and is today, one of the most knowledgeable people in the world on the subject of weavings, especially Navajo weavings. We had become acquainted at the Institute for the Emerging Self, where he bought and sold weavings from an office he rented in the same building. We liked each other, and he watched me working to get back on my feet. He agreed to share his apartment with me, while I continued to try to put my life back on "solid ground."

Tyrone drove a brown 1976 Cadillac El Dorado, and from time to time, he would send me on errands. As I drove the car, I would visualize having a similar car. It was one of my earlier learned prosperity techniques. The idea was to imagine it, as if it already *is*, and it *will* be. Sometime later, as I walked to work one day, I saw a brown 1976 Cadillac for sale. It wasn't quite the cherry Tyrone's was, but it looked good to me. The sign on the window said the owner wanted $1,400 for it. I had about $300 saved. I decided to ask the owner if he would hold the car for me, until I raised the rest of the money. I told him I would give him the $300 down. He agreed to sell me the car and said that I could pay him $200 a month.

Then, surprisingly he said, "You can go ahead and drive the car. I have liability insurance on it for now, and I'll give you thirty days to get your own."

That night, as I parked the car beside Tyrone's, I noticed that both cars had the same left rear hubcap missing. Had I, unconsciously, visualized a missing hubcap?

While employed at the Regent International Hotel in Albuquerque, as bar manager, I was offered the position of room service captain. The room service department was a mess and was losing money, I was told. It was my goal to fix it. Within days, I discovered the whole department was involved in stealing. I caught one waiter pocketing order slips (guest checks) and money. Under threat of arrest and in tears, he confessed the scheme was being used by every waiter there. I offered to let him simply resign, if he would sign a statement implicating the other waiters. He did.

I hired Renee, a new waitress for the department, and told her what I was facing. I explained that I intended to terminate everyone in the department; that I needed someone to roll up their sleeves, and work around the clock, and help me make the room service deliveries while I hired and trained new waiters. She agreed to join me. I called each member of the wait staff into my office, one at a time, over the next two days. I showed them the letter and asked each one to sign a resignation. Meanwhile, Renee and I worked day and night. I interviewed and hired during the slow times.

I spoke briefly to Helen about the number of hours I was working. I told her I just hoped I could find and train help before I dropped from exhaustion. She responded by telling me a story about how Ben Franklin would take little catnaps and wake refreshed and inspired after only a few minutes of sleep. She said the key was to set one's intention; that is, go to sleep telling oneself, "I will sleep deeply for twenty minutes (or whatever period of time was available), and I will wake up fully refreshed and inspired." I took to sleeping under some stairs in a tiny closet. I taught Renee the trick, too. It worked miraculously well. Helen had said we are never given more than we can handle; that we are always given the resources necessary, when we are committed to doing the right thing.

Within two weeks, we had turned the department around. At the monthly staff meeting, we discovered the sales had quadrupled. And, just like Theodore's, we had created a staff that was honest, respected each other and took pride in doing a good job. Everyone knew we had done it together, and everyone was acknowledged. A palpable sense of well-being was generated and felt by the members of the room service staff.

Several months later, I began to feel frustrated by the fact that, regardless of my success in room service, I had not been able to move up any further into management. Again, I talked to Helen. She asked if I had worked through the proper channels in asking for a promotion. I answered affirmatively. She asked if I was sure I had gone the extra mile in every way. Again, I said I had. Helen then said, "In my opinion, you are not being properly appreciated or compensated for the level of commitment you have shown. This is a sign that it is time for you to move on. You may want to consider quitting." I was surprised.

"Shouldn't I find another job, first? I mean, wouldn't this be like 'tempting the Lord, thy God,' again?"

"No," she answered. "This is a case where you have done your best. When you are giving all you have to give to something, you are building inner substance, and that substance will support and sustain you. You can have faith, when you have built the inner substance." She then quoted scripture, "Faith is the substance of things hoped for; the evidence of things not seen."

"I have no doubt you will be guided to another place, where your services will be more fully appreciated," she continued. "And, whatever you do next, make sure your compensation is increased. Spiritual law requires that you be properly rewarded for your services."

I left the hotel and launched a new business. I decided I knew the keys to turning a business around. I believed it was primarily the staff. They were the building blocks that made it possible to succeed. With the right people and by treating those people with respect and by sharing a vision of success, I believed I could turn other businesses around. I named my management consulting business Building Blocks.

Also, I now had a two bedroom, fully furnished apartment. This more gradual process of building substance seemed to be just what the doctor ordered. I was beginning to understand now. Indeed, the word substance means "stands under." I could sense a feeling of something more solid growing within me. As in Corpus Christi, in the landscaping business, doing my best and going the extra mile were giving me this good feeling, this feeling of substance.

At any rate, I had one more lesson to learn, before I would have the keys to turning businesses around. I learned it from the owner of the first restaurant to hire me as a consultant. My business, Building Blocks, was not a consulting company that simply advised. My vision was one of assuming the management of a business for a period of time, long enough to clear out problem employees, and hire and train new ones, who were fully subscribed to the turnaround. I would then make plans, set goals and proceed to implement the vision, step-by-step. Finally, I would train a manager behind me, and move on.

What I didn't understand yet was that people might say they wanted to turn their business around but not be willing to exercise the discipline necessary to do so. The owner of the restaurant that first contracted me expressed great enthusiasm for the idea. She also turned out to have an agenda that was in direct conflict to the turnaround. She was spending the business money on all sorts of personal matters. And, she didn't give me full access to the books.

Meanwhile, I followed the rest of my formula. I managed to rid us of the mediocre members of the staff. I hired new, enthusiastic help. Ronnie West, who was now living in California, came to visit me and stayed to help me again in the early days of this turnaround. I enrolled everyone else in the idea that, together, we would bring this business back to life; we would create a success, and it would be enjoyable to be a part of this. Formerly, the restaurant had been open only at night, and now we began to open for lunch. We called on everyone in the community and asked them to try us out - and they came.

Within two months, we had doubled the business. The owner, however, claimed that other costs had escalated. She had one emergency after another, for which she claimed she had to have money. Finally, I discovered she was using the business cash flow to fund her emergencies. Then, despite the fact that cash flow had doubled, I found we had not paid all our vendors. Companies began to require us to pay cash, rather than allowing us the normal thirty days. This was another burden on the cash flow. I knew we could make it if the owner would agree to stop draining the cash. She promised to do so, but she still wouldn't give me unfettered access to the books. She secretly kept on with the very behaviors that had hurt the business before. She was unconsciously sabotaging herself. It was a case of "killing the goose that laid the golden eggs."

I was also very attached to being successful with my first endeavor. I stayed far too long, attempting to succeed in spite of her. Eventually, I allowed myself to see the lesson clearly. I would never again take a contract without being given access to the books and a large degree of control over cash flow. My ability to effect turnarounds increased dramatically. Building Blocks became my first sustained success in business and served me and others for years.

The inner teacher in me remained underground during this period. I was counseled by Helen to keep my mouth shut, and to be frank, that was fine with me. I was now enjoying the role of student. I became the most committed student at the Institute. I managed the volunteer staff for Helen. She placed more and more responsibility in my hands. I was required to be present and to coordinate almost all of her events, including regular Sunday services. She told me that I was not to forget that the priority was my spiritual work. My career was simply the proving ground, where I was to demonstrate the spiritual principles. She held the attitude that if a business wouldn't let me have the time off I needed to assist her, it was not the right place for me, and I should move on.

Amazingly, standing firmly on my commitment to the Institute as my priority never cost me a position or a contract, even when she announced a pilgrimage or a retreat that she expected me to attend - and Helen loved to plan retreats and pilgrimages.

We spent a week with Preston Monongue, the adopted son of Grandfather David Monongue, Keeper of the Keys of the Hopi prophecies. While there, our small group experienced a phenomenal spiritual manifestation while participating in a ceremony at Prophecy Rock. Prophecy Rock is considered a sacred place and is where petroglyphs convey ancient prophecies about a coming time of enormous change. It depicts, among other things, the idea that some of the white race will unite with the native race in choosing a new and more harmonious way of relating to life and, more particularly, to Mother Earth.

During the ceremony, light rain began to fall. This, in itself, is considered a very positive omen, in the arid land of Hopi where rainfall is rare and is seen as the gift that nourishes life in the manifest realm. Then suddenly, the rays of the sun flowing through the raindrops cast before us the most vivid double rainbow I have ever seen. It is the only double rainbow I have experienced where both arcs were complete and brilliant.

While working on this book in 2011, I was contacted by another of those who had gone on this pilgrimage and with whom I had not spoken in over twenty years. He said, "Mark I remember it as a *quadruple* rainbow. The brilliant double rainbow was reflected as another, less vivid, double rainbow." At any rate, it was breathtaking in its radiant beauty and appeared directly before us. No one spoke a word, as we were captivated by this phenomenon of nature.

It was so phenomenal that Preston, a renowned Native American artist, decided he had better take us up to Grandfather David, and tell him about it. I believe Grandfather David, who was known and highly respected by the whole of Native America, was 114 years old at the time, and blind. His mental and spiritual faculties, however, were still finely tuned. As we entered Old Oraibi, the oldest, continuously inhabited community in North America, we could see Grandfather David moving down the street with a cane.

"What is going on here?" he was saying. "I feel something important has happened. Someone needs to see me. Who is it?"

As we gathered in his home, Grandfather David listened carefully to Preston telling him about the event. After hearing Preston's report, Grandfather David conducted another ceremony in acknowledgment of the fact that an important event and a significant connection had been validated by the wondrous forces of nature.

Helen also led pilgrimages to Peru where we visited Machu Pichu, the Nazca lines and Cuzco.

On the relationship front, my pattern continued. I had a number of short-term relationships. I made no commitments. I hoped this stance would keep me out of the really painful circumstances. One evening, as I expressed this belief to Helen, she offered another in a long series of the confrontational lessons I had, by now, learned to roll with. She said, "Mark, you are offering women something you are not able to give."

It only took a moment to see that this was true. I was sending a message saying, "I am available to love you." But that was not the whole truth. I was only willing to give as long as it didn't become too painful. I was incapable of fulfilling any durational commitment. In my heart, I had known all along that many of the women I had been with had been hoping for more from me. I quickly saw and admitted this to Helen. She wasn't satisfied, though.

"Don't assume that being even more up-front about your intentions lets you off the hook. You have been given much, and to him who is most aware falls the greater responsibility. You must learn to be discerning. It is up to you to see the truth about the women you meet. Just because they are willing to be with you doesn't mean it is right. Look deeper. Listen to your deeper wisdom. And stop offering that which you cannot deliver." This little talk curtailed my sexual activity.

My relationship with Sig Paulson evolved during this time, too. Sig and his wife, Janie, were on the Board of Directors for the Institute for the Emerging Self, and they visited us a number of times. On one such occasion, Sig gave his signature twist to an already popular story, as follows:

Some researchers set up a maze with hidden cheese. Mice were released into the maze and would run around, looking confused, smelling the cheese and looking for it. Eventually, they found the cheese. The next time they were released, the mice would remember where the cheese had been and would run straight to it. The researchers would then move the cheese. The next time the mice were released, they would run straight to where the cheese used to be. Then, again looking confused, they would back up once or twice, and come back to where the cheese used to be.

Eventually, realizing the cheese must be elsewhere, since they could still smell it, the mice would begin the search anew, and run up and down the maze until they found where the cheese had now been placed. The researchers concluded that mice must be more intelligent than humans, because humans will return over and over and over to a place where there is no cheese, because they believe the cheese should be there. In fact, they said, humans will continue to run to where they believe the cheese should be, even when there has never been any cheese there.

"I guess you could say that the Kingdom of Cheese is within you," quipped Sig, at the end of the story.

Another mysterious event, involving Sig, took place during the third of my four years in New Mexico. I was working on the turnaround of a Rax Restaurant in Las Cruces, New Mexico. Helen called and reminded me that the International New Thought Alliance's annual conference would be held in Houston that year. It was scheduled for the next week. "It will be at the Adams Mark Hotel," she said. "And," she added, "Sig will be there." I could tell she was hinting that she thought I should be there. She rarely gave me direct advice anymore, though. She expected me to know for myself.

At that precise time, I was in the middle of what I considered a crucial stage of a turnaround. I had the staff I wanted, and they were trained, but the week the I.N.T.A would be held was the week we had coupons coming out in the paper. That meant, if the coupons were successful, we would get slammed with business. I knew that taking care of the business was crucial to earning the trust of new customers. I didn't feel at all comfortable going. I told Helen so. She made no further overture.

"You'll just have to follow your own guidance," she said, and we hung up.

I noticed I felt uncomfortable with my decision. I sat up in bed at the motel where I was staying and entered a time of meditation. Toward the end of the meditation, I had a vision of Sig. I was looking at him and thinking that I really needed some healing. I was imagining that he knew I had a lot of underlying stuff - unresolved issues, impurities, that kind of thing. In the meditation, Sig walked up to me and looked down, as if peering down into my head. Then he said, "I think everything is just fine."

After the meditation, I decided I should go to Houston. I called Helen back and talked to her some more. She said, "Mark, who do you think is responsible for the success of your ventures?"

I answered, "God."

She said, "Don't you think this Power is great enough to solve your little problem?" Then she reminded me, "Your first priority is spiritual. I know you are trying to do the right thing by the business. Yet, if you fail to follow your spiritual guidance, you will be cutting yourself off from the foundation of your success. A way will open for you, if you keep your priorities straight."

I appointed an assistant manager that week and charged him with the responsibility of handling the business in my absence. The first day I was in Houston, I saw Sig in a hallway, talking to someone. The hall was filled with conference participants. Sig, who is quite tall, exited his conversation and walked up to me.

"How are you, Mark?" Strangely, he seemed to peer down into my head, just as he had in my vision. He quickly answered his own question.

"I see everything is just fine." Then, turning on his heel, he returned to his original conversation.

The rest of the week was enjoyable, yet somehow anticlimactic. One more surprise awaited me on my return, however. As I drove up to the restaurant, I winced as I saw the parking lot was full of trash. There were paper cups and bags strewn in every direction. My heart fell. As I entered the back door, I saw my new assistant, hunched over his nightly paperwork. "What in the world? How long has it been since you guys picked up the parking lot, Brent?" I was angry.

"Don't you say another word," said Brent, "until you see these numbers. We have been cleaning the lot every night," he continued. "The reason it looks like it does is because we've been raking it in. I looked it up. Our previous high in weekly sales, before this week, was $6,700. Tonight closes this week, and we did $12,400. That's nearly double," he beamed.

The spiritual teacher in me had taken a four-year sabbatical, gone underground for understanding, and understanding had translated itself into at least some spiritual and material substance.

## Chapter 22
## Santa Fe: Setting the Stage for a Big Surprise

In early 1987, Helen asked me to take a look at her daughter's restaurant. It was losing money and had become a burden. Helen's daughter, Karla, and her husband, Glen, and I worked out a contract, and I moved to Gallup, New Mexico, to manage the restaurant. While there, I was still expected to continue my duties as coordinator of volunteer help at IES. I would close the restaurant on Saturday evening, drive 140 miles to Albuquerque, and oversee the setup of the banquet room at the Sheraton Hotel for the Institute's Sunday services. Helen called these services Serendipity Sunday.

After services at the Sheraton, I would often have lunch with Helen, and I would visit her at her home in Corrales from time to time. On these evenings, we would discuss spiritual principles, and I had the opportunity to bring up any personal issue I wanted. One Sunday night, I told Helen that I was experiencing a lot of conflict about my relationships with women. I really hadn't had any relationships at all lately. A part of me wanted one. Yet, the pain I had experienced, time and again, had given me cause for much hesitation. I had been reading a lot about yoga and other Eastern approaches and was wondering if maybe I should give up the idea altogether, and commit to a life of celibacy.

After explaining these things to Helen, she said, "Mark, I may not be the best person to talk to about that. I suggest you talk to Sig and Jack (Dr. Jack Holland, another of the board members of the Institute). They will both be coming to our next retreat in Santa Fe at the Bishop's Lodge." The retreat at Bishop's Lodge was called a Celebration of the Teachings of Joseph Murphy. Joseph Murphy, now deceased, had been a leader in the New Thought Movement. We were going to honor his contributions to our field. His widow, Jeanne Murphy, had agreed to attend.

Helen had spoken with both Jack and Sig and had asked them to make some time for me. I did airport runs and picked up Jack at the airport in Albuquerque. As it turns out, Jack had chosen celibacy after a long and fruitful marriage. He told me he hadn't started out to take the route of celibacy, but he had loved his deceased wife so much, he couldn't really imagine another relationship. The choice had been made long ago, he added, and if he had it to do again, he might well choose to have another relationship.

I would have to wait to talk to Sig, as I was scheduled to take him back to Albuquerque, after the conference. Meanwhile, I got a glimpse of Helen as a human being, for a change. Our relationship had always been one of student to teacher, which had been fine with me. On this particular occasion, Helen was in one of the banquet rooms we were using for presentations. Sig, whom Helen referred to as her preceptor, was sitting at the center of a dais at the front of the room. Helen was chatting away about this, that and the other thing, when suddenly, I heard her say something critical. Having heard her own words echoing back to her, she looked up toward Sig and said, "I guess I better watch my idle words...."

Sig immediately responded, "It might help to remember - there are none."

I thought I saw Helen flush, just a mite. We all laughed, though, and moved on. Sig's way was always the way of fewer words. He both practiced and preached through an economy of words. One of my favorite one-liners that exploded through Sig was, "An open mouth reveals the contents of the mind behind it." A truth that could cut either way, I thought.

At the end of our conference, Sig and I drove south toward Albuquerque. We made a stop at Sunrise Springs, another spiritual retreat center just south of Santa Fe. Sig had heard this retreat center had a multi media chair, with audio and video wired into a single unit. The participant could relax, and allow the music and colors to wash over him. After Sig tested out the consciousness-altering contraption, we took a walk. Actually, I had a number of questions I had been saving for this time. I decided to save the relationship issue for last.

"Sig, how do you relate to prosperity teachings? You never seem to struggle with it. How do you see the manifestation process?"

"To me, it seems that life is like a stream of consciousness, and our job is not so much to struggle, as to wait for the spiritual vision, and be true to the vision. Most of the time, I find that it is my place to catch the vision, and hold it. What happens is that a portion of the stream of consciousness is crystallized or made concrete. The greater problem isn't really manifesting what we want, though. It is knowing when to release that which no longer serves and allowing it to dissolve back into the stream."

My next question involved my attempt to understand the deeper meaning of the crucifixion and the resurrection, as a pattern in my own life. I had died a lot of deaths, spiritually, and I had been lifted again many times. I posed my question a little more like a statement. I said, "It seems to me that the key is to accept the crucifixion, with less resistance. I mean, we are all crucified over and over, in a way, aren't we?"

Sig's eyes had a glint in them, and his face broke into a smile.

"That's true, Mark. But some people get off the cross, and then insist on dragging the damned thing around with them."

We both exploded with laughter. Our subtle attachments to our sense of victimhood had been made graphic in a single moment of time. The image I had of how we hold onto that which no longer serves has remained with me, indelibly impressed upon my consciousness by a burst of laughter.

On the road again, I told Sig about my relationship issues. I told him about the inadequacy that arose, again and again, when I attempted to enter into a committed relationship.

"Mark, we are all wounded. I suspect our wounds are part of what make us who we are. I may have never told you, but my mother committed suicide, when I was quite young. For many years I carried the feeling that I should have done something more. In fact," he continued, "I can still feel a stirring right now, as we speak about it." With that, he placed his hand over the center of his chest (Heart Center). "When it comes to relationships, we just have to listen within. The real question is, 'What do you *really* want?'"

I hesitated momentarily, thinking about that same question again. What do I really want? Finally, I answered, "I guess I really would like someone to share my life with, but I don't have much to share."

Sig looked up in surprise.

"What do you mean? You have your *life* - and there is no greater gift."

Tears entered my eyes, as I felt something deep within me shift. At some hidden level, I had still been judging my worth by material measures and had never even considered the fact that my *presence* was a gift. His words seemed to penetrate me. This set the stage for a big surprise.

# Chapter 23
# India:
# Opening into Grace and Casting New Roles

During the first week of September, 1987, I received a long-distance telephone call from Helen. She was at the annual Teton retreat, and I was at work at her daughter's restaurant in Gallup. Helen had been planning a pilgrimage to India, and I felt I could not afford to go. "Mark, I've been thinking, and I've decided I want you to accompany me to India as my co-host. I realized I had better call you and let you know right away, because our departure date is October 1st. Since we'll be gone three weeks, you may need to make some plans at work to cover yourself while we're away."

"Helen, you know I used to have a burning desire to go to India, back in the '70s, but I really don't feel a need to go anymore."

"That's good," she replied, "because we're not going to fill your needs. We're going to pay homage to our spiritual roots."

That statement, in my opinion, explains the reason our pilgrimage was an experience of an almost continuous flow of grace. Helen's attitude set the tone for the trip, and those of us who joined her did so by joining her in consciousness. We adopted this attitude from the start.

I have known many pilgrims who traveled halfway around the world to India to seek spiritual wisdom, only to return disappointed or confused. India is a mysterious place, and she does not give up her spiritual treasures to those who are unprepared. In my view, the difference between seeking and paying homage is the same as the difference between attempting to get something out of a sense of lack, and giving something out of a sense of abundance.

One of the strangest statements in scripture, when viewed literally, is Jesus saying, "To him that hath, even more shall be given, and to him that hath not, even that which he hath shall be taken away." It is not so strange, after all, when viewed as an expression of spiritual principle. When we come from the Source of Being (abundance), more is added. When we come from the egoic sense of separation (lack), we experience more lack.

Helen had aligned with and set an intention for the flow of grace. The restaurant in Gallup was now operating in the black. It was no spectacular success, but it was no longer a financial drain. I told Karla and Glen I had to go to India. I put things in order and flew into New York City on September 29th. I was staying at an inexpensive hotel, while Helen was in a suite at the Waldorf Astoria. I was to meet her there for cocktails and a discussion of my duties as co-host. It seems Helen had been told things would tend to unfold much more easily for us in India if hotels and airlines dealt with a male, rather than a female group leader. So, outwardly, I became the group leader and her liaison.

Somehow I knew, even before we left on this trip, we were in for some dramatic changes. I remember thinking on the long flight that nothing would ever be the same. Yes, India is a mysterious place, and she would unveil herself to us in ways we could not have imagined.

We had a full day and a half scheduled at leisure in Bombay, to recover from jet lag. After a number of excursions to holy sights in the Bombay area, our little group of seven gathered for an evening meal the night before departing that city. I recall the participants asking Helen if she would perform a Kriya Yoga initiation for us at some point on the trip. Helen had been authorized by Roy Eugene Davis to convey this initiation, and a number of us who had experienced the initiation with her in the past were hoping to do so again. The ceremony and the spiritual experience were nearly always uplifting to all. "We'll see," was her only response.

Within minutes, we began to observe a phenomenon that would show us that ceremonies might not be required for uplifting experiences. One of our group, Ray Anderson, an accountant from Canada, began to shake uncontrollably in his chair at the dinner table. I had noticed it from the moment it began, because I was sitting directly across from him and had just been talking to him. At first, it was a subtle, almost imperceptible shaking. Then I noticed his eyes rolled upward toward the third eye or sixth chakra. Immediately, I began to recall my own experience, so long ago in Tucson - the one I always thought of as my "mini-samadhi." Someone started to reach out to him as if to comfort him, and Helen quickly prevented it.

"Let him be."

The shaking grew more obvious, and tears started to stream down his cheeks. "He is experiencing an awakening of the kundalini," Helen explained. "We need to respect the process, and watch over him. These experiences can be disorienting, at times."

That was certainly true! For the next two days, Ray was floating on a cloud. He could barely relate to the physical world. When we arrived at our next destination, he had no desire to go anywhere or see anything.

"Where could there be to go?" he asked me. "It's all already here."

We traveled next to Ganeshpuri, the headquarters for Siddha Yoga. The ashram is huge, with many structures, and it appeared to be efficiently run. Compared to most of India, it is lavishly furnished and decorated. We were there to celebrate the fifth mahasamadhi (yogi's conscious exit from the body) of Swami Muktananda. Years later, the irony of Ray's comment, "Where could there be to go?" occurred to me, as I discovered the title of one of Swami Muktananda's books was *Where are You Going?*

Ray felt no impetus to move back into the world. He was absorbed in a state of ecstasy. Although he eventually became a bit more grounded, he remained in an altered and heightened state throughout the trip. He would not be alone.

I felt no particular resonance with Swami Chidvilasananda, more popularly known as Gurumayi, the new leader of the Siddha Yoga tradition. I did pay homage to her, as I understood she had been appointed personally by Muktananda to succeed him. It was not at the ashram, but in the little village of Ganeshpuri, where I would make a more conscious connection to the grace that had begun to flow amongst our group.

Swami Muktananda's guru, long passed from the body, had been a peculiar man with a big belly, named Swami Nityananda. He had been known to entertain cobras and speak incoherently at times. I told Helen I had heard there was a little temple devoted to Nityananda in the village of Ganeshpuri, and I wanted to visit there. I asked her to accompany me.

We discovered a very small, humble temple devoted to Nityananada. A single disciple, a tiny man at least 70 years old, was attending to the care of the temple. When we arrived, he was dusting the walls and sweeping the floors with a small short handled broom. There was a placard at the entrance explaining that this direct disciple of Swami Nityananda's had taken a vow of silence and had devoted his life to the care of this temple. Prasad - tiny, white, sweet pellets that symbolically represent the sweetness or ecstasy that is the grace of the guru - was freely offered to those who might wish to receive it, the placard explained.

The little man watched with a glint in his eye and a smile on his face, as I approached the altar of the temple. I knelt before two silver sculpted feet, a replica of Swami Nityananda's feet. As I leaned over and kissed the tiny silver feet, I placed a few rupees on the altar. I could feel a shift in consciousness begin to take place. Tears entered my eyes as I realized, at a deep level, that to reach the feet of the guru is to touch my own deepest essence. Meanwhile, the disciple-caretaker had transformed himself into the disciple-priest. He held out his hand and offered me prasad. As I swallowed the prasad, I understood I had accepted the grace represented by the act.

I fell prostrate to the ground and wept uncontrollably during the following minutes. Then a deep peace filled me, and I was transported into further ecstasy; a sense of wonder beyond any I had known since Tucson. Again, all that had seemed to be outside of me was now a part of me. The disciple-priest seemed to be an old, forgotten inner friend. I imagined he knew what was happening and had seen it many times. His smile was one of compassionate understanding.

Helen, too, seemed to be an old, inner friend; a part of me. And she, after having followed me to the altar, now stood by the door, watching reverently, until at long last, I rose from the floor. My next inner impulse caused me to empty my pockets of all the rupees I had with me, and lay them on the altar. The little disciple-priest and I bowed slightly toward one another. He returned to sweeping, and I stepped out into the sunshine of one of the most glorious days I have ever known. Helen seemed to know it was not yet time to speak of it. We remained silent as we returned to our lodge. This conveyance of grace and the expanded state of consciousness remained with me, to a somewhat lesser degree, throughout our pilgrimage. Next would be Helen's turn. Her experience would prove less comfortable. It would be no less life-changing, however.

Our next stop was Bangalore and the Puttaparti Ashram of Sai Baba. Sri Satya Sai Baba, the "man of miracles," was revered by thousands as an avatar, as God incarnate. He is reported to possess miraculous powers, which he uses to heal the sick; interpret the meaning of dreams without being told of them; appear in more than one place at a time; and manifest objects out of thin air in front of large crowds. One of the most common manifestations is the creation of *vibhuti*, a fragrant sacred ash.

The ashram was extremely crowded, and, although Sai Baba appeared on a number of occasions, he was always at least 100 feet from our little troupe. We could see him handing items to people, which he appeared to materialize as he wished. I was unimpressed, yet I have learned to remain open to these things. I was already in a heightened state of consciousness and didn't mind, one way or the other, what happened.

On the final day of our visit at the ashram, as we departed, I noticed Helen seemed to be a little off balance. Normally confident and take-charge in her actions, she now appeared shaken. When I asked her about where and when to gather for the next leg of the journey, she shook her head, as if to indicate that she didn't wish to be bothered about that just now.

I did my best to coordinate with everyone else, and we gathered for a flight to New Delhi. On the flight, Helen confided in me, "Something very strange happened. Sai Baba appeared to look me in the eyes, and when he did, I saw fire coming from them. At that moment, I saw that I am spiritually stuck, because I have remained in a marriage without love. I had known I was not growing anymore spiritually, and I had asked Sig about it. Sig told me that, by asking him about it, I had already opened up to the next stage. He said that the way would be revealed. Now I know I have to leave my marriage if I want to grow again. I had always felt I was staying until the kids were all grown. They are gone now, and I have stayed in the marriage. I realize I have been afraid to leave, because I have never really had to take responsibility for earning money before. My husband has always been the provider, and a very good one. Please keep this conversation confidential for now, will you?"

This was a big change. The teacher had revealed her humanity, even her fallibility. The teacher-student relationship would now change, I knew. I felt a spiritual calling to offer whatever support I could.

"Whatever I can do, let me know."

In New Delhi, we climbed aboard a brand new Mitsubishi minibus. In India, this is the equivalent of riding in a Rolls Royce. It was beautiful and had air conditioning and a stereo sound system with speakers, front to back. Helen seemed to regain some of her equilibrium, but she was not the same Helen, by any means. I was still in a heightened state, as was Ray. Everything seemed to fall into place. Even if we seemed to make a wrong turn, it would always lead to something wonderful.

Our next stop was to be Agra, but on the way I saw a sign for Vrindavan, formerly Brindaban. This, I knew, was the birthplace of Krishna, the Hindu equivalent of the Christ. I told Helen we should make a stop there, and she quickly agreed. While in Vrindavan, we paid homage to the birthplace of Krishna in a small temple, where tiny silver feet at the altar symbolized the feet of baby Krishna. Again, I led the way to the altar, and Helen followed. I pointed out the tiny feet to her and knelt and kissed them, then rose to my feet. Helen, too, knelt and kissed the feet, then began to cry. It was a gentle sobbing. I sensed her sadness. Later, she explained that she felt a sense of profound relationship with India and yoga, beyond any she had previously imagined.

Next stop, Agra, the home of the Taj Mahal. Beautiful as it was, the Taj was not the point of greatest impact for us. It was the Agra Fort, next door to the Taj, that would be the scene of the next stage of Helen's serial awakening. It was Helen's turn in the spiritual barrel. While there, she had a vision of herself in a position of royalty and rulership. I only learned of this later, but she entered this state of consciousness while there. I knew something had happened to her. It was most evident as we left. A large crowd of tourists were streaming toward us, coming up a ramp leading into the fort. Helen seemed unconscious of her surroundings. She was walking right down the center of the ramp, with head high in the air. The crowd was parting, as if they unconsciously sensed they should make way for her.

Later, when Helen told me of the vision, she said the important part of her realization had been that, in the consciousness of royalty, she felt no love for the people. She thought it might have been a past life, and if so, she said, it was one where she had everything except love; and the result had been a profound feeling of loneliness and isolation. She further confided that the truth was, she was having the same problem in this lifetime, to some extent. She felt she had access to a great deal of wisdom, but actually felt very little love.

The teacher was now lost from sight. I realized Helen had opened up to a new stage of growth, and she would need me as a friend, not a student.

Our next encounter of substance would occur in Rishikesh. Rishikesh literally means "city of seers" and has long been considered a holy city. It was made better known to the West through a visit by the Beatles, during the early days of their spiritual search. We were most interested in a visit with Swami Rama. We were graciously received by him for a private audience as a result of Helen's relationship with Roy Eugene Davis.

Swami Rama is the subject of a wonderful biographical work entitled *Swami* by the author, Doug Boyd. Doug documents some of the research projects that Swami Rama submitted himself to at the Menninger Foundation. Swami Rama is also the founder of the Himalayan Institute in Pennsylvania. In the studies done at the Menninger Foundation, Swami Rama revealed rather amazing abilities to control his breath and the rate of his heartbeat. He claimed to have developed these abilities during a lengthy period of intense meditation practice under the tutelage of Himalayan masters.

As our group of seven gathered in a tiny room with the Swami, he closed his eyes and entered a short time of meditation, after which he asked us what he could do to serve us. When no one immediately replied, he suggested we might have questions.

I began. "Swami, what do you feel is the primary difference in the consciousness of the East and that of the West?"

Again, he closed his eyes for a moment. "In the East the tendency is toward the subtle and subtler, toward Source. In the West the tendency is toward the gross and grosser, toward manifestation." After years considering these words, I believe Swami Rama's answer encapsulated a balanced perspective of essential Truth.

Then the Swami turned to Helen and asked her a number of questions about her life. I recall Helen telling him that she had four children, and they were all grown now.

"Ah," said Swami, "then you are free now!"

The Swami had cut to the core of Helen's issue. His words seemed to her and to me a validation of the idea that she needed to leave her loveless marriage. Before departure, Helen performed a Kriya initiation for us all. Then we boarded a plane for home, a home that would never be the same for any of us. I had been further opened to grace, and Helen had been opened to her pain. There had been many surprises. The really big one was yet to come. If Santa Fe had set the stage, India had cast the new roles.

# Chapter 24
## The City of the Sun:
## A Changing Curriculum

Tucked down into the southernmost edge of New Mexico, about three miles from the United States' border with Old Mexico, is the village of Columbus. It is a tiny town with a population of about 300 in the summer and 500 in the winter. Columbus' primary claim to fame resides in the fact that it is the only place in the continental United States ever to be invaded by a foreign national power. The famous Mexican revolutionary, Pancho Villa, and his followers raided the village in 1896, provoking an Old West style manhunt. Gen. George S. Pershing was dispatched by President Theodore Roosevelt. He led the army into and throughout the northern states of Mexico in a search for Pancho Villa that lasted for years. It was entirely unsuccessful. Today, Columbus acknowledges this nearly forgotten page of history with a little state park named the Pancho Villa State Park.

On the northern edge of Columbus is an even smaller community. The City of the Sun, with a population of between fifteen and thirty, is all but ignored by the world. It is located on private land, originally donated to the City of the Sun, a non-profit organization, by Wayne Taylor, the founder. Wayne claimed to have been spiritually guided to this location for the purpose of establishing an intentional spiritual community. When I met Wayne in late 1987, he was quite elderly and failing in health. He never tired of telling me his story, though. He had been part of the early "light groups," spiritual study groups, which formed in the early 20th century to seek spiritual light or awareness. More than anything else, Wayne believed this area of land was a place of healing. He said he had received spiritual guidance that told him

148

there was a dome of light over the area that both protected and healed those beneath it.

The City of the Sun would play a vital role in the next stage of my development by providing the locale for an important and surprising shift in the curriculum of my spiritual education. When Helen and I returned from India, we outwardly resumed our lives as usual. Privately, we were discussing Helen's decision to leave her marriage, and since I had agreed to support her decision, we were brainstorming about how we could manage it. Although Helen's household income was high, she had no control over any of the finances. Afraid of confrontation with her husband, Helen told me she wanted to leave home and let the courts handle divorce and settlement proceedings. This meant we would have virtually no financial resources. Since I was working for Helen's daughter in Gallup, Helen felt I would have to leave that job in order to keep her daughter from being in a conflicting position between her parents' interests. So we were looking for a place to ride out the storms of divorce and await the settlement Helen was expecting.

The third or fourth week after our return from India, we were holding what we called Community Sunday. Once a month, after the Serendipity Sunday service, everyone was invited to stay for brunch in the Sheraton Hotel's dining room. We sat at round tables of between six and eight persons each. Helen and I were seated side-by-side at one of the tables. To my left was a tiny little woman, about seventy years old, named Dorothy Rayburn. Dorothy said she had been waiting to ask us for some help. She wanted to know if we would pray for her to sell her house. She then pulled some pictures from her purse and showed them to us. The house, she explained, was located in a small, spiritual community, and the real estate market in the area was all but nonexistent. She said she had lowered the price three times and was willing to sell it for even less. She just wanted out so she could move back to Albuquerque.

As Dorothy continued, I glanced at Helen and telepathically communicated to her that we might want to do more than pray for the sale of the property. Perhaps, it might serve an immediate and practical need, which only the two of us knew existed. I asked Dorothy where the house was located. She said it was in a place called the City of the Sun, just outside of Columbus, New Mexico, and could be reached by car from Albuquerque in about four hours. She then revealed that one of the biggest obstacles to selling the house was the fact that anyone who might be interested in buying it must become a member of the City of the Sun. The City of the Sun, she told us, was operated by a set of by-laws that called for the majority of the community to vote on acceptance of new members, and new members were required to pay a one-time membership fee of $600.

We promised to pray for the sale of Dorothy's house. Privately, I inquired when she might be available to show it. She said she would be there beginning the next day. This encounter provided the final catalyst for Helen's departure from her home and her marriage. She never returned home again. We left the service that day and drove to Columbus. Helen had no clothes, almost no money and no real plan. Despite all the lessons I had been given by Alan, my guru of plans, I didn't have a plan either. Life, however, did have a plan of its own. The love offering from the services that morning contained a check for $2,300. It was made out to Helen and was accompanied by a note expressing the giver's desire that Helen receive it, personally, as a tithe.

In Columbus, Helen and I walked out on the land surrounding the City of the Sun. Helen was terrified about having left. She was dressed in a green sweater, blue jeans and cheap tennis shoes we had purchased at K-Mart. I don't believe Helen had ever shopped at a K-Mart. I know I had never seen her in such inexpensive garb. I told Helen to lie down on the ground and feel how the earth was there to support her - to just let go and let life hold her up.

She did let go, and as she did, she began to cry. As she wept at length, I glimpsed a dome of light over the area. The auras that had slipped from view in my youth had been obvious to me again for years. In fact, experience now tells me that most people can easily be taught to see them. In any case, all spiritual phenomena are just that - *phenomena*, fleeting and destined to pass away. This includes seeing auras and ecstatic states and the deflations that follow all spiritual inflations. But at this still early stage of awakening, it was not given me to realize this or even remember it much of the time.

As Helen gathered herself again and stood, she said she felt this was definitely the right place for us. We agreed there seemed to be a healing quality to the area. The City of the Sun happened to be holding a monthly membership meeting the next day. At the meeting, we were unanimously approved for membership and paid our one-time fee. In the meantime, Dorothy agreed to sell us the house for $17,500 with no money down and $300 a month, pending approval of our membership. The next day, we signed a simple real estate contract and traveled back to Albuquerque and Gallup to wind up our affairs. I gave notice to Karla and Glen. They agreed to release me that week, since they now understood my presence there could pose conflicts within the family.

Helen asked me to present the final Serendipity Sunday service for the Institute for the Emerging Self, as she did not plan to attend. For the first time in over four years, the teacher in me was called forth to speak again. It was a sad service. It had fallen to me to deliver the news to her students that Helen was filing for divorce and exiting her public ministry - all at once.

In late November, Helen and I bought used furniture from a number of thrift shops in El Paso, kitchen and house-ware items from Walmart, and groceries from Safeway. We moved into the house on a Wednesday. The next day, Thursday, was Thanksgiving Day. This was our first day in our new retreat house and a time set aside for grace and gratitude. We cooked turkey and the trimmings. By nightfall, we knew our relationship had been irrevocably altered. There was no discussion of marriage. We did, however, make a commitment to stay together, to share the spiritual path together, and to do all we could to help each other grow. And we promised to love each other.

To say this was a big surprise is an understatement. I was shocked by the developments. I felt impacted in a number of ways and knew I would now be required to make major adjustments. Fortunately, I did not yet know the degree or the depth of the adjustments that would be required.

For one thing, I had lost my spiritual teacher. The confident dispenser of wisdom had disappeared. Helen had expressed her desire for further spiritual awakening, and her prayer had been answered. Now her persona had cracked and broken. My years in the therapeutic process had shown me that opening up emotionally, being vulnerable, could lead to deep healing and a greater acceptance of one's self. I believed Helen simply needed a safe environment in which to process these feelings, and I wanted to offer containment.

In the place of the teacher, another aspect of the mystery of Being arose in Helen - a vulnerable and fragile girl. I had bought an old Norman Rockwell collector's plate at one of the thrift stores the day before. It pictured a young girl on a bench in a train station with a suitcase beside her. If memory serves, it was entitled *Leaving Home*. This plate, which I kept beside me for the next decade, would remind me that I had joined, less with a teacher of wisdom, and more with an innocent woman who wished to know love.

Also I felt, for the first time, I had something to give that was not only valuable but also needed. Something had shifted within me when Sig had reminded me that my life was a gift worth sharing. Unwittingly, I had entered into the territory in consciousness that would require further healing for me. Regardless of the hidden or unconscious aspects that were functioning in our coming together, I also knew this was happening for our highest good. The Mystery of Being, in its march toward awakening from the belief in separation and identification with form, takes many forms. The sacred curriculum was now, outwardly, a changing curriculum.

Over the next two years, Helen and I wandered in a spiritual wilderness. Her divorce and settlement proceedings were, as she had predicted, difficult and protracted. During this period, I attempted to earn money and support us, but my ability to do so was limited. At one point, I went to San Diego to find work and couldn't find a job. I was living in a cheap motel, paying weekly rent. I submitted dozens of applications for jobs in management, and I waited. And I waited. I was at a complete loss as to understanding why nothing seemed to work. Finally, I decided I had better just take any job. Then, I reasoned, perhaps I can work my way up by applying my usual high standards of performance on the job.

I told Helen, who was struggling to keep up with her bills back at City of the Sun, to come on out to San Diego and join me. She did so. I took a job at a large hotel on Harbor Island as a part time busboy and part time dishwasher. I remember the interview that got me the job. The personnel director told me she had no positions available but would keep my application on file in case anything opened up. Of course, I knew what that meant. Nothing. Adios. Good-bye.

I said, "I have never seen a hotel this big that didn't at least have need for a part time dishwasher or busboy."

"That may be true, but you are overqualified for those positions, and I don't think you would be happy in them."

"Ma'am, I need a job. And I need one badly. I would be very happy to take any opening you have. All I ask is that management watch my performance, and if they like the quality of my work, promote me when openings occur. I can promise you I will always be at work on time. I will always wear whatever uniform the job calls for, and my grooming will be immaculate. I will display a positive attitude and will not complain about anything. In my opinion, you have little to lose and much to gain if I turn out to make a positive contribution here."

The personnel director asked me to step into a waiting room while she made some further inquiries around the property. When she called me back in, I had a job as dishwasher and busboy. Over the next few weeks, I was promoted to cashier, then waiter, then to assistant manager of the restaurant. At one point, the hotel furnished Helen and me a $100 a night hotel room as a temporary incentive to keep me there. Helen had received a sum of money as part of her settlement, and we had decided to return to Columbus. The food and beverage director listened to my reasons for wanting to leave and offered me the hotel room and another promotion to restaurant manager.

I was under consideration for the assistant food and beverage director's position when we finally left. In a matter of four months, I had moved from making less than $200 a week and living in a cheap one-room weekly rental, to earning $40,000 a year and living in a $100 a night, 12th floor luxury hotel room overlooking the Pacific Ocean. Yo-yo should have been my middle name.

More wilderness days were waiting, though. Helen and I returned to what we now referred to as the retreat house in the City of the Sun. While there, Helen and I sought spiritual guidance as to what we should do next. We had little doubt we would be called to serve again. The problem was, we had no idea about what form that service might take. The feeling was one of not belonging anywhere. We prayed about it, and we fantasized about it. There were no answers forthcoming.

We eventually came to understand that this is the nature of a spiritual wilderness experience. It is a time when one is called to turn away from attempts to control life (as if one ever can). It is a time when one is called into a deeper surrender. As Kahlil Gibran puts it in *The Prophet*, "Think not you can direct the course of love, for love, if it finds you worthy, directs your course." We were wandering in the wilderness and waiting for our course to be directed.

# Chapter 25
## Washington DC: Accepting Holy Orders

As Helen and I continued the process of surrendering and seeking guidance about where and how to serve again, I happened to read a book by Joseph Murphy entitled *Prayer is the Answer*. In this book, Dr. Murphy offers a mystical interpretation of the holy sacraments. One chapter particularly caught my interest. It was the chapter on Holy Orders and is devoted to unveiling the deeper meaning of ordination. The outer ritual is intended to reflect an inner commitment by the individual to practice the presence of God continually. This is accepting Holy Orders, and when this is done, "You are now a moving, healing force. You are ordained."

(You may recall that it had been at a celebration of the teachings of Joseph Murphy that the stage had been set for this new relationship with Helen, and that Dr. Murphy had performed Helen's ordination many years before.)

According to Dr. Murphy, this decision to inwardly accept Holy Orders, to devote one's life to Truth, is symbolized by the outer ritual or sacrament of ordination. According to Dr. Murphy's book, receiving Holy Orders inwardly means making a commitment to devote one's hands to giving spiritual gifts; one's feet to going on spiritual missions; one's eyes to seeing the sacred in all life; one's ears to listening for divine guidance; one's tongue to speaking truth; one's mind to spiritual understanding; and one's heart to expressing an unconditional or divine love for all creation.

As I read the words in this book, I felt I had already placed myself under Holy Orders. I knew I wanted to express this commitment outwardly. I wanted to experience a formal sacramental ritual of ordination. That central question, "What do I *really* want?" had been answered again, and the answer had provided the guidance and the impetus that began to move Helen and me out of the wilderness and back into service.

A little research revealed that minor amendments to the by-laws and articles of incorporation of the Institute for the Emerging Self would make it legal for the Institute to confer ordination. Helen was in full agreement with the idea. We contacted the board of directors of the Institute, held a special board meeting via conference call and gained approval for the amendments. All members of the board agreed to participate in my ordination. Since we all planned to attend the annual International New Thought Alliance Conference in Washington DC that year, it was determined the ceremony would occur there.

Each of these board members had played a significant role in my life. Janie Paulson was my first prosperity teacher, while I was studying at Unity Village. She was also responsible for placing the final stamp of approval on the Theater of Prosperity, allowing me the opportunity to bring it into visible expression. J. Sig Paulson was my teacher's teacher, and he became both a teacher and a friend to me. I know he would be the first to decline credit for any personal achievement and the last to claim arrival at any final destination in consciousness. Sig recognized the value of the human and the divine, as aspects of a single, sacred dance of life. For as long as I've known him, Dr. Jack Holland has been at the forefront of the true givers in our society. After experiencing a dramatic spiritual healing, he devoted his life to uncovering and expressing the relationship between the scientific and the spiritual. And, of course, Helen Brungardt has given me more than words can say.

These four and I gathered in a small meeting room at a luxury Hotel in Washington DC. There, I was charged with and accepted Holy Orders. As Sig had said, "In the long-run, our lives become the tithe." We are called to give much more than one tenth. Our lives are not really ours, anyway. We are the formless Life expressing Itself as form.

# Chapter 26
## A Return to the Neighborhood:
## Visions and Manifestations

Helen and I took the southern route home from the I.N.T.A. conference in Washington, DC. We picked up Interstate 10, then traveled west to Houston. I planned to introduce Helen to the Montrose District, the old neighborhood that had been the setting for so many of my early spiritual experiences. We toured Montrose and took a walk in Memorial Park, where I had walked to strengthen my leg after the collision on Pope Street in Corpus Christi. It had also been while walking in Memorial Park that I had received the initial inspiration to launch the Theater of Prosperity.

On this day, as we strolled through the park, I had a vision. The face of Babaji, the East Indian Guru who, according to Paramahansa Yogananda's *Autobiography of a Yogi*, had revived the ancient art of Kriya Yoga, appeared on the screen of my mind. As in the case of my earlier vision of King Tut, the face appeared alive and radiant. He spoke seven words, "It is time to write the book."

For some time, I had felt that I ought to record my spiritual experiences in a book. I had not spoken about the idea to anyone. I knew, without a doubt, that this was the meaning of the words I was now hearing. I felt a sense of encouragement and inspiration. At that time, I thought of the book as a compilation of the highlights of my spiritual experiences. In my mind I called it *Autobiographical Notes*. The reason I had not acted on the idea was that I felt I still lacked enough understanding to make the book valuable to others. That may have been true. However, if it were not for my writing these early chapters and filing them away, I would almost certainly have forgotten some of the important details of the experiences. Indeed, the book I was about to write was less a book than it was a set of autobiographical notes; notes which have served me in recording this account and in remembering experiences that were transforming, and which characterized the path toward further awakening.

I told Helen I believed we should stay in Houston. I told her I felt being in Montrose would serve in remembering the experiences I was now being guided to record. I suggested to her that we should rent a little garage apartment, like those I had lived in during the '70s. It was obvious to both of us that the neighborhood was no longer the vibrant spiritual center it had been in days past. In fact, much of it now appeared neglected and run down. Nevertheless, Helen agreed, and we set out to look for an apartment we could rent on a month-to-month basis.

The following day, after several phone calls rendered no viable possibility, we stopped at a bank of pay phones to make more calls. As we sat in the car, I suggested to Helen that we might want to exercise the prosperity principle of imaging as taught by Neville, the author of *Your Faith is Your Fortune*, *The Law and the Promise* and *The Miracle of Imagination*.

This principle says that, if one can imagine being in the specific circumstances one *wishes* to be in, and if one can achieve and sustain the *feeling* that would be his or hers in that circumstance, then the circumstance must manifest accordingly. Neville teaches that, to manifest our dreams, we should travel in consciousness to a place where the dream is a *felt reality* and remain there, in faith, until the dream is made manifest. In this sense, it is said, "To travel is the privilege, not of the rich, but of the imaginative."

Neville teaches that it is important to employ all the senses in the imaginal experience, *seeing* and *feeling* and *hearing* the details of the imagined experience. I found the teaching similar to Sig's, as he had conveyed it to me in Santa Fe, when he said he felt that the key to prosperity is simply waiting for the spiritual vision and holding or being true to the vision until it comes into manifestation. So, Helen and I decided to attempt an experiment along these lines. We decided we wanted a large, two-story garage apartment, behind one of the old Victorian homes in Montrose, in order to replicate more fully my early days and ways of living in the '70s. We imagined floor-to-ceiling windows and an old, claw-foot bathtub. We envisioned the apartment to be a combination of my favorite color, hunter green, and Helen's favorite, yellow.

Having noticed some of the run-down pockets in the neighborhood, Helen also insisted the apartment be in an area with friendly neighbors. Finally, in order to better employ the senses in the imaginal experience, I visualized us walking around inside the apartment, looking at an old claw-foot bathtub, and walking upstairs where we encountered huge, floor-to-ceiling windows on every side. I then imagined myself lifting Venetian blinds and saying to Helen, "Look at these wonderful windows," whereupon I imagined I felt the hot sun strike my arm through the window.

We sat in our car and played out this vision, in detail, several times. The imaginal experience became more and more real for me. Once I felt a sense of conviction, I opened my eyes, and we proceeded to study the classified ads again. I exited the car and walked toward the bank of pay phones to make another call. As I stood at one of the pay phones, I glanced across Alabama Street and noticed a large, Victorian home. It was *yellow* with *hunter green* trim and had a red and white sign in one of the windows with the words, "Apartment for Rent." Even though I had felt a sense of conviction in my vision, I still shuddered when I saw it.

I walked back to the car and pointed out the sign to Helen. She said she had goose bumps. We drove across the street and into the driveway. Before we could knock on the door, a Latin American man and his young son came out to greet us. In halting English, he explained that, yes, the apartment was still available. We then walked to the rear of the house, where we found ourselves standing before a two-story garage apartment with twenty-two, floor-to-ceiling windows. Like the house, the apartment was painted yellow with hunter green trim.

Inside the apartment, we found a large, claw-foot bathtub in the upstairs bathroom. I then walked toward the windows that faced out from the front of the apartment. I said to Helen, "Look at these wonderful windows." As I said this, I reached up and bent the Venetian blinds and felt the warm sunlight hit my hand and arm....

Earnesto, the resident of the house, told us he was from Nicaragua and was only helping the landlord rent this apartment. He assured us, however, it would be okay to rent on a month-to-month basis. In the excitement of such a positive response to our imaginal exercise, I had forgotten Helen's final criteria, that the apartment had to be in a friendly part of the neighborhood. Nonetheless, as we were preparing to leave, Earnesto's little boy said something in rapid-fire Spanish. Although I speak some Spanish, I didn't understand him. I looked questioningly at Earnesto.

He said, "He wants me to tell you, he wants to be your friend."

Over the following days, I wrote a first draft of the initial chapters of these autobiographical notes. Memories emerged in vivid detail, and the words flew from my pen. While writing, I knew that the book would not be completed until I reached greater spiritual maturity. I had been given the visions, though, and the manifestations had followed, as surely as day follows night.

# Chapter 27
# A Return to the City of the Sun:
# A Movie and the Ministry Behind the Ministry

Back at the retreat house in the City of the Sun, Helen and I turned our attention to seeking guidance as to how we might serve again. There was no question in our minds about what we were meant to do. We believed we were meant to minister. The question was more a matter of where or to whom.

One evening, I rented the movie *Resurrection,* starring Helen Burstyn and Sam Shepard. I had seen it at an art theater in Houston during my time of recuperation from the auto accident in the early '80s. I had been touched by this movie and wanted to share the experience with Helen.

In one sense, the movie tells the archetypal story of the wounded healer. A woman experiences a clinical death and has a spiritual vision. She is then drawn back into her crippled body, which has sustained irreparable nerve damage. She eventually discovers she has the ability to heal herself. She then attempts and is successful in extending this healing to others. The implication is clear. Having been wounded herself, she has been opened to being able to transmit this gift.

Two scenes are particularly significant, in a mysterious way. The first occurs after the woman is released from the hospital, as she is being driven back to the Midwest from California by her father. They stop at a quaint, old service station in the southern California desert, where an old man with a glint in his eye attends to them. A sign painted on a hubcap is visible on the side of the station. It reads, "God is Love and Versa Vice." Upon realizing the young woman is crippled, the old man attending the station casually places one hand on

161

her head and one on her hands, looks her in the eye and says, "Arrivaderci, young lady. You go in peace, and remember, when life gives you a bunch of lemons, you just make yourself a batch of lemonade."

The second scene occurs at the end of the movie. The young woman, having encountered a number of problems, including a great deal of resistance to her healing gift on the part of some of her Midwestern neighbors, decides to leave. A time elapse camera shot informs the viewer that many years have passed.

The final scenes are set in the southern California desert. An RV, with a couple and an obviously sick little boy, pull into that same quaint, old service station. On the side of the station sits the old sign on the hubcap, "God is Love and Versa Vice," now cracked and peeling. Our protagonist, the wounded healer herself, now much older and gray-haired, is the attendant. She entertains the couple and the little boy in much the same fashion as the old man had entertained her, so many years ago. After asking and discovering the little boy has terminal cancer, she gives him a little puppy and extracts payment for the puppy from him in the form of a hug. The last scene is a freeze-frame in which she now lays her hands casually on him in an embrace we know will somehow mysteriously facilitate a healing and extend the gift of healing.

Over the years, I have watched this movie on many occasions, and its significance continues to unfold for me. On this occasion, in the late '80s, it spawned an idea that would become and remain the real essence of ministry for me. I called the idea that occurred that night the Circle K Ministry. It is symbolic to me of the ministry beneath all ministry. I will explain it, as I understood it at that time.

First, I sensed a similarity between the awakening and healing that occurred in the film and my own initial early awakening. My auto accident and healing in Corpus Christi also seemed to follow this pattern. Secondly, I also resonated with the idea that we are eventually called to give back to others that which we have been given. I had begun to appreciate the possibility that *wounding* is often the means by which we are opened up spiritually. The wound can be the metaphorical crack through which the light emerges into awareness and expression. Finally, I sensed that a certain spiritual maturity had occurred by the end of the film. The protagonist now trusts life to organize the events and circumstances necessary to the conveyance of her gift. There is no longer any attempt to control or explain or justify the gift. It is simply given, wordlessly, to whomever life places before her.

As you may know, Circle K is the name of a large chain of convenience stores. In my experience, most people enter and leave convenience stores in a hurry. Often, no real contact is made with the clerk, who may, at times, be viewed as an automaton.

My idea was, rather than encountering others unconsciously, one could choose to be conscious of the underlying spiritual essence or spiritual nature of anyone, anytime, anywhere. The key, as I saw it at the time, was simply to allow Life to organize the circumstances and to remain conscious as they occur. In my view, as it began to develop while watching this movie, there is no need to announce one's qualifications for ministry, nor is there a need for a building or a congregation. All that is really required is a commitment to remembering the Infinite Invisible Truth of Being, which commitment I had made by accepting Holy Orders.

That night, an idea had been born within me that would enrich me for years to come. I no longer needed to wait for a job or guidance about who or where to serve. The ministry beneath all authentic ministry is always calling all who have ears to hear. It is always *here* - and it is always *now*.

# Chapter 28
## A Return to India:
## All Our Tomorrows Have Their Own Ways

What may be the largest spiritual gathering on earth occurs every twelve years in the city of Allahabad in India. It is the Kumbha Mela, a religious fair. The Kumbha Mela is held in the lunar month of Magh (January-February) every three years, and its location rotates among four cities: Hardwar, Ujjain, Nasik and Allahabad. Although each is held on the banks of a river, it is the Kumbha Mela in Allahabad that is considered the most important. It is held at the confluence of three rivers: the Ganges, the Yamuna and the mythical Saraswati, or invisible river of Spirit. Saints, sadhus, ascetics, yogis and other pilgrims gather at the Kumbha Mela to gain spiritual merit, by bathing at the point of confluence at this auspicious time.

The Kumbha Mela has ancient roots. The Chinese Buddhist traveler, Hsuan-tsang, records a visit to the Allahabad Kumbha Mela in the 7th century, in the company of the emperor, Harsavardhana, who distributed religious alms on the occasion. In the eighth century, Sankara, the founder of the ancient order of Swamis, exhorted all sadhus to meet at the Kumbhas for an exchange of views.

The myth that underlies this famous pilgrimage claims that the gods and the demons fought over a pot of elixir - *kumbha of amrita* - that rose up from their joint churning of the ocean. In order to retain possession, the gods ran off with it. On their return to heaven, they rested the pot at four locations, thus sanctifying the four sites of the Mela.

In interpreting this myth, we may view the ocean as the vast unconscious realm, in which the dark and light forces of our relative being struggle. The redemptive result of this struggle is that the

164

spiritual nectar (Transcendental Source of all opposites) is extracted from it. Visiting the sight of the Kumbha is a form of symbolic redemption or awakening from the struggles of the individual with the dual forces of life.

My relationship to the Kumbha Mela began in the late '70s, when I first read *Autobiography of a Yogi*. According to Yogananda's account in this book, it is at the Kumbha Mela in Allahabad that Babaji appears to Lahiri Mahasaya, the yogi he authorized to teach Kriya Yoga. Lahiri Mahasaya finds Babaji there, demonstrating humility by washing the feet of a renunciate. It was at a Kumbha Mela, that Mahavatar Babaji first appears to Sri Yukteshwar, Yogananda's guru. Here, Babaji expresses his interest in seeing an exchange and a balance of Eastern and Western virtues. It was for the fulfillment of this desire to contribute to the exchange between East and West that Yogananda was trained by Yukteshwar.

I had calculated and knew the Kumbha would start again in Allahabad in January of 1989. I felt a strong desire to make this pilgrimage. Helen, who had been authorized to carry on the tradition of Kriya, felt a strong attraction to the idea, as well. So we made plans to go. This time, there would be no students to accompany us. We felt it more appropriate that the two of us make the journey alone. On the second day of January 1989, Helen and I boarded a flight in Los Angeles bound for Calcutta. The following words are a combination of the recorded entries in my journal of this pilgrimage and some additional remarks, written after our return.

*Jan. 5:* "We arrived in Calcutta this morning. We think our primary purpose is to attend the Kumbha Mela. The East has a way of deciding for itself what the purpose of its visitors is, however. It behooves us to keep a very open mind."

These words would set the tone for a journey filled with delays, canceled flights, lost reservations, synchronicity and surprise. Later that morning, I would make this entry in my journal: "...we are reminded that God is in charge.... It turns out neither the local tour agency nor we have any air tickets for the next leg of our journey. According to our itinerary, we are to fly to Bhubaneshwar tomorrow morning.... Today we are scheduled to visit Belar Math Temple on the Ganges River."

My next journal entry reads, "Well, Belar Math is canceled, and Dakshineshwar Temple, which was to follow, is canceled, as well. At this time, it appears our flight to Bhubaneshwar is fully booked. However, the plan is to go to the airline in the morning anyway, and Tamas, our local tour guide, will attempt to get us tickets. We are having a great time on our pilgrimage, which has now taken us on a 2-1/2 hour tour through the slums and prosperous neighborhoods of Calcutta. I found it difficult to differentiate between the two.

"We were told that one outstanding characteristic of the Calcutta people is their tenacity in the face of problems. This is characterized, it was pointed out, by the citizens hanging on to the sides of buses, trucks or whatever, in an attempt to traverse the city. We are now enjoying tea at the tour agent's office. It has been decided that, as a last resort, we may hold on to the side of our plane, Calcutta style, and thus overcome our apparent problem."

*Jan. 6, 12:45 p.m.* "We still have no idea what to expect next. We'll see. We may fly to Bhubaneshwar, and we may not. God only knows, and even He or She may not. As Joe Cocker, the musician sings, 'All our tomorrows have their own ways....' And as soon as I know, I'll let you know."

*Jan. 6, 2:24 p.m.* "We are now sitting at the airport in Calcutta. We have our tickets. Our baggage is checked. Whether we board our plane and fly to Bhubaneshwar or not remains to be seen. The appearance has changed, though. We are now assured by the travel agent that we are going. Also, they have contacted our U.S. travel agency, and the rest of our airline tickets for travel within India are being purchased and will be given to us on Jan. 10, when we return to Calcutta on our way north to Varanasi and Allahabad for the Kumbha Mela.... We'll see...."

*Jan. 6, 5:07 p.m.* "We arrived in Bhubaneshwar. Our next local travel agent, however, did not meet us at the airport according to schedule. So we negotiated a taxi. It is a little, three-wheeled, open-air job. The price we settled on is 20 rupees ($1.40 US). The other taxi drivers attempted to intimidate us and our driver. They wanted us to take a larger, traditional taxi, saying our taxi driver didn't belong to the right union. Neither we nor our driver succumbed, however. When at last he pulled out of the airport for the hotel, Helen and I applauded him for his tenacity. He simply beamed.

"At the hotel, we asked the clerk to call our local travel agent, which he did. While the clerk was on hold on the phone, the travel agent arrived at the hotel, apologizing profusely. He agreed to pick us up at 9:00 a.m. for the drive to Puri tomorrow. After he left, the desk clerk informed us, 'Your travel agent answered the phone and put me on hold. While I was holding, he jumped into his car and drove quickly to the hotel. He is afraid you're mad at him.' Everyone at the desk laughed uproariously at this revelation. Isn't this fun?"

*Jan. 9, 7:55 a.m.* "We arrived in Puri, Orissa on schedule. Our main intent is to visit the seaside hermitage, founded by Sri Yukteshwar. It is there that Yogananda underwent much of his training. It is there Yukteshwar entered mahasamadhi, a yogi's conscious exit from the body, some 53 years ago. It is there that his body was buried and enshrined by Yogananda. We had some difficulty in locating the hermitage. Puri is a popular pilgrimage destination and is the location of many ashrams and temples. We decided upon visiting any temple or ashram we could find and asking for information which might lead us to the one we sought. After some two hours, we found it. It is now (1989) called the Kriya Yoga Meditation Center.

"The meditation hall, lined with pictures of the masters, is altogether unostentatious, reflecting the simplicity of the truest of yogis. The Swami in residence greeted us with a warm smile. We received permission to walk and enjoy the grounds. We have visited the ashram, also called Karar Ashram, each morning and evening now for three days.

"Our hotel, the Southeast Railway Hotel is situated on the beach of the Bay of Bengal. It is a pleasant surprise. Its architecture is English Colonial with huge verandas. Our room is upstairs and overlooks the beach. The service is delightful. There are probably two workers for every guest, and all are cheerful, attentive and courteous. Helen and I usually tip a 10 rupee note (.65 cents US) for any small service - delivery of tea, mineral water or whatever. The gratitude they express is nearly incredible. One fellow, today, literally bounced up and down on his toes with glee over a 10 rupee tip. I have a feeling most guests don't tip here. If not, it is too bad, as they are missing a special opportunity to experience the joy of giving.

"The outside workers all wear white bamboo hats, shaped like a Hershey's chocolate drop, coming to a *point* at the top. They remind me of a cartoon image on the cover of the Harry Neilson album, *The Point*. In case you aren't familiar with this work, the *point* of *The Point* is that there is a *point* to the existence of each of us, regardless of who we may seem to be in the world of appearances... no matter how *pointless* we may seem from any given *point* of view. And there is more of a *point* to our meeting these workers than has yet to be *pointed out*. At any rate, the pointed hats of each of these friendly workers at the Southeast Railway Hotel have a number painted on them. Two of these gentlemen offered their special services to us, bringing prawns and lobster for dinner, taking us out in a fishing boat or anything else we might imagine we wanted. These two call themselves Number 4 and Number 8. Helen and I have taken to calling them Mister 4 and Mister 8. They are comical characters, probably sixty to seventy years old, running around the property with almost lunatic grins on their faces."

*Jan. 11, 10:45 a.m.* "A Puri lesson has finally unfolded. Yesterday, on our final day in Puri, we began to be confronted by all our friends. They wanted us to give them money. It all began with our rickshaw driver, Jaganath. Jaganath was hired on our first day in Puri, to drive us back to the hotel from the ashram. After some checking with our guides, we realized that his charge of 20 rupees was extremely high from a Hindu point of view. However, we still felt comfortable, since Jaganath was young, strong, courteous and prompt. So we had scheduled all our rides with him while in Puri. We wanted to leave for the ashram each morning at 5:30 a.m., and Jaganath was always outside, waiting. He was clean, while many drivers exude a degree of unpleasant body odor. He was a non-drinker, while many rickshaw drivers use alcohol to dull the pain of this strenuous form of livelihood. At any rate, such was our rationale.

"Toward the end of our stay in Puri, Jaganath began to hint to us that he was very poor and was supporting five people in a household, where everyone depended on his income. We, on the other hand, he said, were rich Americans. He, therefore, would like a nice gift upon our departure. The workers at the hotel took this same position and began to make similar overtures. Helen and I both agreed that we were uncomfortable about this. The more uncomfortable we became, the more the hints became direct overtures. An apparent vicious cycle had been created. We became more and more unhappy with these overtures, and as we did, we were confronted more often and more directly.

"Finally, two of the workers entered our room and suggested we make a gift for all the workers in the hotel. They held a book, which they said was used to record these donations. To me, it appeared to be a device for increasing the pressure on us to give. They pointed out that other rich guests had given 1,000 rupees at the end of their stay. I was now angry. I wrote 100 rupees into the book and shooed them out of the room.

"Helen and I discussed all this at lunch, in a somewhat more objective manner. We attempted to discern what the lesson must be. We began, of course, with the assumption that, if we were upset - and we had definitely been upset - then we needed to learn something, rather than blame the outer world, in the form of seemingly ungracious and ever more demanding workers. Slowly, it dawned on me that I had allowed a subtle false belief to take up abode in my consciousness. The hidden and ugly side of my consciousness was that I had allowed myself to view these workers as less than equal to us.

"Following this realization, I suddenly shifted to seeing the truth. These people are not victims. They are personifications of the Divine, playing out a drama on the screen of consciousness for our benefit. The mirror of life is perfect. I had felt victimized by their behavior. The instant I realized the mistake and that the drama of the Self was just that - a drama - the picture reversed itself. Suddenly, the beggars and the beggar-like behavior dissolved before my eyes. In the place of beggars and victims, I now saw that the Presence manifests as all creatures, great and small. The workers returned to their humble, grateful, smiling selves, and all wished us well on our trek further into the consciousness that is India. The pointed hats had presaged an exquisite lesson. Indeed, they had a *point!*"

*Jan. 11, 1:00 p.m.* "We are back in Calcutta now. According to an inner prompting, we are coming to ancient Benares, now officially renamed Varanasi. The feeling building within me at present is one of great good impending."

*Jan. 11, 5:05 p.m.* "We are now at the Calcutta airport. We arrived here at 1:45 p.m. for a scheduled departure to Benares (Varanasi) at 3:25 p.m. Our flight was delayed to 3:35 p.m., then again to an estimated departure of 6:00 p.m. I'm reminded of a short poem I wrote, a few years ago. Let me place it in context. A friend and I decided to go out one night for a bus ride. It was drizzling rain in Houston, Texas. The idea we had was to just jump on the first bus we saw, regardless of destination, and enjoy going wherever. When we climbed on the bus, we heard the bus driver tell another passenger, 'We're on schedule.' And now the content:

> *One rainy any-night*
> *We rode a bus of light.*
> *Who cares, wrong or right?*
> *The bus driver says we're on schedule.*
> *Who could know better?*

*Jan. 12, 8:30 p.m.* "One may surmise, from the fact that we watched the sun rise from a boat on the Ganges River in Varanasi this morning, that we did actually leave Calcutta last night. In the same way, and only in this same way, I've been able to determine the same fact.

"Varanasi stands regal and eloquent on the banks of this famous river, as perhaps the oldest known civilization in this part of the world. Its structures speak vaguely of their ancient knowledge. It seems to me that no pilgrim can be fully justified unto himself without at least one visit to Varanasi. Here, the Ganges runs south to north, due to a 180-degree bend in the river. For this reason, it is said that bathing in the Ganges cleanses the individual, not only of those sins which one has consciously committed, but also of those which one may not be aware.

"We met a gentleman, later in the morning, who had devoted himself purely to preparing himself for death. He felt he had fulfilled his worldly responsibilities as an engineer and a householder. Now he is grateful for the opportunity to release the things of this world, and to turn his attention entirely to God. Although he acknowledged us briefly, he immediately returned his attention to the inner realm.

"On the street, we met a blind and deaf, saffron-robed renunciate. Only a little perceptive ability was necessary to recognize an inner state of joy emanating from within him. I perceived in this one a ready willingness to express his joy in an acknowledgment of God as present in the world and in himself. Amidst the throngs, he stood as a seeming bulwark of God as *joy.*

"A certain famous saint, it is said, found his guru and at once removed certain obstructions of the ego on the steps of a bathing ghat, here in Varanasi. After bathing in the Ganges, he was moving up the steps of the bathing ghat for morning devotions in the temple, when he encountered the sweeper, sweeping the steps of the ghat between the river and the temple. Being of the high Brahmin caste, the saint-to-be became incensed with the sweeper, yelling, 'What are you doing, trying to cause me to be unclean, sweeping this dirt in front of me? Can't you see I am performing my morning rituals? And here you are, a low-classed sweeper, sweeping dirt in front of me. Get out of the way!'

"The sweeper looked calmly back and replied, 'Sir, you have not completed your bath. Please return to the river, and clean yourself fully.'

"The saint-to-be was even more angered. 'Who do you think you are, a lowly sweeper, telling me I am not clean and presuming to direct my actions?'

"The sweeper again replied, with calm authority, 'Please return to the river, and complete your bath. You are filled with anger and with ego and are, therefore, unclean and not fully prepared to enter the temple. I, myself, am a lowly sweeper, as you said, but I am making nothing dirty but am instead cleaning your way to the temple, which duty is my karma to perform in this lifetime.' Our saint-in-training, it is said, surrendered, causing the dissolution of ego. He then took the sweeper as his guru."

*Jan. 15:* "On the way to Allahabad, we stopped at Ananda Moyi Ma's Ashram in Varanasi. Mataji, as she was affectionately called by her devotees, was considered an incarnation of Divine Mother, or in Western terms, the embodiment and personification of the unconditional love associated with the Mother-image. Our visit to her ashram was an extraordinary experience of love for both Helen and me. I do not know exactly what Helen's experience was, but judging by the tears streaming down both our faces, I assume we were touched by the same One Love.

171

"Vishnu, a disciple of Mataji, arrived on the scene and took us through the ashram to view a temple, the grounds and the rooms that had been occupied by Mataji. Throughout the tour, he issued an exposition of the teachings of the great lady and realized being, now deceased. Almost from the moment he began his talk, I felt a movement of energy rising up my spine, culminating at a point just above and between the eyes. The unconditional love of Divine Mother welled up within me. The wondrous sense of love, the movement of energy up my spine and the words of Vishnu all seemed to be related. Vishnu smiled at our tearful appearance and bowed toward us. We bowed to him in return, silently conveying the universal blessing, Namaste, meaning, 'I, as the Presence Itself, bow or acknowledge you, as this same Divine Presence or Undivided Being.'"

*Jan. 16, 10:00 a.m.* "We arrived in Allahabad in the afternoon of January 13th. We had hired no guide for this leg of our journey. Not knowing what to expect, with some twelve million pilgrims anticipated for this largest religious festival in the world, we assumed we should just trust God for these four days, and let things unfold on a moment-by-moment basis (as if we could stop them from doing so). After checking into a small hotel in a residential district of the city, I returned to the front desk to ask a question, and there I encountered another Westerner, a rare sight in Allahabad thus far.

'Hello, where are you from?'

'Boston,' he answered, without looking up.

'What's your discipline?' I asked. I assumed any westerner in Allahabad for the Kumbha Mela was a disciple of some teacher or teaching.

The man appeared agitated by my question but seemed to consider it, nonetheless. He replied, 'I believe that meditation without service is either selfish or ignorant, and service without meditation is mostly futile.'

"It was an unexpected answer that had, in a single sentence, expressed a penetrating perspective on the value of balance. We invited our new acquaintance from Boston to dinner. There, we learned his name was Seth Friedman. Seth was on his fifth trip to India and had arranged for a car, driver and English speaking guide to accompany him while here. He also had a fair working knowledge of the city and invited us to join him for bathing the next day and other excursions thereafter. Thus, our guidance problem - if indeed there ever had been a problem - was solved, in a manner surpassing anything we had thus far pre-arranged.

"On our first day, we agreed to rise at 3:00 a.m. to go for our holy dip at Sangam, the point of confluence of the three rivers. Even by 4:00 a.m., the crowds were amazing. In an aura of spiritual reverence, thousands were flowing, from every possible direction, toward the holy point. A thick fog hugged the ground, adding a further mystical quality to the scene. This day, January 14, 1989, we are told, is considered a most auspicious one, since a particular astrological configuration is reflected in the heavens for the first time in 144 years, bringing even greater benevolent influences into play in an already fully sacred place and time. I cannot document or prove any of the above information. All I can say is, in typical Indian fashion, 'this is what is said....'

"Although I did my best to maintain an attitude of reverence during the ceremonial baths, I must confess, it was difficult for me, as a westerner, to strip off my clothes in the midst of people pressing on all sides, walk off into what is known to be one of the most polluted rivers in the world at a time when it is being even further polluted, almost beyond belief (from a rational point of view), bathe myself in it at freezing temperatures and, at the same time, realize all the spiritual significance inherent.

"Later that day, we entered the fairgrounds. After having already walked some four or five miles through the noisy crowds, we found ourselves before the temporary camp of Ananda Moyi Ma's disciples. As we entered the camp, I felt as if I had entered the manifestation of respite. In contrast to the noise, dirt and mayhem, this little place was clean, quiet and peaceful. As we sat to pay our respects in Mataji's shrine, I felt a cool breeze blow, and once again the sense of pure benevolence that is unconditional love rose, as if from within me and yet all 'round me. *Respite*. Helen's eyes were brimming with tears again as we exited the shrine. I could only bow to that ineffable *something* that had graced me again. Whence cometh this peaceful power? I still do not know. Perhaps we are not really meant to know too much."

*Jan.17:4:00 pm:* "This day began with a stunning revelation. Our new friend, who was providing us with transportation, guidance and companionship, explained a reference he had made to life having been difficult recently. It also explained his apparent gruff manner at the registration desk, on the day we first met. 'My wife and child were killed in an airline crash last month. They were on Pan Am Flight 103 over Lockerbie, Scotland, when a terrorist's bomb exploded on Dec. 21st. They had been heading to the United States for the holidays.'

"My first feeling was one of being inadequate. I had known the darkness, but nothing compared to what I was now confronted with. My heart felt as if it was breaking, and a sense of compassion seemed to flow through me. It wasn't a human sense of compassion. It seemed to arise from a place within me and yet beyond the personal. I told Seth I was sorry and that I knew any words were inadequate. He said he had planned this trip to the Kumbha Mela some time ago and had discovered, after the incident, that there didn't seem to be anything more important to do than continue on the pilgrimage.

"Later, we took a boat ride down the Jamuna River to the sacred point of confluence, and once again, we bathed at this holy place. This time, I had no difficulty entering the appropriate devotional mood. I was having a problem relating to the shocking news imparted by Seth this morning, and the opportunity to give myself to the river in prayer was an attractive one."

My journal entries end here. I do recall that, at our next stop in Lucknow, we would again be required to deal with lost hotel reservations, a canceled tour and a tour guide who never materialized. In New Delhi, our final destination before returning to the U.S.A., we were not met at the airport, as had been planned. India had provided new depth to the idea of learning to "go with the flow."

Seth would become a friend for life, and we would come together, time and again, to explore the spiritual dimension. We have shared the mystery that is death on another occasion... but that will have to wait. My tomorrows are, as yet, unknown to me.

# Chapter 29
## Las Vegas: Lightening Strikes Twice
## and a Lucky Meditation

Helen's divorce became final in 1989, and she was awarded the family home, as a part of her settlement. We moved into the house. It was located along the Rio Grande River in the little village of Corrales, New Mexico, just north of Albuquerque. We put the house on the market. While there, we began to hold classes in the home. These classes, which were based on *Autobiography of a Yogi*, attracted a diverse group of students. We had two former nuns, one former priest, an elementary school teacher and several other students of Kriya Yoga. The classes met on Sunday mornings.

One Saturday evening, a wild thunderstorm hit Corrales. The night sky was brightly lit, again and again, by lightening bolts exploding all around us. The morning after the storm, we found the yard, which had been immaculately landscaped and shaded by huge cottonwood trees, now a disaster scene. Enormous limbs from the cottonwood trees were covering the entire two acres. The limbs were so large and heavy that I couldn't budge them. It appeared that cleaning this up would be a daunting task - and expensive, no doubt.

I cannot explain my peculiar response to this circumstance. Helen was depressed. Even with her settlement now final, we were struggling financially. We were renting out extra bedrooms in the home. I was finally applying the lessons I had learned about auto sales from my father by buying and selling cars. We were doing everything we knew to try to make ends meet until we could sell the house. We both thought this mess was the last thing in the world we needed. Then, like a second lightening bolt striking, a very strange idea entered my mind.

"Helen, let's take a vacation. Let's go to Las Vegas and celebrate."

Helen, you will recall, had taught me to be practical. She was the one who had provided a sense of grounding to me. She now looked at me as if I had lost my mind.

"What are you talking about? Celebrate what? This house is our responsibility, Mark, and we have to find a way to get this cleaned up."

"I know, Helen. I know it sounds crazy. But I'm not talking about just walking off and leaving the mess. I'm talking about going to Las Vegas to celebrate the good fortune we are going to have. I don't know how, but I believe this mess will be gone by sunset. And it won't cost us an arm and a leg to get it done. I don't know where it came from, but all of a sudden, I just feel lucky."

"That's fine, Mark. I'm glad you feel lucky. The fact remains, the yard is in horrible shape. How do you propose we get it cleaned up, anyway?"

"I don't know how it will get cleaned up, Helen. Just listen to my proposition, though...."

At this point, Helen was beginning to appear at least slightly receptive to my craziness.

"I say we should assume that something miraculous will take place and the yard will be completely clean before the sun goes down. We should call the airline and make a reservation for tonight, say after 7:00 or 8:00 p.m. If I'm wrong, we'll just cancel and stay here and do whatever it takes to get the yard cleaned. If I'm right, we'll go spend a couple of days in Vegas and celebrate."

"All right," she said. "But remember, we have a class starting in about an hour, so we can't even begin to consider the problem with the yard until after class." I agreed. Somewhere inside me, I had the feeling that having the class was somehow going to help. I went into the back room and made reservations for a flight to Las Vegas, which would leave a little after 8:00 p.m. Then the two of us began to set up the living room for the class and the dining room for refreshments.

We always began every class with a half-hour of silent meditation. The participants would arrive, let themselves in and quietly enter meditation. Everyone knew not to ring the doorbell so as not to disturb those already in meditation. Some twenty minutes into the meditation period, the doorbell rang. I opened my eyes and looked around the room. Everyone in the class had already arrived. I looked at Helen. She looked back at me with a quizzical look. Obviously, she didn't know who it might be, either. I walked to the front door and opened it. Standing there were two men. One wore blue jeans and a plaid shirt. The other was outfitted only in jeans. His naked upper body was muscular and streaked with dirt and perspiration. In his arms, he cradled a large chain saw.

"How'd you like us to cut and haul your cottonwood limbs?" asked the young man in the plaid shirt. With a huge smile, he added, "We only charge $10 an hour each, and we supply the chain saw, the gas and the truck because we can use the wood for firewood. Or, if you want, we can stack it up for you to use. But cottonwood burns awfully fast, and most people don't want to use it for firewood."

"Can you start right away? And can you finish before dark?" I asked.

"I'm not sure," replied the one doing the talking. "There's just the two of us, and you have a lot of wood out there."

I continued attempting to extract a commitment that would allow us to be free to leave for Vegas that night. "What if we get you some help loading the wood in your truck? Could you finish by tonight, then? We need to leave town tonight, and we can't leave with the yard in a mess."

"Sure thing," said God, in the form of a woodcutter. "With a couple of extra hands, we can do it."

"OK, you're hired. I'll see if I can find some extra help. You go ahead and start." I then walked to the back of the house and offered two of our tenants $10 an hour to help load the wood as it was being cut. Both agreed. Helen was grinning like a Cheshire cat now. We were watching a miracle, and we both knew it. Observing this orchestration of events was tickling us to no end. I could barely contain my glee. "What a lucky meditation," I thought. The good luck had only just begun, though.

Of course, I didn't feel I should explain to the class that the real reason I wanted the job completed today was because I'd had this hare-brained idea to go to Las Vegas. No matter. After the class, nearly everyone in attendance stayed and helped haul the wood. It was a good thing, too. The job was bigger than any of us had imagined. We finished just as the sun was setting.

I had made reservations at Bally's, and we packed and made our flight with only minutes to spare. The next morning, as we ate a late breakfast in one of the dining rooms, Helen played a round of Keno and won $250. Watching her bounce up and down, you'd have thought it was a fortune. "What a lucky meditation," I thought.

After breakfast, Helen and I decided to walk down the street to what, at the time, was the newest Hotel and Casino in town, the Excalibur. We had seen its turrets beaming in the sun down the street from Bally's. Distances in Vegas can fool you, however. We walked and we walked, and the Hotel seemed to recede as we went. We finally made it and headed up the long ramp into the casino. We toured the casino, and finding it less appealing than Bally's, we determined to take a taxi back.

On the way out, Helen pointed out a twenty-five cent video poker machine and suggested I play it once. I placed the maximum bet of five quarters and pushed the button. The wheels spun around. When they stopped, a bell began to ring. It took me a minute or so to figure out what had happened. I studied the cards that were now visible on the monitor and realized I had hit a royal straight flush in hearts. I had won the jackpot, and the bell was now ringing to inform management. A few minutes later, I filled out a tax form. I had won $1,487. "What a lucky meditation," I thought. We split the winnings and caught a cab for Bally's.

That evening at dinner, Helen played Keno and again won $250. We were now at the point of almost regretting that our flight was due out the next morning. We knew we had been lucky, and at least this once, I knew it would be foolish to become attached to "more." On the way home, I proposed to Helen, and she accepted. We decided we should return to Las Vegas for the marriage. Las Vegas had been the scene of good luck once, and we hoped it would continue to be a venue where good fortune could be had.

On a return trip to visit on January 26, 1990, Helen and I were quietly married in the living room of a Religious Science minister's home. We knew it was to be an unconventional marriage. But the willingness to be present to one another in our commitment to realizing Truth ever more fully seemed appropriate for us, in contrast to the promises made and the unconscious hopes and fears that move so many to the altar. After the small, informal wedding ceremony, we changed clothes and headed out of town. Helen insisted we stop at Sam's Town, a casino that is popular with the locals in Las Vegas. We ate there, and Helen played Keno. She won $250. On the way out the door, Helen stuck some quarters in a slot machine and won another $100.

## Chapter 30
## From Isla Mujeras to Unity Village Again:
## A Dream of Transformation and a New Curriculum

Helen and I spent our honeymoon on Isla Mujeres, an island off the coast of the Yucatan peninsula in Mexico. It was a beautiful time. I had never seen Helen look so happy. She loved the water but had never learned to swim. Coco Beach on Isla Mujeres is only waist-deep for nearly a quarter of a mile out, and I was able to show her how to float on the water. I recall her eyes glittering with delight, as she discovered that the water would support her. We ate whole baked fish and drank two foot tall pina coladas. We rented a small motorcycle and traveled all over the tiny island. I felt all was right with the world. Once again, I didn't even suspect there was another shoe. Duh...

Within a few months after our honeymoon, I began to feel myself contracting and withdrawing. As mentioned earlier, I suspect intimate relationship can be a transformational path for those mature enough in understanding to recognize unconscious material being projected. I had only some of this understanding, and only some of the time.

Some saving grace in all of this was that Helen and I communicated throughout. We would express our feelings, as best as we could identify them. It always helped. In many ways, we became closer in this process. On the other hand, I didn't really have the tools for this level of self-discovery. I didn't understand the degree to which I was unconscious and projecting the egoic nature or *little me*, as some spiritual teachers put it, upon the screen of the others (Helen). I had told myself that I was in the relationship to give. I had been doing all I could to live up to that *image* of myself. I had not admitted to myself that I may have been seeking something. The degree to which I was identified with an image in the mind was simply unknown to me. The

180

*little me,* the image with which I was still unconsciously identified, was emotionally needy and highly defended against seeing this.

Helen, too, may have had unconscious patterns, but this is not her story. It would be inappropriate for me to speculate on that. My apparent world, or as Jesus put it, the "world of appearances," as it arose in my awareness, was again that of fear and separation. This distorted appearance would come and go. Often, I would awaken again from it and see the Truth - the Undivided One Presence - and then I would fall again into the delusion of the ego's view. This is, of course, what is referred to as *shadow* or unconscious material being projected onto the screen of awareness. Its purpose is to reveal unconscious aspects of being, awaken us from the dream of separation through awareness and Presence. In the end, the *story of me is* the dream of separation. Its only destiny is death or the withdrawal of consciousness from identification with form. At the same time, the egoic nature still had momentum and, at least in my case, quite a lot of momentum.

The only valuable perspective I had to help me during these difficult times came from two of Helen's former students. Marian Sears had undergone a lengthy training under Helen and had been ordained by her, years before. Hal Vaile had also studied briefly with Helen. These two were now a couple, and we began to visit with them occasionally at their mountain home in Cedar Crest, New Mexico, east of Albuquerque.

I remember sharing my experiences of falling in and out of fear with Hal and Marian. They never attempted to teach anything, nor did they counsel. They simply listened and always seemed to respond in open, objective ways. They knew how to listen without judgment. Hal liked to think of this mountain property as a retreat, and both he and Marian voiced the idea that they were glad to be able to give us a place to come for respite.

These visits with Hal and Marian were healing for me. I always left feeling better. I learned that Hal and Marian were attending conferences with Dr. Brugh Joy. It never occurred to me that the unconditional love I felt while visiting them might be related to their work with Brugh Joy and the awakening of the Heart Center. It's amazing to me that I didn't make the connection. I remembered having read the book, *Joy's Way* by Brugh during my hospital stay in

Corpus Christi, but I had forgotten I had felt a healing energy while reading the book. Since neither Hal nor Marian ever suggested outright that I might want to attend these conferences, I never pursued the subject.

When Helen's house sold later that year, we moved back to the retreat house, and we continued to speculate about how to earn a living again. At one point, I took a contract in Hollywood, California, with a new convenience store chain called Pink Dot, which specialized in 24-hour delivery of household items. I had suffered occasional back problems over the last two years, and while there, the back pain became even more severe. I didn't realize these back problems were related to unconscious material, or egoic patterns. I was about to learn, however.

By the summer of 1991, during a trip to Denver to visit Helen's daughter, Linda, I erupted emotionally. I do not recall what precipitated it, but I do remember telling Helen I wanted to spend some time alone. I left Denver and headed back to New Mexico alone. I called her from somewhere in southern Colorado to apologize for my reactivity. As I headed through northern New Mexico, I began to pray for some kind of guidance. I felt at the end of my rope emotionally and believed I needed to find a way to serve again. I was crying and literally begging for some kind of sign for what to do.

After crying, I began to feel a little better. Then suddenly, I heard an inner voice say, "Go back to Unity Village." It came with a sense of power and conviction. I knew immediately what it meant. It meant I was to go to Unity Village and enter the Ministerial Education Program. I was to serve the spiritual movement that had served me in so many ways during my earlier years.

My very first response to this idea was relief. It felt like an answer to my prayer. My second response was a sense of conflict. I didn't think Helen would like the idea. She had already been ordained three times. She had worked to have me ordained, as well. She wouldn't want to go back to school; nor would she want to go to Missouri and wait for me, I imagined. I knew the training would take two years and would be expensive. I fully expected her to react negatively to this idea. I couldn't have been more wrong.

I continued on across New Mexico to our retreat house in Columbus, attempting to reconcile my feelings about this new spiritual guidance. In Columbus at the City of the Sun, I contacted the Unity School of Religious Studies and obtained more detailed information on what is required for entry into the Ministerial Program. I discovered I might not qualify because I had not been actively involved in a Unity ministry for years, and I would need a recommendation from an active Unity minister in order to be considered. I had felt this kind of intuitive guidance before, though, and knew that, if it was meant to be, I would be accepted. The larger question was still about how Helen would relate to this idea. I called her in Denver and explained what had happened on the road.

"I've got goose bumps, Mark. I think you've got it. I don't think I ever told you, but Unity was my first love, spiritually. I always knew they had the best training for ministers. I couldn't go before, because I was raising the children, and our businesses were in New Mexico. Let's go to Unity Village, and check it out."

At Unity, we already knew, despite her three previous ordinations, Helen would need 50 credits from the Continuing Education Program in order to qualify for entry into the Ministerial Program. I had taken some 139 credits during the '70s and didn't require the credits, but I enrolled with her, anyway. Halfway through the classes, my back began to act up again. Day by day, it became worse and worse, until I could barely walk upright. It finally occurred to me that I was a candidate for spiritual healing. The Unity teachings point out that the root cause of our suffering lies in consciousness. My body was in great pain, and I began to entertain the very real possibility that there might be something about my consciousness that needed attention.

I sought spiritual counseling from one of the staff members at Unity School. During our session, I began to feel my back pain worsening. The counselor told me she felt there was a part of me, probably an unconscious part, that needed to be loved. She suggested I try to come up with an image of this wounded aspect of my being. She suggested I also come up with some image of the Christ or other spiritual aspect, and using active imagination, allow these two aspects of being to dialogue with one another. I began to experience so much pain during this counseling session, I had to cut it short and leave.

Helen and I were staying in a motel room on the grounds of Unity Village. I returned to our room and lay down. Within a few minutes, I discovered that I was unable to move from the bed. I had been attempting to do the exercise that the counselor had suggested to me. While doing this, I saw an image of a young man covered in armor, complete with breastplate, helmet and carrying a spear. He appeared to be about fourteen years old. His face and arms were covered with cuts and bruises. I sensed this image represented my successful attempt to build a persona to defend myself against the emotional pain of my youth.

Across from the image of the young warrior, I saw another image of a young boy. This image was clothed in light. This second image was holding out its arms to the first. I began to cry uncontrollably. I began to feel the fear and insecurity I had buried long ago in reform school. I knew the second image in my vision was an offer of healing and love, but I could see the warrior was still quite reticent. A part of me was reaching out to heal another part; yet the part that needed the healing did not trust the process.

Helen returned from her classes to find me nearly paralyzed with physical pain. My emotional blood-letting hadn't stopped, either. During this process, I realized I had not been fully honest with myself or with Helen about my motives for marrying. I saw that I wanted to be loved and that I sought the financial stability I believed would be mine by marrying her. These realizations were covered in shame. Yet, I now felt that hiding these things from myself or from her were part of the reason I was frozen with pain. I began to tell her. It wasn't that I didn't love her. I did. It wasn't that I didn't want to be with her. I did. It was that these other, less altruistic motives had been hidden in me, as well.

Helen left the room later that afternoon to attend her classes. When she returned, she brought Rev. Chris Chenoweth, the minister from the Unity Village chapel, back to the motel room. He prayed with me for healing. After the prayer, I told him about the internal process I was going through. He told me that he was sure I was supposed to be a Unity minister, and knowing I needed a recommendation from an active minister, he said, "I feel guided to recommend you for the ministry, Mark. I believe you are destined to be accepted by the school." This was quite a statement from someone who had just met me, particularly in light of the fact that only a small percentage of those applying each year are accepted. Still, I was unable to move from my bed.

We decided we had better take me to the hospital. Helen helped drag me to the car, and I crawled into the back seat. The doctor immediately scheduled an MRI. "You have two herniated discs," he informed me, "L4 and L5. You will almost certainly need surgery. There is a slight possibility that you could achieve some healing without surgery but you would have to lie in bed for several weeks, and be very still (note the spiritual advice *"Be Still"* being dispensed as practical advice). Assuming you would be willing and could take the time to stay in bed, there is the possibility that surgery could be avoided, possibly for years."

That night I had a dream. I was holding a suitcase up and across a high voltage power line. On the other side of the high voltage line was Boomer Esiason, a former quarterback for the Cincinnati Bengals. I am struggling to hand the suitcase to Boomer. Boomer has one hand on the handle of the suitcase and is holding his other hand beside his mouth, as if to amplify his message, yelling, "You can let go now, I've got a good grip!"

I awoke with some understanding of the dream. Dreams are the language of the unconscious, attempting to bring awareness to the surface mind. Its language is symbolic. As one awakens, it becomes more and more apparent that we are, allegorically speaking, living in a waking dream. Every moment, every appearance in form is reflecting to us exactly what is needed to serve consciousness awakening to Itself. Grace, it seems, will use all manner of forms to awaken us. These include both the "carrot" and the "stick."

Synchronicities and/or so-called miracles stand out, simply because they show this to us, and these special events seem special, in that they disrupt and awaken us from our more limited perspectives and our beliefs in separation. Actually, the miracle is Life, and the more extraordinary fact is that most humans are able to avoid seeing the connectedness of all things and the spiritual dimension, which is always already here and now and shining in, through, and as all form.

However, the surface mind only sees the third dimension and creates an entire belief system based on appearances. The collective belief in the world is so strong that it casts the spell of delusion upon nearly all who inhabit the planet. In fact, historically, the individual is seen as a fool for believing in an invisible dimension. Rather than rewarding those who penetrate the veil, the collective has been more likely to persecute, punish or kill these individuals when they have attempted to reveal what has been seen.

The suitcase, in my dream at Unity Village, represented my emotional baggage; those aspects of my being that needed to be released; or limiting beliefs, with which I was still identified. The high voltage power line represented the spiritual power of transformation. Boomer Esiason, the quarterback or leader of these internal forces, represented the booming voice of God or the Higher Power, the One Presence in charge of this transforming process. "You can let go now, I've got a good grip," was a message from the unconscious to my conscious mind, reminding me that I cannot heal myself; that I must let go, and let God or the Transcendental complete the work. As I interpreted it, these words were also intended to assure me that my healing is in good hands.

The next morning, Sig Paulson called. He and Janie had recently returned to Kansas City. When I told Sig about the dream, he said, "Grip - G.R.I.P - God Really Individualizes Power." We laughed. In his economy of words, Sig was saying again, "You can trust the divine power individualized in you and as you to heal the body."

Helen and I rented an apartment in one of the old brownstones near the famous Plaza in Kansas City. I spent the next six weeks on my back in bed. While there, I began to hear the inner voice speaking to me, time and time again. This inner voice was reassuring me that I was being healed. After receiving one of these reassurances, I asked, "What can I do to help?"

The inner voice responded, "Nothing, please. You are to *be still* - and do *nothing*. If you did anything to help, you might get the idea that *you* were doing the healing, and we can't have that, can we?" It seemed this deeper wisdom wanted me to understand the ultimate powerlessness of the ego. By late September, I was walking again and was pain-free.

Helen and I had filled out and submitted what is called a pre-inquiry form to the Ministerial Education Program. In early October, we were approved and were sent applications, which we completed and forwarded to the school. We had made the first cut. That day, during meditation, an image appeared in awareness. An image of Jesus Christ arose in me and an inner voice said, "I have written my name in your heart and your name in the registration for the

Ministerial Education Program." These words provided me with a sense of conviction about the application process. I now knew I would be admitted to the Program.

By November, Helen and I had rented an apartment across the street from Unity Village, and we moved our possessions from both the brownstone in Kansas City and the City of the Sun. In January of 1992, we received notice that we had made the second cut. We had been invited to interview with the screening committees. Still, we were being told that only about thirty applicants, of some sixty or seventy due to interview, would be accepted into the school. Although my confidence was still strong, I could feel some of the old egoic nature stirring, as we were told the interviewing committees could be very confrontive and might ask difficult questions.

Each candidate would go before two separate committees. It was generally believed that a good showing at both interviews would be necessary to gain admittance. After the interviews, I still felt good but less certain. Helen also admitted that the interviews had been tough, and she felt uncertain, too. Actually, I can't imagine anyone interviewing at the time could have felt complete confidence in their acceptance.

The next day, we were given individual letters and asked not to open them until we were in a place of privacy. Since over half of the candidates would be dealing with disappointment, it would be inappropriate to celebrate in front of those who were declined admittance. So we took our letters and drove across the street to our apartment. When we pulled into the parking lot, we realized Chris Chenoweth had pulled in behind us. As he stepped from his car, he had a huge grin on his face.

"Well," he said, "how does it feel?"

"What do you mean?" I asked.

"Oh, no," said Chris, looking down and seeing we hadn't even opened the letters, "I didn't realize you hadn't opened your letters yet. But I wanted to be the first to congratulate you."

"You mean we have both been accepted?" I asked.

"Of course." said Chris.

School began in the summer of 1992. We were informed that our class would be the first class of ministerial students enrolled in a new curriculum. It was referred to as the Transformational Curriculum and encouraged the student to uncover and identify his or her core wounds. Instead of an intellectual approach to our preparation, we would be confronting our need for healing at depth, and working toward that healing throughout the program. In one of the first classes, Robert Brumet, the Chairperson of Psychological Studies and Skills, drew a little cartoon on the blackboard. It was a smiling face, bisected, showing the separation in the development of the psyche between the conscious mind/persona and the unconscious mind/shadow. Further, it depicted the means by which the unconscious mind projects the hidden psychic material onto the outer screen of life. (See Figure)

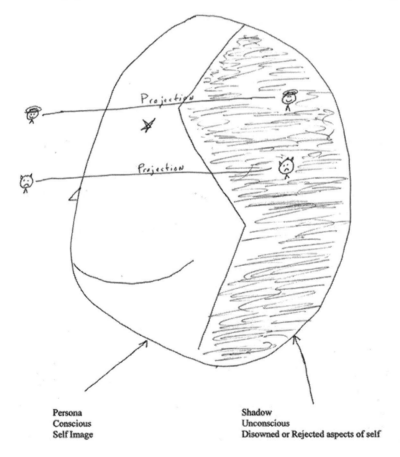

Persona
Conscious
Self Image

Shadow
Unconscious
Disowned or Rejected aspects of self

Shadow work would no longer be a theory or an occasional choice, but nearly a requirement to move forward in this program; not that I hadn't understood the principles involved in the projection of unconscious material. Now, however, the graphic image before me caused me to accept more fully the need to embrace the process of making the unconscious conscious. The school, especially through this cartoon image, had shown me a map I could understand. The following, from notes taken during conference work later with Brugh Joy, seems appropriate at this point:

*Projection is the internal mechanism by which the unconscious seeks to make itself conscious. This mechanism (projection) is not under the volition or control of the personal will. The primary and unmistakable clue that one is viewing projected unconscious material is emotional charge. That is, when one feels a positive or negative emotional charge, one may be certain that what one is seeing is unconscious psychic material, projected onto the screen of awareness. This is expressed quite simply and directly by the ancient Oriental teaching that says, when one is pointing the finger at another, whether one is positively or negatively impressed by what one sees, there are always three crooked little fingers pointing back at the one doing the pointing. In identifying one's unconscious material it is crucial that one not judge the material. Becoming conscious itself is spiritual awakening, and the material is best seen as simply that which needs to be, not only made conscious, but redeemed. Therefore, such awakening requires compassion and awareness, not judgment.*

## Chapter 31
## Unity Village Again:
## Humility, Grace and the Transcendental Tap Dance

Both my entry into the ministerial program and the process of the training there emphasized a life lesson for me. My back pain and the hidden emotional issues I discovered through the pain were experiences in humility. I discovered, again and again, that surrendering brings grace.

My preparation for ministry confronted me with my worst fears as a public speaker. We were required to deliver our inspirational lessons in front of faculty and a peer group containing many already accomplished speakers. I spent long hours preparing my talks, only to discover that, unless I was able to surrender inwardly before speaking, all the preparing in the world didn't really help.

The role of a spiritual teacher is, in many ways, a fool's game. To be effective, one must enter a heightened state of consciousness and speak from that state. At the same time, the heightened state cannot be reached by any act of will. It can only be reached by surrendering the personal will and opening to these higher forces. So what happens when these heightened states don't show up? We are left doing our transcendental tap dance, with nothing transcendental behind it. Everyone knows, in a visceral way, when a speaker isn't really inspired. So, we stand up and present ourselves, and we rely upon (read hope for) the Transcendental to arrive and flow through us. Every time we stand up, it has the potential of being a very humbling experience.

The first presentation I was required to make during the ministerial program seemed to be about as easy as it could be. The staff intended an easy initiation. We were asked to choose a subject we knew well and tell how to do something, in a five-minute presentation. I chose How to Make Cajun Gumbo. It is a subject well known to me. I showed up for the talk equipped with my props, including all the right utensils, and I was perfectly prepared. When my turn came, I stood up and became almost speechless. Unreasonable fear overwhelmed me, such that my hands and legs began to visibly shake. I dropped utensils, left and right. It was one of my worst nightmares come true. I made an absolute fool of myself in a room with staff and two of the best public speakers in our class. I thought I was going to die of embarrassment.

Humility. My life seems to revolve around this lesson. Looking back through my story, it is not difficult to see that humility has paid me many visits. Although I have rarely greeted her with excitement, she has always led me to grace. The Sunday lesson I chose to deliver to the full staff and student body for my "chapel talk," one of the more significant fires of initiation through which the candidate must pass on the journey to graduation, was entitled, "Out of Humility, Grace," and reflects this life lesson. Of course I still didn't know, at the time, how many more rounds of learning there were in store for me. As it has been said, I was teaching what I needed to learn.

Outwardly, the curriculum at the school was comprehensive and included studies in comparative religion, Bible history and interpretation, communication skills, psychology and counseling skills. As previously mentioned, the hallmark of this new curriculum was the expectation that, as students, we would discover and identify our core woundedness. The idea was, having been humbled and having glimpsed into our human limitations, we would be less likely to project our woundedness onto those we would serve professionally.

This inner curriculum of identifying our core woundedness set the tone for our class. Gay members identified themselves publicly - came out, to use the vernacular - early in the first quarter. Blacks held the first Black History presentation at Unity Village. Many tears flowed as we opened up to one another as best we could. Marriages were either dissolved or strengthened, and most all of us were humbled in some way.

During this period, I developed the habit of withdrawing for a day prior to any presentation I was scheduled to give. I would write my presentation in the form of a script, as we were trained to do. Then I would pray for surrender. I got varied results. For the most part, I could sense a somewhat expanded state of consciousness while speaking, and I was certainly grateful for these times. At other times, however, I would inexplicably feel flat or empty. I had shown up and was left doing my transcendental tap dance, while the Transcendental seemed to have taken a vacation.

## Chapter 32
## Puerto Rico: A Floating Ministry Comes
## to be on the Ground and on the Air

In the summer of 1994, Helen and I graduated and were licensed and ordained. It was a happy occasion. We were also about as happy to leave as we had been to arrive. Most students were chomping at the bit to get out of the gate.

Unlike many religious movements, Unity ministers are not assigned to churches. They must apply, and if a church is unwilling to hire a minister, regardless of ordination, that minister must find other means of making a living. The process works as follows. One forwards one's resume, and if a church is interested, references are asked for, and telephone interviews generally follow. If a candidate is still found favorable, he or she may be invited to visit the ministry as a candidate. The recommended policy is for churches to screen down to three candidates. If invited, the candidate then travels to the church, conducts a Sunday service, expresses a vision for ministry and usually facilitates a workshop or teaches a class. Further interviews may follow.

After the three candidates have undergone this process, the church will either extend an offer to the candidate chosen through another process which involves input from a search committee and the congregation, or the church begins the process of looking further. Once a candidate has been approved by the search committee, etc., a salary package will be negotiated, which includes all the terms of employment.

Paul Hasselbeck, who was scheduled to enter the ministerial program during the following year, entered our ministerial class one day to convey a message from his home ministry, the Beacon of Light

Unity Church in San Juan, Puerto Rico. They were in the process of searching for a new minister. He would also be available to meet with interested parties later that day in the cafeteria, he said. Helen showed no interest, but I felt a stirring.

We participated in the meeting with Paul in the cafeteria that afternoon and made a few notes. We discovered this church had evolved out of a much larger Spanish speaking church in San Juan. A group, which had wanted to worship in English, had asked for and received permission from the larger Spanish speaking ministry to begin a new church. This new church was only a couple of years old, and although they had hired two different ministers, both had left after only a short time. Also, it seemed that money could be a problem, since San Juan is quite expensive and the church relatively small. Still, I noted my inner stirring.

Later that summer, Helen and I were invited to try out at the Beacon of Light Unity Church. We were quite well-received. Since we were the final candidates scheduled to try out there, the board met and determined to offer us the position. The offer, though, fell short of what we had determined would be necessary to live there, so we declined. I felt a bit heavy of heart. We had been so appreciated by the congregation, and I felt we could be successful there. Nonetheless, we could not agree to work for the money offered.

As we prepared to leave, we received a phone call from the board president, asking how much we needed to go there. We gave her a figure we felt would bring the speculation to an end, as the figure was substantially more than the original offer. Within an hour, she arrived at the apartment where we were lodging. She said certain members of the church had told her to give us what we needed. They had pledged to make up whatever was necessary. There had been a unanimous vote that we were the right ministers for them. Again, I had a vision and heard a voice, which had that sense of internal power to it, saying, "I don't know where you're going, but this is *my* ministry."

Thus began the adventure of what we came to call the *floating ministry*. Not because it was on an island, but because we moved from meeting place to meeting place, about as often as a floating crap game moved as a measure against the players being arrested for gambling. Two months into our contract, all was going our way, when we arrived at the meeting room in the back of a popular restaurant where we held our Sunday services. We were quickly informed that the restaurant had decided to discontinue renting us the facilities. Furthermore, we learned that no lease had ever been signed; therefore, no notice was due us. This was at 10:00 a.m. on a Sunday morning, and our service was to begin in one hour.

This was a potential disaster, in my mind. However, as I stood there, not knowing whether to laugh or to cry, I noticed a Best Western Hotel next door to the restaurant. Within minutes, we had secured a banquet room for that day and the following Sunday. The conference rooms were booked solid beyond that, we were told. Stationing a person at the door of the meeting room at the restaurant that had dismissed us, we set up church in the banquet room of the Best Western. Meanwhile, our lookout at the restaurant redirected the congregation. The congregation found the situation much more amusing than I did. Helen and I would soon discover that commitments were interpreted loosely by the culture in Puerto Rico.

Since we could only meet at the Best Western for two Sundays, we proceeded to rent a meeting room from the San Juan Convention Center. We had to station lookouts at two locations now, as many congregants only attended church occasionally, were not on any email list or mailing list, and we could not afford to lose congregants. Now we had to begin the Sunday service at 11:45 a.m., even though the scheduled time was still 11:00 a.m. We had to wait for everyone to find their way from both former locations. The Convention Hall was anything but ideal. First, it was too expensive for our budget. Our congregation of about one hundred was now meeting in a room designed for five hundred or more. And second, ambiance - there was none. So we continued to look.

Two of our most active members were a young couple from the States, who lived on a sailboat and were planning to continue on a long voyage after the winter. They recommended that we investigate the San Juan Yacht Club, as a possible meeting place. The Yacht Club, it turned out, is a small building about the size of a restaurant or bar - which is what it was - situated at the end of a long, wooden pier. It was financially reasonable and was closed for business on Sunday, so we were able to rent the space. There would be no lease, but we needn't be concerned that we would lose the space, we were told. Also, for ambiance, the San Juan Yacht Club had windows opening in every direction to the Caribbean waters. Given our ability to announce this most recent move in advance, only one lookout would be required. We laughed that we had now manifestly become a "floating church." Everyone was happy - except Helen and myself.

Having to set up a church service with a movable bookstore, sound system and hymnals, then having to break it all down each week, can become a tedious affair. We were compelled to buy a dolly to help move these things across a parking lot, a road and down the lengthy pier. After every service, we had to load it all back up again. While we were happy to be situated, it was far from ideal. To address this issue, Helen and I initiated a building fund with the idea that we really needed our own church home. This was so, not only to relieve backs; building and growing a church requires office space for counseling, midweek classes and a fellowship area, at the least. We looked at property after property after property. Most were too expensive. San Juan real estate runs on the high side. Also, parking in San Juan is a huge problem, particularly on the weekends. Most rental space has no parking provision.

One day, Helen was reading some Catherine Ponder prosperity material, suggesting that if one is having difficulty manifesting a particular desire, one should look in one's own backyard. The principle was saying that what you were looking for may be so near you are overlooking it. Ultimately, this is an understatement, since the roots of all manifestation are always within, and all that appears to us is a projection of either one's personal belief system or the collective belief system.

Helen and I were living on the ninth floor of a high-rise apartment building, situated on a hill. Helen loved the views of the ocean out all our front windows. The back of our apartment was simply a door opening into a hallway, where the elevator was located. Stepping out this back door, peering out and down through a hallway window, Helen spied a For Lease sign in the window of the building next door to us. In our own backyard, we had found a church home. An enormous parking lot adjacent to the building accompanied it. All we needed now was the money to remodel.

A member of the congregation approached me and told me that he had become wealthy through the application of Unity principles. He had been raised on the *Daily Word*, the inspirational Unity publication that reaches around the world. He wanted me to know that he would provide whatever was necessary to establish the church on firm ground. Soon thereafter, Lolita San Miguel, wife of our board president, Hiram Cintron, introduced me to Bubo Rodriquez, one of the wealthier citizens of Puerto Rico, whom she said was a philanthropist and who owned an English speaking radio station. Bubo offered to set up an interview for me with the station manager. The station manager interviewed me on a morning talk show. Next, I was invited to air regular inspirational messages with a trailer to advertise our ministry. Our floating church had docked - and now we were *on the ground* and *on the air.*

## Chapter 33
## Sedona: Engaging the Mystery of Death

During a class break, while still in the ministerial program at Unity Village, Helen and I had ventured to Sedona, Arizona. We had heard that the church there was struggling. We had called to offer ourselves as guest speakers on a Sunday, the January before we graduated. We privately hoped for a ministry in the southwestern part of the country, since we both loved the area. While in Sedona, we discovered the church had hired a new minister that very week. We still did the presentation that Sunday and had breakfast with Max Lafser, the new minister. Max had served in many field ministries, and he told us he was only planning to stay in Sedona for a few months to help get the troubled ministry back on its feet.

"Do you think you'd like to serve here after graduation?" Max asked.

"We're certainly open to that," I answered.

On my way out of town an inner voice said, "This will be your ministry." The words came with such power, that I felt sure we would apply to and be offered this church upon graduation. However, as the Great Mystery had it, the church exploded in growth, and we heard through the grapevine that Max had been asked to stay and had agreed.

At no point in my life have I heard inner guidance, such as that which I received about the Sedona church, and failed to see it manifest. At any rate, in the fullness of our time in Puerto Rico, this was all but forgotten. As the time for our contract renewal in San Juan approached, Helen began to express misgivings about staying. At one point, she put her foot down, saying, "We have to leave. I cannot stay here any longer. Don't ask me why." Just as she had gone along with my guidance on many occasions, I felt I should follow her lead on this.

Informing the church was difficult and brought some grief. We had worked together and built a successful ministry. We had grown together, in many ways. Now we were leaving, and we couldn't really explain why. We didn't know, ourselves. Eventually, the members of the Beacon of Light church accepted this and sent us off with much grace and good wishes.

Now what? We returned to the retreat house in Columbus, once again, arriving in time for Thanksgiving. It was exactly one decade after our first Thanksgiving in this little house in the desert. At that time, we had come here, having released Helen's marriage and ministry, to face an unknown future. Now, we had returned to face the unknown again. The only plan we had was to work on a rewrite of Helen's book. The publisher had asked her for it. *Contemplation: The Activity of Mystical Consciousness* was to be renamed. The new title was to be *For the Aspiring Mystic.*

By January, we were making progress on the book and beginning to look ahead. We planned to begin our search for a new ministry soon. Before we could begin, we received a phone call from Michael Catalano, a close friend during ministerial school. He was now serving as minister for Unity of the Hills in Branson, Missouri.

"Weren't you guys once interested in the ministry in Sedona?"

"Yes," I answered.

"Well," he continued, "you know the position is open. Max left, and they are interviewing right now."

Helen and I acted immediately to update our resumes. I called the church and was informed that their deadline for receiving new resumes was only three days away. We forwarded ours for consideration. On a follow up call to the church in Sedona, a board member seemed to suggest that it was so late in their selection process they couldn't offer much hope. I found out later the church had all but agreed upon hiring another minister who had already visited the church as a candidate.

Nevertheless, the Great Mystery being what it is, we received an invitation to come to Sedona as their final candidate. We were extremely well-received, were offered the position, negotiated an acceptable salary package and signed a contract, within ten days. The

Unity Church of Sedona would be my greatest professional success to date.

This success would be partly due to the influence of a highly skilled church administrator, Kathryn Olson. From the first meeting, I recognized Kathryn as a person of integrity. I knew, intuitively, she would be of great assistance to our work there. As it happened, she had many skills. We would later learn she had formerly been the manager of a nonprofit organization in California with a multimillion dollar budget.

Although I had worked for years in management, I was not fully skilled at the budgeting process for non-profit organizations. Kathryn would teach me how to justify every line in a budget, on the income and expense sides. We should reduce the projected income by five to ten percent, and expand estimated expenses by the same amount, she explained. Her strategy would give rise to the goodwill that flows from reporting a budget surplus every year we were there.

My success in the church would also be due to a shocking development.

During the first week of May, Helen began to experience some back pain. Her chiropractor theorized that she was dealing with "blocked energy" and was treating her accordingly. I had no reason to think otherwise. On Mother's Day of 1998, Helen gave the Sunday service, despite the fact that she had back pain regularly by now. We had decided to visit her eldest daughter, Karla, in Gallup, after the service. While in Gallup, her back pain worsened. She was nauseous. She asked to go to the chiropractor, rather than the emergency room, as she was fully subscribed to a Sedona chiropractor's theory that her pain was the result of blocked energy. The Gallup chiropractor suggested we return to Sedona, as soon as possible, and continue treatment there.

On the side of the road between Gallup and Sedona, Helen and I sat on the desert floor and had one of our most heartfelt conversations ever. She reminded me of her realization in India that, despite all the spiritual wisdom she had dispensed and all the training she had, it was not until her relationship with me that she had really known love. And she wept.

On May 18th, I went to work alone. Helen was still experiencing back spasms and was scheduled to see her chiropractor again. I hoped that, since she had been able to be so vulnerable recently, she might have a breakthrough soon in her treatment. A little after lunch, I called her. I had cleared my desk and told her I planned to come home early to be with her.

"Thank you, for calling. I'm glad you're coming home. I love you, you know."

"I love you, too, Helen."

Five minutes later, I received a phone call at the office from Helen's sister, Charmayne, who was visiting with us. Apparently, she had just returned to the house.

"Mark," she said, "I think Helen is gone."

"Oh," I responded. "She's probably at the chiropractor's office. She had an appointment."

"No, Mark," she exclaimed. "She's here on the bed. I mean she's dead."

I do not remember much detail of what transpired after that. Helen had died of cardiac arrest, about two minutes after we had hung up the phone expressing love for one another. I called Seth Friedman first, remembering that he knew about shocking loss and death. He arrived immediately from Boston. Michael Catalano flew in from Branson to conduct the memorial service. Helen's students, many of whom are themselves ordained ministers, came, as well as many of her friends. Her children were, of course, in the greatest shock.

Death is an unfathomable mystery and a transformation. It is also potentially an experience of awakening for those left to ponder its mystery and the fleeting nature of all form. I feel that Helen had sensed her time was near. That's why she insisted on coming home from Puerto Rico. It had allowed her more time with her children, who all live in the Southwest. For several months, she had been expressing interest in purchasing insurance policies that would have paid off her credit cards, in the event of death. I had talked her out of this.

Of the many internal changes that were initiated in me by Helen's death, the most immediately evident was in my public speaking. I realized I had always held myself back, to a certain extent. After all, Helen had been my teacher. She had always been the teacher. It was as if some part of me had remained a student to her. Now it seemed I had no choice. What I had to say seemed to come more directly from the heart now. I was no longer so concerned about tap dancing alone.

After a period of time grieving and attempting to respond to others who were grieving as well, I decided one afternoon to get out and do something. I packed an overnight bag and stopped at the ATM to withdraw some cash. After completing the withdrawal, I sat contemplating... and wondering... Where should I go? What would I do? I began to see that I really just needed to have an authentic conversation with someone who wasn't so deeply engaged the drama of death and grieving. I remembered Kathryn Olson had told me to call if I wanted to talk. Of all the people I knew, I sensed she was the most balanced and authentic. I called her and we had dinner that evening. Our connection that night would lead to the beginning of the most transformational and awakening relationship of a lifetime. Kathryn and I knew there had to be a mysterious destiny to our meeting.

During my time in Sedona I began to pursue further spiritual development, in new ways. I began to attend conferences and retreats with Journey into Wholeness, an organization founded by Jim and Annette Cullipher, based on the psychological model of Carl Jung. This model had been and would continue to be of significant value for me. Through Journey into Wholeness, I met and was particularly influenced by Robert Johnson, the author of some of the most readable and understandable renderings expressing the Jungian approach. Two of the more well-known are *He* and *She*. Robert Johnson's autobiography, *Balancing Heaven and Earth,* impacted me as well.

It was Robert, who first caused me to more fully understand how it is not only the negative or painful aspects of the psyche that are cast into the shadow or unconscious. We also reject the gold, or that material which is too wondrous for the ego to allow into awareness. He said Jung felt that it was easy to uncover and face our more limited or non-ego-enhancing material compared to the ordeal of coming to terms with the transcendental (gold) within oneself."

I began to see more fully how the egoic nature in me had attached itself to both negative and positive experiences. In either case, the *little me* operates to appropriate anything to keep from being seen to have no real substance. Egoic inflation occurs quite naturally when transcendental forces operate. One can say that the heightened energy or expanded states that are being expressed through the individual are not *me,* 'til the cows come home. Meanwhile, beneath the surface, the ego can continue to function in this way.

During a vision quest with Robert Johnson, another Jungian analyst named Barry Williams, and others, on a remote island near Temagami, Canada, north of North Bay, I realized I was being called away from the ministry. The inner voice simply said, "It is time to go now." Once again, the need to let go was asserting itself from a deeper place than that which may have been attached to some outer success.

I resisted and rationalized and suffered. I finally relented and gave notice to leave the Sedona ministry, effective January 15, 2000. Again, I had absolutely no idea what I would do next. I had engaged the mystery of death. I had experienced a transformation. That is, the form of my life had changed, but these changes were still only another beginning. It would require about nine months to even glimpse what this next chapter of life would look like.

## Chapter 34
## Paulden, AZ:
## Rediscovering the Significance of the Heart

Kathryn Olson and I entered an intimate relationship and were married. We began to participate together in all manner of transformational experiences. She is, by nature, highly reserved and private. I tend to be almost foolishly open. Opposites attract.

Out of respect for Kathryn's tendency toward privacy, and because I do not have words to adequately express the nature of our relationship, I will share very few details about Kathryn in these pages. Still, it should be known that behind these words, behind any service I ever give, and behind the writing of this book, her presence shines. She is in the story that now unfolds... as an unfailing love that endured all that is reported here, and endures to this day as the greatest love of my life and my best friend. Sense into and behind these words... sense into the nature of what is known as the significance of the heart. She is that.

Thus, I begin a chapter entitled *Rediscovering the Significance of the Heart*.

When I first left the Sedona ministry, I used my new found freedom to pursue greater health. After a few months I began to feel disquiet. I had many ideas, but none was accompanied by the inner stirring I knew would validate a new direction. As it turns out, grace was seeking me and would find me. And would move me into a new chapter of service and further glimpses into awakening.

In early October of 2000, Hal Vaile and Marian Sears sent me a new book by Brugh Joy. Shortly thereafter, Marian called and said she felt inspired to tell me that Brugh Joy was planning two or three more conferences and then would be taking a lengthy sabbatical. I felt something stir. I looked up Brugh's website and found there was a Foundational Conference coming up immediately. Following that, he would conduct a Darkside Conference. I was attracted to the Darkside Conference, as I believed that my greater transformation would occur through bringing the dark, hidden or rejected aspects of nature into awareness. However, reading further into the description of this conference, I discovered these words: Prerequisite - Foundational Conference.

At first, I thought I should call and ask for an exception, since "foundational" sounded, to my surface mind, like a conference for beginners. I now realize that my request might well have been granted, and I count it as grace that I never made the call. The so-called Foundational Conference was not a beginner's conference, at all. Rather, it was a conference in which the foundation for all later conference work is made conscious.

I would attend both conferences and benefit hugely from each. The Foundational Conference was, however, the most powerful group process in which I have participated. It would provide me a clearer and more conscious understanding of the Source of Grace as Unconditional Love. During this conference, this Love would be ignited in me anew. During this time, I would be granted the first glimpse into a new form of service that was now on the horizon.

It is also at this stage that a fuller understanding of the teacher-student relationship would come into awareness. Much earlier, I had encountered an explanation about how the transmission of *shakti,* flowing through Swami Muktananda, could result in the initiation of awakening or "a blessing from just being present." In scripture, one may read of the woman who touches the hem of Jesus' garment and is healed.

Brugh Joy had been trained as a medical doctor at Johns Hopkins and Mayo Clinic. Therefore, embracing both an appreciation of science and spiritual teachings as two perspectives of Truth, he explained the teacher-student relationship through a principle he called *induction.* The term literally means "to introduce, to initiate or to lead." In his second book, *Avalanche: Heretical Reflections on the Dark and the Light,* Brugh speaks of the many avenues whereby induction may occur, explaining the principle, as follows:

*The word "induction" has another important meaning, related to the phenomenon of electrodynamic induction in physics, in which a current is created in one electrical conductor when it is brought near another conductor in which current is flowing. This analogy can be applied to experiences we have with people and certain situations. Induction occurs, for example, when I sit in the presence of a Spiritual Teacher.*

This explanation by Brugh clearly articulates one of the means by which spiritual awakening can occur in the field of relationships. From an absolute perspective, the One Undivided Presence is dreaming a dream of separation, and the Awakened Teacher is the form that consciousness takes in the dream. The Awakened Teacher is Grace shining into the dream and beckoning to those aspects of Itself, which are still dreaming the dream of separation, saying in various ways, "Its time to wake up now." For most of us, still partially caught in the spell or trance of egoic illusion, this *waking up* takes time, even though, in deepest Truth, there is no time.

Well, my story is still caught in time and in the trance or spell of separation, regardless of the fact that grace has reached in, on numerous occasions, to nudge me toward awakening. This grace has, as I have said, used its allegorical carrot and its stick. Ultimately, I will see that it is believing this story - the *story of me* recorded here - that is keeping me spiritually asleep. I want to reach into the story, from where I sit in 2011, and say to this contraction called *me* in the story, *"Smile - You're on Candid Camera."*

The archetype of awakening is embodied in the stories of awakening, but also hidden from the uninitiated by literal interpretation. As Joseph Campbell so eloquently articulated, "Everything in the phenomenal world is a reference to the Transcendental." Or as another has said it, in the more negative expression, "Literalism is idolatry."

I am grateful for the many teachers who have entered my awareness. Many teachers, including yours truly, express spiritual gifts and heightened states, but are not free of attachments; or in terms articulated by the spiritual teacher, Adyashanti, are not living in an *abiding state* of awakening. So the responsibility lies with the student to develop discrimination. One can partake from a teacher, when the teacher is in a heightened state, without demanding perfection from the teacher. Spiritual maturity only begins to occur when we understand that all teachers are but projections in the mind of the one to whom they appear. From whom are we demanding perfection?

These disclaimers and perspectives aside, *my story* continues...

The retreat center, where we met for the Foundational Conference, was located in some foothills, completely out of sight of roads and dwellings, near Paulden, AZ. After checking into my room, I climbed the nearest mountain, where I had a spectacular view of the valley and sat watching the rain clouds in the distance.

Each participant had received a letter, with directions and certain instructions, intended to assist in preparation and to set the intention of awakening. In particular, we were asked to release all ties to everyday life. We were asked to complete all business, so that we could be unencumbered by such concerns for the twelve days of the conference. We were asked to leave all computers and cell phones at home. Messages from outside the conference were to be limited to a life and death circumstance only. Participants were to be aware that this work is life-renovating. The Foundational Conference was described on Brugh's website in only a paragraph. Essentially, it said that this is the conference in which participants would be formally initiated into the wondrous resources of the Heart Center.

My first contact there was with Henry Miller, my roommate. Henry was a light-skinned black man, remarkably resembling Muhammed Ali. Like Ali, he had Parkinson's disease. I found him to be wise and authentic. Over our time together, we had many conversations on the nature of life, death, love and what is truly valuable. Henry was very clear about these matters for himself. He felt our time alive is precious. In his words, his disease had taught him that "a yard of gold cannot buy an inch of time." So, I began this conference reflecting upon the preciousness of life.

For the next twelve days, I watched lives around me being profoundly changed by Love. I watched tears flow daily. I observed a facilitator, Brugh Joy, who related to each person and the group with unconditional love, compassion and wisdom. I observed a group of adults, most of whom were fairly sophisticated, well-educated and spiritually informed, open ever more fully to an awakening process being generated by and in an atmosphere of trust, because Divine Love was palpable and integral to the environment.

We participated in a number of exercises throughout our time there. Our times of activity were balanced by time apart, rest and periods of silence. The primary focus was continually on the Heart Center. I quote from my journal entry made on the first day of the conference. "We have been instructed to touch the Heart Center (center of the chest) and to ask that whatever is most purposeful happen here... a kind of sacred setting of intention, I think."

Specifically, I will recount a portion of one of the most significant events that occurred during this conference. Please know that words can only point to the experience. One may sense into that which is beyond the words. At the beginning of each session, Brugh would ask the group, "Who would like to call the forces?" In conventional terms, *calling the forces* is akin to an opening prayer. This was, as I understood it, one of the ways of drawing spiritual resources out of the group. I understood it to also model something distinct from the leader-dominated or patriarchal model. However, Brugh would often say, over the years of my acquaintance with him, that it is an error to pathologize spiritual models which served in the past (such as the common, somewhat deriding tone with which many in today's larger spiritual community speak of the patriarchal).

In working with Brugh, everything was to be seen through redeeming eyes or through the eyes of the Heart. In Brugh's words, this hearted perspective is always seeing, not what is wrong, but what serves, or what is right about anything perceived.

One evening, I felt my hand go up, volunteering to call the forces. When I opened my mouth, I heard a new voice, expressing new words with a new power. It was still my voice. The language was English, but the use of my normal, prayerful terminology was absent. I can only liken the power to the experience at Unity Village, when the inner teacher first emerged. Still it was different from that. The forces I felt flowing through me were closer to what I imagine would be a Priest-Priestess archetype. Images consistent with the words being spoken emerged in awareness as I spoke. Brugh's response was, "Whoa... this guy could be dangerous." The group laughed loudly. It had been clear to the collective that a heightened state had been expressed.

I had no idea what was going to happen when I felt my arm going up that day. The pattern for the next stage of awakening and service had been made conscious and set. Over the next months, I would go on to explore this gift and to learn more and more to trust it. My service outwardly, for the foreseeable future, would now be expressed as "being in service to the awakening or induction of the Heart Center."

I could not see yet that the so-called Heart Center is only a relative perspective. The infinite invisible or formless nature of Being is also Unconditional Love and Grace. When Ramana Maharshi equates, as he consistently did, the Self with the Heart by saying Self/Heart, he is not pointing to a place in the physical body. The so-called Heart Center is, in microcosm, the entrance to Self/Heart beyond form.

Such was not necessarily appreciated yet, though. I was still in the predicament of having an egoic nature, which would inflate itself around every possible awakening moment and call it *mine*. Of course, I *knew* this Power wasn't *of me*; that it was flowing from a Transcendental Source. Nonetheless, seeing and knowing are not the same as realizing this. In some sense, it appears that the consciousness appearing as *me* was destined, not only to transmit certain heightened states, but also to make almost every conceivable error the ego can dream of making. Of course, for the egoic nature to remain operant, it must do so in a way that isn't seen.

Ego can only function in the shadow of unconsciousness. One way of understanding this is expressed by Adyashanti in his book *The End of Your World*, in which he points out the many subtle ways the ego continues to operate after initial awakening. It operates, he has said, as a kind of shape shifter - taking on or appropriating every experience to itself. Of course, the sign that ego is operant is always some form of apparent separation from what is being seen. Well, let me stumble on through this dream of awakening that is already being incorrectly perceived again in this *chapter* of the story of a *me* that never really was....

# Chapter 35
## Lone Pine, CA:
## Learning to Consciously Deflate the Thief

*"I see you've been wounded by success."* ~ Carl Jung

In early September of 2001, we gathered for a six-day conference with Brugh, at the former property of western mystic, Franklin Merrill-Wolf, at the base of Mt. Whitney near Lone Pine, California. This was a very different atmosphere and type of gathering. There were participants who would experience Brugh's teaching for the first time, and there were those who had known and worked with him for over twenty years. This conference had no prerequisites. Some stayed on the premises. Others lodged at motels in Lone Pine. Kathryn and I had chosen to stay in a motel.

In recent months, I had begun my new work, timidly at first. I held small *sacred circles* in our home in Sedona. I was discovering that the gift of induction was evident in the circles. People could feel the essence of Love. I had also given my first public lecture at the Sedona Creative Life Center and had followed it with a series of gatherings, which ended with my conducting, for the first time, formal rituals initiating the Heart Center.

Then, little by little, I re-entered a more public life, traveling as a guest speaker and conference facilitator. I usually felt uplifted and inspired during these presentations. Prior to the time I was to present, I would often be filled with fear and self-doubt. At times, my experiences were somewhat reminiscent of that first experience during the Easter Retreat at Unity Village, when I had been afraid I wouldn't make it to the podium.

After the presentation, I would still be in a heightened or expanded state of consciousness. The heightened state would then fade or

210

contract. Sometimes this process of "coming down" would take place within hours, and sometimes it would occur over the next day or two. My best understanding at the time was that the heightening came for the purpose of serving. But, the hidden desire to attach to or identify with these heightened states was still functioning.

I began the practice of putting on a bracelet and a ring before serving, as a ritual act of placing myself in service. Then I would go to my hotel and kneel, removing the bracelet and ring, this time ritually releasing or detaching from the heightened experience. I was training myself to let go, because I now knew that the consequences of attaching to heightened states would be a painful deflation, at a time not necessarily of my choosing.

On the second day of the conference in Lone Pine, I awakened and consulted the Tarot regarding what I might want to be aware of that day. The Tarot is an oracular device used to consult the deeper levels of the psyche regarding what it might serve the surface mind to know. It is symbolic of reaching into the unconscious and making conscious that which the unconscious delivers up. One cannot draw the wrong card, for in Truth, we are always drawing the most appropriate possible card in life, allegorically speaking. Tarot can be understood as a means of utilizing the principle of *synchronicity*. As has been mentioned previously, Carl Jung, who is said to have coined the term, defined it as the *acausal connecting principle*. In other words, in drawing prayerfully into the deck, we are reaching beyond the linear world of cause and effect.

I was using the Voyager Deck, which utilizes more modern symbology than older, more traditional designs. "What might I want to be more aware of today? What might want to be made conscious?" I asked that morning. I drew the Sun card, on which is pictured, among other things, the golden illuminated face of young King Tut. A rising sun occupies the background of the card. In simple terms, this card represents illumination and awakening. My interpretation was that these energies wanted to be made conscious. Having worked with the deck and having drawn the Sun card on numerous occasions, I didn't suspect that drawing this card would necessarily portend anything dramatic. I had no reason to get excited - or inflated.

Kathryn and I arrived a little late for the first gathering of the conference. By the time I reached the building, I could hear the sounds of *Mahogany Nights,* the music being used during meditation times. It has a haunting quality to it. The music playing also informed me that the meditation had begun.

The policy was to remain outside once meditations have begun, so I drew up a lawn chair, turned it to face the morning sun which was about to rise, and entered meditation. Almost immediately, the life force or kundalini began to snake up my spine. I felt the warmth move very easily and gently up into my head. I opened my eyes and saw the outer sun rising. As the sun continued its outer ascent, the inner movement continued its ascent. The experience was one of growing clarity, well-being and ecstasy.

As the meditation time closed, I entered the gathering and sat comfortably to await the start of the session. As we began, I realized immediately that I had entered into a degree of telepathic rapport with Brugh. I instantly knew every word he would utter, as he would speak. He seemed to know, too, as he glanced at me often, smiling. Brugh is a master of the understated and would never have drawn attention to this. I - yes, its still always about *me* - was simply overjoyed to have been so lifted in awareness. After the session, Brugh caught me alone and simply said, "I see we're being visited by the transcendental this morning," and he smiled and walked away.

My heightened state continued. It was September 11, 2001, and as the morning unfolded, Brugh received news of the World Trade Center attack. I began to have images of the Tower card flash in my mind. This card represents the deflation of the ego, among other things. The image is one of a tower on fire, with a figure jumping from it. Above the tower is the image of the sun. This image invites deflation or coming down to earth. The tower is the edifice of the ego. The word "arrogant," when viewed without judgment, may be seen to simply mean "from the air" and suggests one may have gone too high and needs to come down. The card is a call to re-balance.

Brugh determined that we should descend from the foothills around Mt. Whitney and visit a friend of his in Lone Pine to watch this event as it unfolded on television. I began to see that the event was reflecting a collective deflation of ego.

This perspective was, of course, not the first to occur to most, even those in the conference. Much later, I would listen to an audio interview of Eckhart Tolle, recorded this same morning, entitled

"Even the Sun Will Die." In slightly different language, he is saying the same thing. Although Eckhart and I are making the same point, only one of us is still inflating while seeing it. And his name is not Eckhart.

In this case, I could actually see the ego inflating. I could see that the *me* was attached to this heightened state. From this heightened vantage point, I knew I could see more clearly than those around me (the very belief that they are *other* is the clear indication of ego operating). I became conscious that inflation was underway.

Brugh had said, on more than one occasion, that we cannot prevent the ego from inflating. That, he said, is what ego does - it inflates. If not around some heightened state, then around some negative state of consciousness, termed *negative inflation* in Jungian terms. Until we have entered the state of abiding awakening, the ego always inflates when heightened states are visited upon us.

One redeeming perspective of this pattern is called the Divine Thief. This archetype is symbolized by Hermes in Greek mythology. It is the pattern of consciousness entering into the unconscious realm and then emerging, to make conscious that which had been lost or unseen. Hermes, in various renderings of the myth, steals from his father, who is a god, then uses the stolen goods to serve. In one version, he uses the ill-gotten goods to create music, which then serves to express divine harmony. Hermes is also a messenger or deliverer (image of winged feet). So, he enters the unconscious and comes back to report or deliver what has been found. The image of Hermes, with his winged feet, is the symbol adopted as the logo for the Greek postal system.

For those who use astrology in an archetypal or deeper sense, we see that the planets are not *out there* but are representatives of archetypal patternings. In my chart, it can be seen that Mars (masculine polarity) and Venus (feminine polarity) are both in Gemini, which is ruled by Mercury, the Roman name for Hermes. It appears, from a transcendental perspective, that the relative "I" had no choice but to steal and to make unconscious errors, all for the purpose of delivering back these warnings to those drawn toward awakening. Part of what I am attempting to convey by telling these stories is, "Look out for the tricky nature of the ego and its unconscious machinations."

213

There are also other values to be brought back into awareness, not the least of which is the *hearted* perspective I have mentioned, which sees everything through redeeming eyes, as a Divine Mystery Play or *lila* (in Hinduism). So, one cannot prevent or control ego, as that would still be ego, pretending to want to wake up. Ego often shape-shifts into a sincere seeker, and it is one of the ultimate tail chases, as many have discovered and many have not.

Any glimpse into expanded consciousness is viewed as awesome to the ego and, since it knows itself to be fundamentally powerless and inadequate, it naturally seeks to bolster its position with any resource it encounters. The ego is, to be blunt and direct, a liar and a thief. The trick is to simply see this, or make it conscious, without judgment. So, a developmental stage of relative awakening is often referred to as attaining the *witness* state of consciousness. However, as this story portrays, the witness, though valuable in beginning stages of awakening, is still a state of separation.

As I sat in the living room a little later that day, I began to remember a story I heard Robert Johnson tell about Jung's inner circle. One member of this inner circle, a woman who had come to study with him in Switzerland, had to present a paper to the group. A lack of confidence had motivated this woman to work long and hard on her paper. Her presentation was enthusiastically received. Amidst the congratulations and accolades, she became quite pleased.

Sitting down the next day with her psychospiritual mentor, Carl Jung, she found him peering over his glasses, studying her carefully.

"I see you've been wounded by success," he remarked.

Understanding the lesson and taking it to heart, the woman and her roommate formed the practice of ritually emptying the garbage when inflation was seen to be underway. This was a ritual act, intended to restore balance or consciously deflate the ego.

As I sat contemplating this story, I began to look around the room for some garbage to empty. Brugh walked by, glanced down and cautioned me, with a smile and these words, "Level flight, Mark, level flight." I responded that I had just been thinking about the story above, which I was sure was familiar to Brugh. Continuing to smile, he said, "Well, stop thinking about it, and get up and empty the garbage." I did.

At this point in the story of *me,* I am learning, to some extent, to be aware as the ego structure becomes inflated, without identifying with either the egoic movement or the witnessing presence. Having a spiritual gift flowing through one in service is certain to bring many, many opportunities to inflate. The failure to learn this lesson is guaranteed suffering.

*Life is living us.* Neither the highs nor the lows belong to anyone, because there is no separate self for them to belong to. This is why detachment is such a central lesson in relating to the experiences that unfold in and through us. If we discover that life has brought us to balance in a disconcerting way, we should avoid identifying with or clinging to the unhappy feeling that may be associated with such a deflationary experience, for this is just another round of yo-yoing, about to begin. Wile E. Coyote, always tricking himself, is the cartoon character that personifies ego.

A helpful practice, as taught by Brugh Joy, is to shift consciousness back to the Heart Center, in order to detach and witness with compassion. According to Brugh, the Heart Center is the Center of centers. It sits midway between the seven major spiritual centers for a reason. This fourth level is the place of balance and compassion and unites the personal to the transcendental, or heaven and earth. Brugh often said that consciousness awakening and living through the Heart Center is the "acme of human spiritual development."

To quote from his first book, the bestseller, *Joy's Way*:

> To be quickened by Love, the unconditional radiance that emanates from the heart chakra moves even the most skeptical person into the Transcendental Process. It is the energy that uplifts downcast eyes, heals the pain of years of struggle... this Love is non-emotional, non-sexual and non-mental. It has the power to spiritualize instantly, imbuing the individual - not a separate person but an individualized expression of the Undivided One - with an expanded experience of universal relationship and universal values. The sensation is one of Divinity, and it does not matter whether rational states comprehend....
>
> This Love is sensed as intrinsic and fundamental, and once ignited, it requires no external source, for its propagation. Every religion of the world has, at its center, this awakening

experience, the reconnection to the whole. Sexual, emotional and mental love all require externals for continuation, but not Love, the fourth level of awareness, where Love stands alone, totally inclusive, unconditioned and unconditional.

Whether we relate to the Heart Center or not, nearly all mature spiritual teachers prescribe detachment as a central lesson in relating to the experiences that unfold in and through us. The ego actually prefers suffering to waking up. This should be apparent to those who are beginning to awaken. I am reminded of the words of Sig Paulson, spoken so many years ago, "Some of us get off the cross, but insist on dragging the damned thing around with us."

At essence, awakening is that which cannot be simpler. Yet, that is the problem for the surface mind, with which human beings have become so identified. This simplicity cannot be comprehended nor grasped with the intellect. Essential Truth cannot be found in the world of form. Instead, Essential Truth is this Invisible or Formless Presence, which animates and gives rise to all form. We are called to return attention to this, which is the Source of all things.

In scripture, this is pointed to by the parable of the foolish man, who builds his house upon the sand (the ever-shifting, ever-changing, ever-fleeting forms) and the wise man, who builds his house upon the rock (that which is eternal and unchanging). We are this formless essence, expressing in form and presently awakening from our belief in a separate *me*. What a ride!

# Chapter 36
## Delphi & Santorini: A Greek Drama
## and the Transcendental Ground of Being

*"Own your shadow - or your shadow will own you."*

In the summer of 2002, Kathryn and I attended a Foundational Conference with Brugh Joy, in the high desert of southern California. It would be Kathryn's first Foundational. Brugh asked me to assist in the performance of the formal initiation rituals, and this experience further awakened my Heart Center. I felt the current of Divine Love pouring through me, as I placed myself in service.

Directly from the conference, Kathryn and I flew to Greece for my birthday. In Greece, the transcendental arose into awareness and informed me throughout the remainder of our excursion. In Delphi, we toured the famous Temple of Apollo, originally devoted to Mother Earth or Gaia. Here, a priestess was said to have sat atop a tripod and utter prophecies for kings and leaders of nations.

It was in the temple grounds of Athena, however, that I began to feel a sense of resonance. In the center of the grounds of this temple complex, I felt particularly drawn to a smaller structure called the Temple of Tholos. This structure had a round base with columns rising around it, supporting the frame of what must have once been its ceiling. Now the base, the columns and the frame were all that remained. I had determined to spend the night of my birthday in meditation. I felt called to sit for this meditation in the Temple of Tholos, so I planned to return that evening.

Later, we learned that the grounds were locked overnight. Signs were posted, warning of severe penalties as punishment for trespassing. As I contemplated the situation, it occurred to me I had spent a lifetime breaking the rules. Doing so now, in a foreign country, on a spiritual pilgrimage didn't seem the way of wisdom. So I sacrificed my plan in favor of simply meditating during the evening. Later that night, after a short period of meditation, I fell asleep, only to awaken an hour or so later. Again, I entered meditation but could not quite settle down. I felt somewhat agitated. I decided to draw a Tarot card, to see what the unconscious might wish to make conscious.

Using the Voyager deck, I drew a card that has often had strong significance for me - the Priestess. As I looked at the card, upon which are a number of images, I was suddenly struck with the realization that one of these images was the small, round structure of the Temple of Tholos - the very structure I had been drawn to earlier that day.

My body shivered with the synchronicity. I now believed I was being called to follow my earlier urge to return and meditate there, despite the rules. I found a flashlight and walked to the Temple grounds. There I climbed the fence and made my way to this tiny temple within the temple grounds. In meditation, I was lifted in consciousness into a highly impersonal and detached perspective. From this perspective, I began to see certain patterns, which were functioning within me.

I once saw a bumper sticker, which said, "Own your shadow - or your shadow will own you." As has been mentioned previously, the depth psychospiritual model shows that personality development occurs through splitting the psyche into persona and shadow; self and not-self; or me and not-me. A great deal of energy is trapped or contracted below awareness in this developmental process, which is essentially the creation of a false self through denial of a portion of the Mystery of Being. Of course, the shadow or unconscious will continue to function and manifest until it is seen. The immutability of spiritual law requires it.

The manifest world is a field of opposites, and clinging to or identifying with one side will always require the individual to project its opposite onto the perceived other, and move toward it or against it. In other words, the shadow owns us until we see it. On the other hand, becoming conscious of such trapped material frees this energy. A lighthearted perspective within me might say this about unconscious or shadow material, "Thars' gold in them thar hills."

I want to mention two particular patterns or pairs of opposites which were made more conscious within me while in Greece. Although both patterns are revealed throughout these chapters, in Greece they were being made even more conscious. The first pair of opposites is *freedom/containment*.

I could see that I had been driven to seek containment in relationships and circumstances. Then I would feel imprisoned by the very containers that held me and protected me. Then I would seek freedom from containment. The following is largely being expressed from the detached and impersonal perspective, which was informing me at the time.

The individual is drawn into relationship by the attraction of these pairs of opposites. One side of the pair will be unseen, at first, by the conscious or surface minds of both individuals in relationship. If the underlying ground of the relationship is rooted in the transcendental, then the relationship can serve to awaken both from unconscious identification with one side of these opposites. This is the deeper meaning of the word "healing" from the same root meaning as "wholeness." Otherwise, turmoil, conflict and suffering will characterize the relationship.

When two individuals are unwilling or unready to awaken, the only way they can function within the relationship is to deny a part of their larger *beingness*. This model of *persona* and *shadow* is another way of seeing the root-cause of what is often termed co-dependency. Brugh found the term co-dependency distasteful, however. As he put it, using such a word can be a way of placing a pathological label on the Mystery of Being, rather than fully appreciating it. He would point out that life will awaken us when we are ready, and in the meantime, the relationship, no matter what its form, is serving.

As I have mentioned earlier, one of Brugh's most common pointers was to say to the individual undergoing the process of redeeming shadow material, "You should ask yourself, not what is wrong with this, but what is right about it." This question, he taught, cannot be answered by resorting to the surface mind's limited perspectives, but only by seeing from an expanded state of consciousness. Therefore, the question is *a call to awaken*.

More personally, I saw I was still being driven by this pair of opposites, which were causing me to seek containment, and then reject that containment in favor of freedom. Today, I see that both seeking containment and its opposite, seeking freedom, are movements of ego. The question seems to be, who is the seeker of anything perceived to be *out there*.

The second pair of opposites I was becoming more aware of in Greece was that of the *saint/sinner*. Previous to Greece, I had no sense that this pattern was living through me or that such a pattern existed. In ministerial school, when feeling bored, I would doodle irreverent cartoons, usually related to whatever subject was being taught. I would then sign these cartoons, "Markelangelo," and draw a smiley face with horns and a halo. Eventually, I began to doodle this image on thank-you notes or greeting cards. Then, in ministry, I often wore black. In my personal circle of acquaintances, at times, I expressed a dark humor, so that some jokingly called me Irreverent Pope. During a conference with Brugh in Scottsdale, he had made this pattern even more conscious for me, when teaching about it, by confessing his own previous experience:

*When the saint is in charge of my consciousness, the sinner wants nothing to do with all that light and peace stuff. He's outta there. When the sinner is in charge, the saint drops to his knees, praying, "Please God, let this be over quickly." Ultimately, both the saint and the sinner must kneel together, before the Heart.*

In a sense, pretty much everyone who knew me well had seen this pattern at play through me. Now it became time for me to see it better. On the island of Santorini, the Transcendental continued to convey Itself. I again heard an inner voice, "Prepare to enter a wider arena of service."

Though I had no specific idea of what this meant, I sensed that mine would continue to be a life of travel and further surrender into service. I knew personal attachments would have to be dissolved. In fact, the transcendental experience which had lifted me into this expanded state of clarity was partially doing just that, freeing me from unconscious attachments and identities.

Later, while still on the Island of Santorini, I felt guided to undergo a ritual baptism. I found a deserted spot near the water, where I entered the sea through a gaping hole in the ground. I experienced the passing through this natural opening in the earth as a symbolic return to the womb or seeking of new birth. I submerged myself in the turquoise waters and offered myself to the Divine, in as much a surrender of attachments and identities as possible. As I rose from the water, an inner voice spoke words, which were enlivening and inspiring and deepening. Once again, the boundary of inner and outer seemed to dissolve, as I experienced the waves and the appearance of Greek fishing boats as movements in awareness. All was lit up with Divine Love.

My journal from this period is filled with exclamations of gratitude and appreciation and wonderment. This journey to Greece would spell the end of my marriage to Kathryn and the beginning of a new form of relationship with her. I entered a gallery in Santorini and heard a song by Chris Rhea, the lyrics of which caused me to know, from that time to this, that the end of the marriage was no ending at all, but an awakening and a beginning of something much more mature. The lyrics through which this certitude came were:

> *Fool, if you think its over, It's just begun*
> *Fool, if you think its over, I'll tell you why,*
> *New-born eyes always cry,*
> *At the first glimpse of the morning sun.*

Although there would be tears shed and further emotional pain in the unraveling of the marriage, this unraveling would lead to the most amazingly transformational relationship I have encountered in my life. I make this comment in August of 2011, not so much to compare my relationship with Kathryn to my relationships with others, as to honor the depth and degree of the impact this relationship continues to have upon the process of awakening for me.

The reconciliation of the drama of opposites, which had become more evident to me in Greece, is reflected in the ancient symbol of the heart chakra. At the center of this symbol are two interconnected triangles united, forming what is often referred to as the Star of David and/or the Seal of Solomon. The union of these two triangles symbolizes the union of opposites. The fundamental pair of opposites is the masculine and feminine.

In this symbol of the heart chakra, we have the triangle which represents the feminine (Earth) in union with the triangle which represents the masculine (Heaven), in balance and union. Both triangles, which make up this "six-pointed star," are contained within a circle. The circle represents the Transcendental which gives rise to all opposites. It does not matter whether these pairs of opposites are perceived as inner patterns or so-called outer patterns. In words spoken by physicist, Fred Alan Wolfe, in the movie *What the Bleep do We Know*, "Really, there is no out there, *out there*, independent of what's going on inside us."

Spiritual awakening is the realization of that which transcends opposites as the Ground of Being. This awakening is what frees the individual from the shadow or unconscious identities and attachments, which have caused the appearance of this Greek drama to be perceived as *out there* and which have caused the suffering that accompanies this perception.

## Chapter 37
## Assumption Abby in the Mark Twain Forest

I have entered the Assumption Abbey in the Mark Twain Forest near Rockbridge, Missouri for a period of solitude, silence and fasting. It is mid October, 2004. I have now traveled in the field of time and space from the Mark Twain Hotel in 1947 to the Mark Twain Forest in 2004. My intention while here, is to complete this book. For the first three days, I have simply suffered a sense of deprivation and craving. Now, there is a peace and a gentle, deep letting-go taking place.

Apparently, the Transcendental intended this, when It birthed me and set me upon the world. It orchestrated a vast collection of individuals within this Mystery Play to parent me, befriend me, guide me, nourish me, contain me, free me from containment and awaken me from the dream/nightmare of separation. Within this Mystery Play, a Love beyond concepts has danced into and out and back into view along this path of adventure, beyond boundaries and beyond conventions.

The leaves are falling now. Their colors are glorious. I have a jack-o-lantern in my window. Propped up beside Jack is a stuffed ghost that says "Boo" on its chest. I assume that is his name - Boo. Hanging above them both is a small rubber bat. He seems to be grinning at me. I have named him Bat Outta Hell. I have always loved Halloween. All Saints Day follows on its heels. I am reflecting upon this Mystery Play, as a play of consciousness and a play of opposites. Halloween and All Saints Day; dark and light; endings and beginnings. A sacred dance of form within the Formless, Infinite, Invisible, Immovable One Presence. Something within me always knew it was all sacred.

223

It seems time to begin winding these stories down. As I do so, I wish to acknowledge another of the spiritual teachers that served in my awakening. Joseph Campbell devoted his life to mythology. He discovered and revealed that the stories and myths and scriptures of all time and all cultures are, in essence, remarkably similar. This, he realized, is because all stories and myths are references to something that transcends our words and thoughts. Eventually, as one awakens, the structures that serve awakening can be released, having served their purpose, just as one gets off the ferry upon arriving at the other side of a body of water.

I am sensing this same truth, ever more deeply...that everything in the phenomenal world is reference to the Transcendental. Let me allow the voice of the inner teacher to speak:

*Literalism is idolatry. To mistake the surface appearance for the Infinite Mystery behind it is to remain spiritually asleep. The Transcendental Ground of Being is the Ground of all Being. The Radiance of an Infinite Mystery shines through and expresses as all life, for those who have eyes to see. If our eyes haven't yet pierced the veil of illusion, if we cannot yet glimpse this, perhaps it behooves us to acknowledge the Mystery of Life and to remain open, rather than draw narrow conclusions, which temporarily satisfy the ego's need to think it knows. What's wrong with a little uncertainty, a little vulnerability?*

*Every face is a mask of the Divine. Every teacher and teaching is a gateway to the Eternal. All ways and paths serve as long as they serve. But let us not mistake the map for the territory. Each face, each teacher, each teaching is pointing to this Transcendental Field, beyond all form.*

*The reds and the yellows and the oranges of autumn appear to be deepening. They are contrasted by the blue sky and the white clouds above them. The earth and the sky stand together, each enhancing the suchness of the other. Together they make a whole. Not a single leaf can be excluded without fracturing existence. A holy Transcendent Light, a radiance shines through it all.*

*Whatever I am seems to be aligned with the desire to point beyond differences that might divide us. Belief systems have proven, historically, to fragment and divide. However, as long as we need to cling to beliefs, let it be so. We need what we need, for as long as we need it. Some individuals may not need to cling so tightly to a belief system, a map, a mask or "the ferry that brought them." Some are now called to awaken from belief and faith into the experience of Being.*

*This is the deepest understanding of the story of Jesus. In the story of Jesus, there is a mercy shining through. It is the story of the sacrifice of the personal will and its attachments to masks and maps, for the sake of Truth. It is the story of birth and death and That which transcends both.*

*The reds and the yellows and the oranges of autumn speak of death; the sun above speaks of a life-giving Source. Together, these two make up the dance of existence, and together they point to a mysterious Transcendental Field, beyond the appearance of birth and death.*

Fortunately, here words fail....

# Chapter 38
## Ava, Missouri: Death and New-Born Eyes

As I was completing this manuscript at Assumption Abbey last October, a woman who knew I had been working on a book told me she felt guided to tell me I had one more chapter to write. My judgmental mind immediately labeled her presumptuous. However, I have learned just a little about letting go of judgments and remaining open. Through that opening came the following.

Harold died on January 1, New Year's Day, 2005. I had just met him in October of last year at his home in Ava, Missouri, very near the Assumption Abbey. Harold knew he was dying then. As is the case with us all, though, he didn't know how long he had. In October, prior to and after the time I spent at Assumption Abbey, Harold and I became friends. He had a heart as big as all outdoors. When we visited, he would cry a little and thank me for coming into his life.

He had no problem accepting that I could be an ex-convict and was now a "different kind of minister." Harold had no strict religious orientation. He just loved people and tried to help, when he was moved to do so. He had grown up in a tiny, poor, rural area of Missouri, and he visited a handful of people he knew there every Christmas. He surreptitiously left $100 bills in his wake.

Harold had built race cars all his life for NASCAR racers. I told Harold I had stolen cars, as a teenager. "But," I told him, "I used to park them near where I stole them, so I wouldn't deprive the owner too much."

One day at the Pizza Hut in Ava, I told Harold I was leaving that day, to return my rental car to St. Louis. Harold quipped, "So now ya rent - instead a steal?" provoking laughter. That was Harold's other gift. Humor. After I left Missouri, I called from time to time to check on him. Eventually, the news came through that his lung cancer had progressed. Now he knew his death was close.

I told him I had had an experience of being out of the body, years before, and that I was pretty sure that dying wasn't the end of it all.

"But," I added, "it's the end of everything we're used to, I guess."

I told him I was coming back to Missouri in January. I could hear him gently crying on the other end of the phone. I knew it was his heart, his love, as much as his sorrow, he was feeling.

"You might have to hurry, Mark," Harold whispered.

We both knew I would never see him again. That's why he was crying. He loved me. That's why I was crying, as well. I loved him, too. Sometimes, we are deeply and profoundly touched and moved by another human being. It's not about how long we know each other; it's more about how open and vulnerable we are willing to be with one another. Death reminds me that all things in this world must pass away, and of the words of Kahlil Gibran from his classic work, *The Prophet*, "Ever has it been that love knows not its own depth, till the hour of separation."

In January of 2005, I returned to Missouri. When I landed at the airport, Barbara, who befriends me and supports my work there and who introduced me to Harold, picked me up in Springfield and took me to dinner at Steak 'n Shake, Harold's favorite restaurant. We ate at Harold's favorite table, and when we left the restaurant, I felt my heart open in gratitude for having known him.

The form of my life continues to change, and I feel continuously called into surrender. Just as in death, spiritual growth calls me to let go of "everything I'm used to." Once again, the words of the lyrics of Chris Rhea float into awareness:

*Fool if you think it's over, I'll tell you why*
*Newborn eyes always cry... at the first glimpse of the morning sun.*

## Chapter 39
## Austin: Ghostly Visitations in the Heart of Texas

March, 2005:

I arrived in Austin, Texas a few days ago, to conduct Heart Awakening conferences. While studying a road map, I noticed that my journey was about to take me within a few miles of Gatesville, Texas. The facilities where I had known the darkest of my days on earth now housed several units of the Texas Department of Corrections for women. I felt an inner prompting to stop and view the place. "Perhaps some old memories that might serve in completing this book will arise," I thought.

Ninety minutes later, I pulled into the town where I had been incarcerated some forty years ago and stopped at a convenience store to ask for directions. Outside the store, I asked a tall, elderly man in a cowboy hat and boots if he lived in the area.

"Yea, sure do. How can I help ya?"

"I understand there is a women's prison located here. Can you tell me how to get there?"

"What unit are ya lookin' for?"

"The Hill," I answered, giving him the name of the unit, as it had been known in my day.

"You mean the Hilltop Unit," he corrected me. "Ya see that water tower yonder?" He pointed to the north. "It's right there. Ya gonna' visit somebody?"

"Well, no, sir. The truth is, I was locked up there myself, about forty years ago, when it was a reform school for boys. I'm writing a book about some of my life experiences. I thought I'd go by and see the old place."

"Is that a fact? You know," he continued, "I used to work there in the old days. I guess it was about thirty-five years ago... just before the courts closed it down. Guess it was a little after your time. It was a hard place, wasn't it?"

"Yes, sir, it was. But I don't have any hard feelings about it. At this point, it just seems like one of the experiences I needed to have. Eventually, I had a kind of spiritual awakening, and now I'm trying to use my experiences to serve others."

"Well, I'm sure glad to hear that. I don't reckon too many came through that place for the better. Fact is, I've always been a little ashamed to have had anything to do with it. I knew what went on there was wrong, but I was young and needed a job. I wouldn't let 'em put me in charge of the boys there, though. I got my job in maintenance, 'cause I couldn't a stood for some of what they wanted us to do for punishment."

The old fellow then went on to ask if I remembered certain guards and inmates he had known there. A few were vaguely familiar. Most were not. Then he asked me if I had known Captain Jack McQuarters.

"Yes, I sure did. He was the guard over B Company when I was there." I didn't tell him that we used to call Captain Jack McQuarters "Rackin' Jack," for being so quick to administer beatings.

"Fact is, I'm on my way to go see old Jack, right now. He's got cancer and ain't expected to have too long left."

"Well, tell Jack you met me. My name is Mark Pope, and I am sure he'll remember me. I was one of the worst back then, and I was in B Company when he was over it. Tell him, for me, that I don't have any hard feelings, and I'm sorry to hear about his cancer. Tell him I wish him the best."

I watched, as a hint of tears seemed to make the old man's eyes shine. After a few moments of the awkward silence that follows emotion felt by a hardened Texan, he said, "You know, they'll probably let you in up there, if you ask. Security isn't too tight, and the warden's pretty friendly. You might just tell 'em what you're up to, and see if they'll let you tour the place. I know they do that, sometimes."

I took the old fellow's words to heart and, upon arrival, asked to speak with the warden, who agreed to give me a short tour of the facilities. She told me, while walking through B Company, that the old buildings, constructed in the late 1800s, make a lot of weird noises at night. She said the women inmates say that the creaky sounds are the ghosts of the boys who used to be there.

Ghosts or not, walking through the place was a haunting experience for me. Old, queasy emotions surfaced, accompanied by a single repressed memory of having been placed in solitary confinement just before Christmas. When Christmas day had arrived, and the pain of my isolation became unbearable, I had told myself that Christmas wasn't really a special day; that it didn't really mean anything. It had been my way of dealing with overwhelming emotions, and I realized that the decision to discount the meaning of Christmas had diminished my ability to celebrate the spirit of that season ever since.

Speaking of ghosts, images of Dickens' classic, *A Christmas Carol* comes to mind. Old Scrooge and I had dealt with our pain similarly. Perhaps in more ways than I can remember, this archetypal pattern has lived through me. Once wounded, closed down, protected and defended, I am awakening to the Power of a Redeeming Love, to which all things are forever and instantly possible.

I have always been deeply moved by this tale of awakening and redemption. I am particularly fond of the 1951 version, called *Scrooge* and starring Allister Simms. Scrooge is forced to look into the past, to see the origin of his wounding and what shut him down. Then he is forced to see a projection of the future, a gravestone, which is his destiny if he remains contracted. Then he is shown the potential for awakening that is always Here and Now.

I can see him, throwing open his window on Christmas morning, overflowing with a grace that sought and found him in the darkness; a grace he now embodies and expresses; a grace that found me in my darkness and altered everything, time and time again.

## Chapter 40
## Leaping into the Non-Linear and Back
## Until All Leaping Ends

*"Return unto me, and I will return unto thee"*

Over the last few years, I have traveled to the south of France, England, Scotland, Egypt and Canada. I continued to speak publicly and served another three and a half years as minister of Unity of Sedona. I left Unity of Sedona, for the second time, in September of 2010.

Brugh and I released one another from the projections of the teacher-student relationship. Some nine months later, Brugh passed away. Brugh's final months were spent openly sharing with his friends and students the process leading to his death via pancreatic cancer.

I was married again, separated a few months later, then divorced. Janis assisted by serving during the second successful turnaround at Unity of Sedona. The purpose of relationships is often something other than we imagine.

I spent hundreds of hours, allowing the words and images of Eckhart Tolle, Adyashanti and a number of other spiritual teachers, to reflect attention back to the non-linear Truth, which is always already *here-and-now*, just beneath the movement of the mind, its beliefs and its projections. They point out that identifying with the *story of me* is what imprisons consciousness and causes suffering. The *story of me* has grown to resemble the character Bill Murray plays in *Groundhog Day*.

It is now, linearly speaking, 2011. I live in Sedona, AZ. Kathryn Olson and I continue to communicate daily. She is the best friend I have ever had or ever hope to have. We live under the same roof, in separate parts of the same house. My mother passed away last month, and Kathryn accompanied me as I went to scatter her ashes in northern Arizona.

During the final days of my writing this, Kathryn had a dream. In her words, "I felt like I lived in a crematorium. There were four boxes of ashes that Mark was to spread but hadn't had time, because of the intensity of his process."

Her interpretation of the dream: "Mark is burning up his false identities, stories and attachments, etc. through writing." She also says she felt the dream was for me to hear, and that it may have meaning to me, as well. I speculate that spreading the ashes may mean publishing the stories, as well as further awakening from identification with them. Linear time will tell.

Ronnie West now lives in southern California. Our stories have been intertwined since 1962, when we met while incarcerated in Gatesville. Along the linear way, we have served each other in the process of consciousness awakening to Itself. Recently, we have visited one another and have spoken often on the phone. It has been partly through these interactions that the inspiration to complete the account of these stories returned to me. Most of the reports were recorded prior to 2005 and now seem like a surreal dream. How wondrous it seems that two criminals would become friends and also serve to awaken one another to That which is beyond the linear story.

One form of the Truth that has been shining into awareness, over recent linear time, has been the book by Adyashanti, previously mentioned, entitled *The End of Your World.* The title of this book is pointing to the end of the apparent world of separation, created by consciousness being trapped in identification with thoughts, feelings and the *story of me*. I have also listened to Eckhart Tolle point out time and time again that the *story of me* does not have a happy ending. It all comes down to the dash between one's date of birth and date of death on a gravestone. Of course, this *me* that dies is not who we are, but the dream of a false self.

Experiences of ecstasy and bliss, as well as the deflations that have followed, are all part of the process of consciousness awakening. It is also evident that all temporary states must eventually give way to That which is eternal and abiding. A friend, Robert Bays, likes to relate the following story of the early life of the spiritual teacher, H. W. L. Poonja or "Papaji," to make this point.

A devotee of Krishna (Papaji) reported his blissful and ecstatic experiences through visions of Krishna to the great sage, Ramana Maharshi.

Ramana responded by asking, "Are you having a vision of Krishna now?"

"Well, no, not right now."

"Tell me," queried Ramana... "what good is a God that comes and goes?"

Of course, temporary states do have transformational value. These experiences eventually give rise to ever deepening awareness. Nonetheless, actual awakening is the awakening from identification with all that is temporary in favor of Eternal and Unchanging Truth.

Consciousness is now awakening in form on earth. This awakening can only ever occur in the non-linear Now. The words of Emma Curtis Hopkins, from The Radiant I AM, are exquisite pointers to this waking up:

> But who has told himself that all the objects he beholds and all their movements, also, are but projections of his own judgment? He seems always to be a learner and a seeker, till at the center of his consciousness, the fact is suddenly proclaimed that he, himself, produced the world, as it appears.... I have let people and objects and activities come toward me and impinge upon me, till I have been over-piled and mountain-covered with thoughts. But now I know that I Am....

The non-linear Truth of Being is always already true Now, and by Grace and through the mercy of a Love beyond conditions, this Truth shines into our self-imposed prisons and liberates us, time and time again, until the end of time and the end of identification with the *story of me.*

In order to report the Truth, one must report honestly. Over the last five years, synchronicities and lapses into unawareness have continued; heightened states of consciousness and contractions have occurred, as well. Uninterrupted awakening, as described by those who seem likely to be expressing it, is not the case for this author. Of course, there is no point in being overly concerned about that. Truth moves to awaken, and it is Truth that is the eternal call and promise behind the words, "Return unto me, and I will return unto thee."

The awareness of Being returns to its Source, which is Itself.

Herein is the final prison break...

*A Wave of Grace,*
Mark Pope
Halloween, 2011

## Afterword:
## Meaninglessness, Mercy and Awakening:

There are two intentions behind the stories in this book. The first is to offer a merciful perspective: Along the so-called path of spiritual awakening, it is not only forgivable to err and fall into temporary periods of contraction, unconsciousness and suffering, it is unavoidable for most. The second intention is to point, and this pointing holds promise: The spiritual dimension, which is always already here and now, can emerge into awareness and change anyone or anything, anywhere, anytime. *One discovers that what emerges is who and what we are.*

During August, 2010, while still employed as minister at Unity of Sedona, I was on vacation in Vancouver, British Columbia, attending a filming session of Eckhart Tolle TV. One day, while sitting on a park bench in downtown Vancouver, something like a flash camera seemed to go off within me. The flash was followed by these words: "It is time to go now. It may be difficult. It may be disruptive. It may be frightening. Do it anyway. Do it now."

I knew this meant leaving my position as minister at Unity of Sedona. It also meant letting go of my identity as a minister or spiritual teacher. Unless I left, I knew I wouldn't be able to see how much I might be identified with such a role.

Then, the flash camera went off again. This time there were no words. An image of myself wearing a baseball cap, sitting in a coffee shop somewhere in Texas, entered awareness. I cannot explain how I knew it was Texas. Somehow I knew this meant I was to go to Texas and be "nobody."

My body quivered with fear. Nonetheless, I rose from the park bench, returned to my hotel, and rescheduled my flight home for the next morning. I called the President of the Board at Unity of Sedona and told her I wanted to call a special meeting where I would be resigning my position.

Three weeks later I left Sedona for Texas. I had broken off nearly all contact with those who knew me as a spiritual teacher or minister. Grace and synchronicity provided a place for me to stay in relative luxury in Houston. Two weeks later I moved into a small one bedroom apartment in the Montrose District in Houston. I was alone. Having left this neighborhood over 30 years ago, except for the return in 1987, I no longer knew anyone there.

For the next few months I sat on park benches and in coffee shops and witnessed the world of people, places and circumstances from the perspective of "nobody." I began to notice that, with no identity of spiritual teacher or minister, I also had no motive to do anything at all. As the months passed, I began to experience existence as essentially meaningless. Barely having the motive to eat, I lost some 20 pounds and became ill several times. I began to suspect I might be dying.

Then, I remembered something I had read in Adyashanti's book, *The End of Your World.* As I remembered it, he had said when the ego begins to collapse, it is like a deflated balloon.

Suddenly, the thought arose, "Oh, I AM identified with this deflated perspective." As I saw this, the perspective began to shift. Then, I could see or witness this deflated balloon-like sense of self again. Seeing this meant consciousness was no longer fully trapped in the deflated sense of self.

I returned to Sedona and slowly regained health and the weight I had lost. Another kind of motive emerged...it now seemed that life wanted to speak, write and report on this yo-yoing process called spiritual awakening. I began to interact with others again and noticed how much more animated I became when speaking, writing and reporting. Eventually, the life force became passionate again.

In July, I was invited to speak publicly. I have now done so on numerous occasions and have enjoyed it. It seems that awakening likes to speak, write and report on awakening.

Last night, I was speaking in a living room by invitation of friends. Afterward, a friend in attendance, who had read one of the final drafts of this manuscript, suggested that readers of this book might be better served if I would add one more report about what had happened during these latter days. Done. ---*Mark Pope, November 8, 2011*

# REFERENCES

Adyashanti. (2008). *The End of Your World.* Boulder, CO: Sounds True

Allen, James. (1948). *As a Man Thinketh.* Camarillo, CA: DeVorss & Co.

Anonymous. (1975). *A Course in Miracles.* Huntington Station, NY: Coleman Graphics

Boyd, Doug. (1990). *Swami.* New York, NY: Paragon House

Buck, Pearl S. (1972). *The Story Bible: New Testament.* New York, NY: Signet

Brungardt-Pope, Helen. (2001). *For the Aspiring Mystic.* Sedona, AZ: Prophecy Rock Pub.

Dass, Ram. (1978). *Be Here Now.* Boulder, CO: Hanuman Foundation

Gibran, Kahlil. (1966). *The Prophet.* New York, NY: Alfred A. Knopf, Inc.

Hopkins, Emma Curtis. *The Radiant I Am.* (See YouTube)

Johnson, Robert. (1998). *Balancing Heaven and Earth.* New York, NY: Harper One

Joy, W. Brugh. (1979). *Joy's Way.* New York, NY: Penguin Putnam, Inc.

Joy, W. Brugh. (1990). *Avalanche.* New York, NY: Random House, Inc.

Lawrence, Brother. (1958). *The Practice of the Presence of God.* Grand Rapids, MI: Spire Books

Mann, Stella Terrill. (1959). *How to Live in the Circle of Prayer and Make Your Dreams Come True.* New York, NY: Dodd; Mead

Muktananda, Swami. (1978). *The Play of Consciousness.* Ganeshpuri, India: Syda Foundation

Murphy, Joseph. (1973). *Prayer is the Answer.* Camarillo, CA: DeVorss & Co.

Neville. (1941). *Your Faith is Your Fortune.* Camarillo, CA: DeVorss & Co.

Tolle, Eckhart. (1999). *The Power of Now.* Novato, CA: New World Library

Wolfe, Tom. (1968). *The Electric Kool-Aid Acid Test.* New York, NY: Farrar, Strauss & Giroux

Yogananda, Paramahansa. (1974). *Autobiography of a Yogi.* Los Angeles, CA: Self-Realization Fellowship

10720094R00148

Made in the USA
Charleston, SC
27 December 2011